Reader's Guide
to
GEORGE ELIOT

Reader's Guide
to
GEORGE ELIOT

S. Dorsch

CENTRUM PRESS
NEW DELHI-110002 (INDIA)

CENTRUM PRESS
H.O.: 4360/4, Ansari Road, Daryaganj,
New Delhi-110 002 (India)
Ph.: 23278000, 23261597

B.O.: No. 1015, Ist Main Road, BSK IIIrd Stage
IIIrd Phase, IIIrd Block,
Bangalore - 560 085 (India)
Tel.: 080-41723429
Visit us at: www.centrumpress.com

Reader's Guide to George Eliot

First Edition, 2009
ISBN 978-93-80106-77-9

PRINTED IN INDIA

Printed at Balaji Offset, Delhi.

Contents

Contents

Preface

George Eliot was the Victorian writer, a humane freethinker, whose insightful psychological novels paved way to modern character portrayals - contemporary of Dostoevsky, who at the same time in Russia developed similar narrative techniques. Eliot's liaison with the married writer and Editor George Henry Lewes arise among the rigid Victorians much indignation, which calmed down with the progress of her literary fame. George Eliot was born in Chilvers Coton, Warwickshire. Her father was a carpenter who rose to be a land agent. When she was a few months old, the family moved to Griff, a 'cheerful red-brick, ivory-covered house', and there Eliot spent 21 years of his life among people that he later depicted in her novels.

Under Eliot's control the *Westminster Review* enjoyed success. She became the centre of a literary circle, one of whose members was George Henry Lewes, who would be her companion until his death in 1878. Lewes's wife was mentally unbalanced and she had already had two children by another man. In 1854 Eliot went to Germany with Lewes. Their unconventional union caused some difficulties because Lewes was still married and he was unable to obtain divorce. Eliot's first collection of tales, Scenes of Clerical Life, appeared in 1858 under the pseudonym George Eliot - in those days writing was considered to be a male profession. It was followed by her first novel, Adam Bede, a tragic love story in which the model for the title character was Eliot's father.

Eliot's translation works include D.F. Strauss's *Das Leben Jesu kritisch bearbeitet,* Ludwig Feuerbach's *Das Wesen des Christentum,* and Spinoza's *Ethics*. Eliot's thoughts of religion were considered at that time advanced.

Author

Chapter 1

Introduction

George Eliot was the male pseudonym of Mary Ann Evans (she would later call herself Marian), born on November 22, 1918 at Arbury Farm in Warwickshire. Her father, Robert Evans, was an overseer at the Arbury Hall estate, and Eliot kept house for him after her mother died in 1836. The Mill on the Floss involves many autobiographical details, and it reflects Eliot's close childhood relationships with her father and her older brother Isaac. Eliot was sent to school as a child and at the age of fifteen and underwent a spiritual conversion to Evangelicism, similar to Maggie Tulliver's pious conversion upon reading Thomas a Kempis in Book IV of The Mill on the Floss.

In 1841, Eliot and her father moved closer to the town of Coventry, which was at that time a centre of radical thought. Eliot made friends with a group of Coventry intellectuals, mainly members of the Bray family, and began reading such works as An Enquiry into the Origins of Christianity. Eliot soon gave up her Evangelicism in favour of a non-sectarian spirituality based on a sense of common humanity. She refused to attend church with her father and began work on a translation from German of Life of Jesus, a rationalist reexamination of some Bible sections. Life of Jesus was published in 1846, and on the strength of that accomplishment, Eliot moved to London after her father's death.

In London, Eliot became the assistant editor of John Chapman's Westminster Review and came into close contact with the leading intellectuals of the time, such as Herbert Spencer, John Stuart Mill, and Harriet Martineau. In 1852,

Eliot met and became close to George Henry Lewes, a writer and an editor of The Leader. Lewes was living apart from his wife, and Eliot's decision to accompany Lewes to Germany, living as a couple, provoked a degree of scandal in London. In particular, Eliot sacrificed her relationship with her brother Isaac, and she depicted the pain of his disapproval in The Mill on the Floss in Tom's disapproval of Maggie's relationships with Philip and Stephen.

Eliot and Lewes lived together, considering themselves virtually married until his death in 1878. With the encouragement of Lewes, Eliot began writing fiction. Scenes of Clerical Life was published in 1856. Adam Bede (1859), her first full novel, was met with critical acclaim, and the public began to wonder what writer was behind the pseudonym of George Eliot. By the time of the publication of The Mill on the Floss in three volumes in 1860, Marian Evans's authorship had been tentatively guessed by a few London intellectuals and friends. Several well-received novels followed, including Middlemarch, the novel now regarded as her greatest artistic success. Eliot died in 1880.

Eliot's most important contribution to literature was in her treatment of realism. Eschewing the caricature fiction of Charles Dickens, Eliot perfected the genre of psychological realism, paving the way for the later work of the American novelist Henry James. Eliot understood that art should be near to life, valuing observed truths and creating a greater sense of sympathy in the reader by coherently and non-judgementally depicting the psychological motives of characters. Eliot's attention to character is mediated by a strong sense of historical and cultural climate. Thus in The Mill on the Floss, Mr. Tulliver's financial downfall is depicted within the larger context of the increased materialism of the British midlands in the first half of the nineteenth century, but it is also portrayed as the result of minute social and psychological actions and reactions of Mr. Tulliver and the characters that affect him, such as Mrs. Tulliver and Mr. Wakem.

The Mill on the Floss marks a break from the earlier work

of Eliot, which was mainly a depiction of provincial life, and it bridged the gap to more wide- ranging later novels, such as Middlemarch, that drew detailed backdrops of the social and economic forces alive in an entire community. The Mill on the Floss is Eliot's only novel to end tragically and the most autobiographical novel.

THE EARLY YEARS

Mary Anne Evans was born at South Farm, Arbury, on November 22, 1819. The youngest child of Robert Evans and Christiana Pearson Evans, she had four siblings: Robert, Fanny, Chrissy, and Isaac. Mary Anne shared an especially close relationship with her brother Isaac — they were inseparable playmates. However, in 1824, Isaac was sent to school at Foleshill, and Mary Anne was sent to Miss Latham's boarding school. At Miss Lathim's, missing the companionship and comfort of her brother, Mary Anne first turned to books as a source of amusement. Those who knew her found Mary Anne a serious, sensitive, and introspective child. She had straight light-brown hair and a plain face. Mathilde Blind described her as "a queer, three-cornered, awkward girl, who sat in corners and shyly watched her elders".

In 1828, after finishing at Miss Latham's, Mary Anne was sent to Mrs. Wallington's Boarding School at Nuneaton. It was at Mrs. Wallington's that she met the woman who was to be the most influential figure of her early life, Miss Maria Lewis. Maria Lewis, a kind woman with strong evangelical beliefs, was a governess at the school. She took an immediate interest in the shy Mary Anne, and marking the exceptional quality of the child's mind, took it upon herself to foster it. By the time Mary Anne was thirteen, she had learned all that Mrs. Wallington's school had to offer.

When she left, however, she maintained a close relationship with Miss Lewis — a relationship they kept up for nearly fourteen years. Upon leaving Miss Wallington's, Mary Anne attended Miss Franklin's school at Coventry. It was here that Mary Anne worked to rid herself of her Midland accent and cultivated the "low, well-modulated, musical voice, which impressed everyone who knew George Eliot in later years". At Miss Franklin's school, Mary Anne became an accomplished pianist, studied French, was admired for her skill at writing, and read widely. She also wrote poetry and fiction.

Drastic changes soon occurred in Mary Anne's life. Her mother had been ill for quite some time. In February of 1839, Mrs. Evans died, and Mary Anne, then 19, left school to take care of her father.

Though not the oldest daughter, Mary Anne had always been close to her father, and she tried to fill in for her mother while continuing her education at home (now Griff House). Robert Evans, proud of his daughter, bought Mary Anne any book she wished to have and arranged for her to receive lessons in Italian and German. In 1841, she and her father moved to a new home at Foleshill.

THE WORLD OF IDEAS

Foleshill was a larger town than Griff, and Mary Anne suspected that her father had chosen it in order to enlarge her social circle, and perhaps help her find a husband. However, Mary Anne felt distanced from those around her. Always serious and shy, she "could not help thinking how much easier life would be to her, and how much better she would stand in the estimation of her neighbors, if only she could take things as they did, be satisfied with outside pleasures, and conform to popular beliefs without any reflection or examination".

Mary Anne had been entertaining doubts about her religious convictions for some time, but she did not have the courage to relinquish those convictions just yet. At Foleshill, Mary Anne continued her studies and spent her evenings reading Sir Walter Scott to her father, whose health was failing.

On November 2, 1841, Mary Anne was invited to the home of Charles and Cara Bray. Mary Anne found in the Brays the same doubts about Christianity that she had been secretly harboring for quite some time and felt she was among kindred souls. In his autobiography, Bray later wrote, "we became friends at once"; in fact, Charles and Cara Bray were to be Mary Anne's most intimate friends for the next thirteen years. In 1842, Mary Anne stopped going to church. Her longtime friend Maria Lewis was disappointed and their correspondence dwindled — though no permanent break was made until Christmas of 1846. Mary Anne's father was even more disturbed by his daughter's heresy and refused to speak to her. Eventually, a truce was effected—Mary Anne agreed to go to church with her father and he conceded that she had the right to think what she pleased (as long as she showed signs of outward conformity), but relations between the two remained strained.

Mary Anne continued her friendship with the Brays. They were open-minded intellectuals, and they brought the shy Mary Anne out of her shell. After five years in their company, she could not be called shy at all. Charles Bray had connections to some of the most important thinkers of the time, and Eliot's acquaintance with him served to bring her closer to "the world of ideas." Mary Anne met many interesting and important people at the Bray's home, including Ralph Waldo Emerson, who was quite taken with her and commented, "that young lady has a calm and serious soul". At Rosehill (the Bray's home), Mary Anne also met some of the people who were to become her closest friends: Sara Hennell, Charles Hennell, and Elizabeth (or Rufa) Brabant (later Mrs. Charles Hennell).

In 1844, Mary Anne began work on an English translation of David Friedrich Strauss' Das Leben Jesu, one of the most influential works of religious thought read in England at the time. This translation took her two years to complete, and while her name did not appear on the publication, it did later bring her some little fame in London when people discovered that it was her work. Meanwhile, Mary Anne's father's health continued to fail, and Mary Anne was his caring nurse. He died in June of 1849. Mr. Evans seemed to soften towards Mary Anne a bit in his final years, but left her little in his will. Mary Anne was twenty-nine.

ALONE

Though emotionally and physically exhausted from nursing her father, Mary Anne agreed to take a Continental tour with the Brays just five days after the funeral. In July, rather than returning home with them, Mary Anne announced her intention to stay in Geneva alone. She returned to England in 1850, and resolved to move to London. She first spent seven months at Rosehill with the Brays, where she came into contact with John Chapman, a London publisher and bookseller. Having read her translation of Strauss, he asked her to write an article for the Westminster Review. Mary Anne finished this article in November. It was an impressive piece. She delivered the article herself to Chapman in London and took up lodgings in Chapman's London home at 142 Strand, where Chapman lived with his wife, Susanna, and his mistress, Elisabeth Tilley.

Chapman was a tall, handsome, magnetic man and a notorious philanderer. Soon after Mary Anne moved into the Strand, he took a great interest in her and they began to spend an inordinate amount of time together, often at strange hours. Both his wife and his mistress were jealous. When Susanna caught her husband holding Mary Anne's hand, things blew up. Susanna and Elisabeth joined forces against Mary Anne and demanded of Chapman that she move out immediately. Mary Anne agreed to return to Coventry.

In 1851, Chapman purchased the Westminster Review. He needed an editor, and he wanted someone who would be willing to let him take all the credit and work behind the scenes anonymously. Mary Anne was his first choice. However, he needed her in London, and knew it would prove difficult to persuade Susanna and Elisabeth to agree. Eventually, he did get the ladies to agree, and Mary Anne moved back into 142 Strand. Things were different this time — Mary Anne saw the true nature of Chapman, and made a vow to keep her relationship with him strictly professional.

This was a vow she kept. Mary Anne edited the Westminster Review for two years and ten issues. Under her direction, it again became the important intellectual journal it had once been under former editor John Stuart Mill. Mary Anne's social circle continued to grow. London had become a centre of enlightened radicalism and there were many parties at the Strand where she met some of the most important thinkers of the time. Though she was physically unattractive, most people who met Mary Anne were quite taken with her. They were charmed by her expressive face and eyes, her gentleness, her beautiful, low voice, and her great intellect.

GEORGE HENRY LEWES

Mary Anne was growing tired of editing the Review and of living in the Chapman home. She became depressed and her health was failing. She suffered from awful headaches. Mary Anne was now nearly thirty-three and feeling lonely. She met George Henry Lewes in October of 1851. Lewes was an unattractive man, but loved by most who came near him because of his outgoing personality and wit. Lewes had married Agnes Jervis in 1841. About eight years into the marriage, Agnes began an affair with Lewes's close friend Thornton Hunt. Both Lewes and Agnes were believers in "free love" and felt that feelings were stronger than legal bonds. So when Agnes gave birth to Hunt's son, Lewes claimed the illegitimate child as his own. In the coming years, she would bear Hunt four more children. George claimed all of them, but he ceased to view Agnes as his wife.

When Mary Anne met Lewes, his marriage had long been over in every sense but the legal one. Lewes came to visit Mary Anne at the Strand often, often enough that by April of 1853, their intimacy had grown far beyond what either of them could have expected. In September of 1853, Mary Anne moved out of 142 Strand and found her own lodgings. This move gave her the opportunity to spend more time with Lewes, and by November they had grown extremely close. In July of 1854, her translation of Feuerbach's Essence of Christianity was published, with her name appearing on the title page. This was the first and last time "Marian Evans" appeared on a work of hers.

In June of 1854, Mary Anne went to Rosehill for the last

time. She knew that her friends Sara Hennell and Cara Bray would not approve of what she had made up her mind to do. Mary Anne had decided to live openly with George Lewes as his lover and spiritual wife. The decision was not an easy one. Mary Anne knew that this bold move would bring public censure and that if George ever left her, she would be alone and outcast. She wrote the following to John Chapman on the subject, "I do not wish to take the ground of ignoring what is unconventional in my position. I have counted the cost of the step I have taken and am prepared to bear, without irritation or bitterness, renunciation of all my friends. I am not mistaken in the person to whom I have attached myself".

MARRIED LIFE

In July of 1854, George and Mary Anne departed for the Continent. They spent eight months in Germany, first at Weimar and then in Berlin, so that George could work on his biography of Goethe. Mary Anne wrote to friends that she was quite happy. Upon their return, Mary Anne took lodgings in Dover, and George went to London to settle his affairs. Mary Anne did not see George for five weeks. She had stipulated that George must separate permanently from his wife, Agnes.

She knew, of course, that a divorce was impossible, but she wanted to be assured that there was no possibility of reconciliation before she would move to London with George. Agnes confirmed that a reunion was not possible. With this assurance, Mary Anne moved to London in April. She and George took rooms as Mr. and Mrs. Lewes, and their "marriage" was officially begun.

Chapman soon asked Mary Anne to take over the "Belle Lettres" section of the Westminster Review at a fixed salary of fifty pounds a year. Mary Anne happily agreed to this extra income. She wrote countless book reviews which gave her ample cause to think about what exactly made good fiction. The couple received few visitors at first, but both Rufa and Bessie Parks broke the taboo and risked their reputations by paying calls at the Leweses.

GEORGE ELIOT IS BORN

In June of 1856, Mary Anne and George moved to Tenby on the coast of South Whales. When Barbara Leigh Smith visited them in July, she remarked that the couple was very happy. At Tenby, Mary Anne began to think more and more about her childhood dream of writing fiction. She felt that she could competently write the descriptive passages of a novel, but feared that she lacked the talent to render dramatic and dialogue passages effectively. When she shared these thoughts with George, he encouraged her to try her hand at fiction writing. In August, the Leweses moved back to London, and on September 23rd of 1856, Mary Anne began to write "The Sad Fortunes of the Reverend Amos Barton," which would later become a part of Scenes of Clerical Life. Despite his avowed confidence in her, George still had some doubts about Mary Anne's ability to write fiction. Those doubts were removed when he read her Amos Barton story.

Her fears were unfounded — she could write good dialogue and she could create drama to stir the emotions. Lewes sent her story to his publisher, John Blackwood, claiming it was the work of a (male) friend who wanted to remain anonymous. The story was published on New Year's Day, 1857, less than two months after Mary Anne's thirty-seventh birthday. Mary Anne then adopted George Eliot as her nom de plume. She later told John Cross that she chose the name because "George was Mr. Lewes's Christian name, and Eliot was a good mouth-filling, easily pronounced word".

In May of 1857, Mary Anne finally decided to tell her family of her marriage to George. At first, she kept the details to herself, but when pressed, she revealed that the marriage was not a legal one. Urged by Isaac, Mary Anne's sisters wrote letters renouncing Mary Anne. She was now an outcast in the eyes of her family. After the publication of Scenes of Clerical Life, there was much talk about the supposed identity of George Eliot, but Mary Anne kept her secret (she didn't even tell Blackwood until February of 1858). In October of 1857 she began work on Adam Bede. The Leweses spent the middle of that year in Munich, Vienna, and Dresden. Mary Anne continued to work on Adam Bede while they were abroad, and finished it in September of 1858, shortly after their return to England. When Adam Bede made it into print, the critics praised the book highly. It was a sensational success. Even Queen Victoria loved it. And the public still had no idea who George Eliot was!

Mary Anne's private life afforded her much joy. She and George were very happy together. He was constantly looking to protect her from her friends and critics alike. In 1859, they purchased their first home: Holly Lodge at Southfields. By this time the secret of George Eliot's identity wasn't very secret. Herbert Spencer and John Chapman had informed many of the members of the literary circle in London that George Eliot was none other than the unprepossessing Mary Anne Lewes. When the truth about George Eliot's identity was firmly established, Blackwood balked at publishing Mary Anne's new novel, The Mill on the Floss. He feared that the controversy surrounding Mary Anne's life with Lewes would keep it from selling. Eventually Blackwood did publish the novel with George Eliot appearing on the title page, and when the book came out, it was a success despite all the worry about the controversial nature of Mary Anne's relationship with Lewes.

Finding their country home too far from town, the Leweses moved back to London in late 1860. Mary Anne became depressed in her new surroundings. Not even George could revive her spirits. Mary Anne attributed much of her depression to the social ridicule she felt. Since she had become famous, her private life with George Lewes had become public business. While the public adored her novels, they often criticized her personally for her defiance of the marriage convention. She resented the fact that she was seen as a violator of the marriage vow while George's unfaithful wife, Agnes, appeared a long-suffering victim. In such a social climate, the Leweses received few visitors (they could count the number of their female visitors on one hand). Rufa Hennell, the first woman to call on the Leweses, also became the first to invite them to dinner. However, the greater part of their social circle remained male, even as it widened with Eliot's increasing fame.

In April of 1861, after the publication of Silas Marner, Mary Anne left for Italy to begin research for her next novel, Romola, to be set in fifteenth century Florence. Mary Anne researched furiously — she often fell into depression because of self-doubt and the overwhelming nature of the task before her. In May of 1862, she accepted an offer from George Smith to publish the novel serially in the Cornhill Magazine. Serial publication proved problematic for Mary Anne, who was very sensitive about her work and easily disturbed by the reviews that came out on earlier parts of her work while she was working on the later ones. Lewes eventually began to suppress almost all negative commentary from his wife. He knew that such negativism would stall her writing, as she was still given to bouts of depression, so he offered her only the good. This policy of Lewes has often been blamed for the "abstruseness" of Eliot's later novels, but without it, she very likely would not have written at all—she certainly was no longer in need of money, having earned nearly ?16,000.

As Eliot's fame increased and her renown grew, her social circle continued to widen. The more popular Eliot's novels grew, the more accepting London society became of her relationship with Lewes. Mary Anne's family continued their silence, but it is apparent that they, too, read her novels and found them worthy of the sister they remembered. Her siblings probably would have been surprised to know how conservative Mary Anne had become by this time, in spite of her unconventional love of Lewes. Mary Anne began serious work on Middlemarch in 1869, though she'd been thinking about this "English novel" for years. Progress was slow, but it was published by Blackwood in parts from 1871-2. The novel was a success with the public. If George Eliot was famous before, she was doubly famous after the publication of Middlemarch.

She was also very rich. Once socially ostracized, now the couple could not get away from a constant stream of visitors. Their dream was to move out into the country so that they could spend time alone with one another as in the old days. They searched for the perfect house for four years without ever finding a permanent residence. By 1876, the public seemed to have forgotten the unofficial marriage status of its beloved author, George Eliot. There were even rumors that her marriage had been made official by the death of Agnes Lewes, but they were false. Agnes was alive and well in Kensington. In 1874, Mary Anne began work on what would be her final novel, Daniel Deronda.

Mary Anne's old fears about the worth of what she was doing returned. She hoped desperately that she was not just "adding to the heap of books". As usual, Lewes did his best to comfort her. Illness followed depression. Mary Anne began to suffer from kidney stones in February of 1874—the pain would plague her until her death. Daniel Deronda came out in 1876. Mary Anne's health continued to falter, and her fame continued to grow. She was now regarded as "the greatest living English novelist". Her fans were wild about her; she received scores of letters from all over the world.

ALONE AGAIN

Eventually, the Leweses managed to stem the tide of visitors to their London home and only saw the few people that they wished to see. One person who was always invited on Sundays was John Cross, their business manager of sorts, whom they referred to as their "dear nephew." In November of 1876, John Cross found a lovely house for George and Mary Anne, and they finally had the country home of which they had been dreaming. They enjoyed their new home immensely, finding their frequent walks in the countryside "so much better than Society!"

In mid-1878, Lewes began to suffer from horrible cramps every night. Though he did not know it at the time, it was a sign of serious illness. The cramps continued to plague him and the attacks were coming more and more often, but he maintained his high spirits, concealing the seriousness of his illness. By November, he could no longer conceal his agony and Mary Anne wrote, "I have a deep sense of change within, and of a permanently closer companionship with death". Mary Anne was right, by the end of the month, her lifelong partner and support was dead. He passed away at their home in London on November 30, 1878. Mary Anne did not leave her room for a week, and did not go to the funeral. She could bear to see no one. Cross pressed her to accept him as a visitor, fearing that too long of a solitude might prove fatal to Mary Anne. She refused, writing on February 7, 1879, "each day seems a new beginning—a new acquaintance with grief". She finally saw him on February 23.

Mary Anne began the task of completing Lewes's unfinished Problems of Life and Mind and decided to establish a trust in his name, the George Henry Lewes Studentship in Physiology. She saw Cross often as he was still helping her to manage her finances. In March, she began to see other friends as well. She and Cross grew closer — they began to read Dante together. In August of 1879, Cross hinted for the first time that he wished to be more than a friend. That November, Mary Anne turned 60 and faced the one-year anniversary of Lewes's death. She still mourned him.

Mary Anne finally accepted Cross's proposal of marriage (which had been extended three times) on April 9, 1880. Cross had just turned 40. The ceremony was in May of that year. In November, Mary Anne turned 61. On the evening of December 19, Mary Anne became suddenly ill. She was diagnosed as having laryngitis, and the doctor saw no cause for worry. A few days later her kidney problem began to bother her again, and she was in much pain. With little warning, she passed away at ten o'clock, the night of December 22, 1880. Her new husband was left alone after only seven months of marriage. Mary Anne was buried in Highgate Cemetery, London, next to her spiritual husband George Lewes.

Chapter 2

Critical Analysis on George Eliot as a Victorian Writer

VICTORIAN PERIOD-A TIME OF CHANGE (1837 -1901)

The Victorian Period revolves around the political career of Queen Victoria. She was crowned in 1837 and died in 1901 (which put a definite end to her political career). A great deal of change took place during this period—brought about because of the Industrial Revolution; so it's not surprising that the literature of the period is often concerned with social reform.

As Thomas Carlyle (1795-1881) wrote, "The time for levity, insincerity, and idle babble and play-acting, in all kinds, is gone by; it is a serious, grave time." Of course, in the literature from this period, we see a duality, or double standard, between the concerns for the individual (the exploitation and corruption both at home and abroad) and national success—in what is often referred to as the Victorian Compromise. In reference to Tennyson, Browning and Arnold, E. D. H. Johnson argues: "Their writings... locate the centers of authority not in the existing social order but within the resources of individual being."

Against the backdrop of technological, political, and socioeconomic change, the Victorian Period was bound to be a volatile time, even without the added complications of the religious and institutional challenges brought by Charles Darwin and other thinkers, writers, and doers. The Period is often divided into two parts: the early Victorian Period (ending around 1870) and the late Victorian Period. Writers associated with the early period are: Alfred, Lord Tennyson (1809-1892), Robert Browning (1812-1889), Elizabeth Barrett Browning (1806-1861), Emily Bronte (1818-1848), Matthew Arnold (1822-1888), Dante Gabriel Rossetti (1828-1882), Christina Rossetti (1830-1894), George Eliot (1819-1880), Anthony Trollope (1815-1882) and Charles Dickens (1812-1870).Writers associated with the late Victorian Period include: George Meredith (1828-1909), Gerard Manley Hopkins (1844-1889), Oscar Wilde (1856-1900), Thomas Hardy (1840-1928), Rudyard Kipling (1865-1936), A.E. Housman (1859-1936), and Robert Louis Stevenson (1850-1894).

While Tennyson and Browning represented pillars in Victorian poetry, Dickens and Eliot contributed to the development of the English novel. Perhaps the most quintessentially Victorian poetic works of the period is: Tennyson's "In Memorium" (1850), which mourns the loss of his friend. Henry James describes Eliot's "Middlemarch" (1872) as "organized, moulded, balanced composition, gratifying the reader with the sense of design and construction."

It was a time of change, a time of great upheaval, but also a time of GREAT literature! The last completed period of English literature, almost coincident in extent with the reign of the queen whose name it bears (Victoria, queen 1837-1901), stands nearly beside The Elizabethan period in the significance and interest of its work. The Elizabethan literature to be sure, in its imaginative and spiritual enthusiasm, is the expression of a period more profoundly great than the Victorian; but the Victorian literature speaks for an age which witnessed incomparably greater changes than any that had gone before in all the conditions of life—material comforts, scientific knowledge, and, absolutely speaking, in intellectual and spiritual enlightenment.

Moreover, to twentieth century students the Victorian literature makes a specially strong appeal because it is in part the literature of our own time and its ideas and point of view are in large measure ours. We must begin by glancing briefly at some of the general determining changes and conditions to which reference has just been made, and we may naturally begin with the merely material ones. Before the accession of Queen Victoria the 'industrial revolution,' the vast development of manufacturing made possible in the latter part of the eighteenth century by the introduction of coal and the steam engine, had rendered England the richest nation in the world, and the movement continued with steadily accelerating momentum throughout the period. Hand in hand with it went the increase of population from less than thirteen millions in England in 1825 to nearly three times as many at the end of the period.

The introduction of the steam railway and the steamship, at the beginning of the period, in place of the lumbering stagecoach and the sailing vessel, broke up the old stagnant and stationary habits of life and increased the amount of travel at least a thousand times. The discovery of the electric telegraph in 1844 brought almost every important part of Europe, and eventually of the world, nearer to every town dweller than the nearest county had been in the eighteenth century; and the development of the modern newspaper out of the few feeble sheets of 1825 (dailies and weeklies in London, only weeklies elsewhere), carried full accounts of the doings of the whole world, in place of long-delayed fragmentary rumors, to every door within a few hours.

No less striking was the progress in public health and the increase in human happiness due to the enormous advance in the sciences of medicine, surgery, and hygiene. Indeed these sciences in their modern form virtually began with the discovery of the facts of bacteriology about 1860, and the use of antiseptics fifteen years later, and not much earlier began the effective opposition to the frightful epidemics which had formerly been supposed to be dependent only on the will of Providence.

Political and social progress, though less astonishing, was substantial. In 1830 England, nominally a monarchy, was in reality a plutocracy of about a hundred thousand men—landed nobles, gentry, and wealthy merchants—whose privileges dated back to fifteenth century conditions. The first Reform Bill, of 1832, forced on Parliament by popular pressure, extended the right of voting to men of the 'middle class,' and the subsequent bills of 1867 and 1885 made it universal for men.

Meanwhile the House of Commons slowly asserted itself against the hereditary House of Lords, and thus England became perhaps the most truly democratic of the great nations of the world. At the beginning of the period the social condition of the great body of the population was extremely bad. Laborers in factories and mines and on farms were largely in a state of virtual though not nominal slavery, living, many of them, in unspeakable moral and physical conditions. Little by little improvement came, partly by the passage of laws, partly by the growth of trades-unions. The substitution in the middle of the century of free-trade for protection through the passage of the 'Corn-Laws' afforded much relief by lowering the price of food.

Socialism, taking shape as a definite movement in the middle of the century, became one to be reckoned with before its close, though the majority of the more well-to-do classes failed to understand even then the growing necessity for far-reaching economic and social changes. Humanitarian consciousness, however, gained greatly during the period. The middle and upper classes awoke to some extent to their duty to the poor, and sympathetic benevolent effort, both organized and informal, increased very largely in amount and intelligence. Popular education, too, which in 1830 had no connection with the State and was in every respect very incomplete, was developed and finally made compulsory as regards the rudiments.

Still more permanently significant, perhaps, was the transformation of the former conceptions of the nature and meaning of the world and life, through the discoveries of science. Geology and astronomy now gradually compelled all thinking people to realise the unthinkable duration of the cosmic processes and the comparative littleness of our earth in the vast extent of the universe. Absolutely revolutionary, for almost all lines if thought was the gradual adoption by almost all thinkers of the theory of Evolution, which, partly formulated by Lamarck early in the century, received definite statement in 1859 in Charles Darwin's 'Origin of Species.' The great modification in the externals of religious belief thus brought about was confirmed also by the growth of the science of historical criticism.

This movement of religious change was met in its early stages by the very interesting reactionary 'Oxford' or 'Tractarian' Movement, which asserted the supreme authority of the Church and its traditional doctrines. The most important figure in this movement, who connects it definitely with literature, was John Henry Newman (1801-90), author of the hymn 'Lead, Kindly Light,' a man of winning personality and great literary skill. For fifteen years, as vicar of the Oxford University Church, Newman was a great spiritual force in the English communion, but the series of 'Tracts for the Times' to which he largely contributed, ending in 1841 in the famous Tract 90, tell the story of his gradual progress toward Rome.

Thereafter as an avowed Roman Catholic and head of a monastic establishment Newman showed himself a formidable controversialist, especially in a literary encounter with the clergyman-novelist Charles Kingsley which led to Newman's famous 'Apologia pro Vita Sua' (Apology for My Life), one of the secondary literary masterpieces of the century. His services to the Catholic Church were recognized in 1879 by his appointment as a Cardinal. More than one of the influences thus hastily surveyed combine in creating the moral, social, and intellectual strenuousness which is one of the main marks of the literature of the period.

More conspicuously than ever before the majority of the great writers, not least the poets and novelists, were impelled not merely by the emotional or dramatic creative impulse but by the sense of a message for their age which should broaden the vision and elevate the ideals of the masses of their fellows. The literature of the period, therefore, lacks the disinterested and joyous spontaneity of, for example, the Elizabethan period, and its mood is far more complex than that of the partly socially-minded pseudo-classicists. While all the new influences were manifesting themselves in Victorian literature they did not, of course, supersede the great general inherited tendencies.

This literature is in the main romantic. On the social side this should be evident; the Victorian social humanitarianism is merely the developed form of the eighteenth century romantic democratic impulse. On the esthetic side the romantic traits are also present, though not so aggressively as in the previous period; with romantic vigour the Victorian literature often combines exquisite classical finish; indeed, it is so eclectic and composite that all the definite older terms take on new and less sharply contrasting meanings when applied to it.

So long a period naturally falls into sub-divisions; during its middle part in particular, progress and triumphant romanticism, not yet largely attacked by scientific scepticism, had created a prevailing atmosphere of somewhat passive sentiment and optimism both in society and in literature which has given to the adjective 'mid-Victorian' a very definite denotation.

The adjective and its period are commonly spoken of with contempt in our own day by those persons who pride themselves on their complete sophistication and superiority to all intellectual and emotional weakness. But during the 'mid-Victorian' years, there was also a comparative healthiness in the lives of the well-to-do classes and in literature which had never before been equalled and which may finally prove no less praiseworthy than the rather self-conscious freedom and unrestraint of the early twentieth century. The most important literature of the whole period falls under the three heads of essays, poetry, and prose fiction, which we may best consider in that order.

Victorian writer, a humane freethinker, whose insightful psychological novels paved way to modern character portrayals-contemporary of Dostoevsky (1821-1881), who at the same time in Russia developed similar narrative techniques. Eliot's liaison with the married writer and editor George Henry Lewes arise among the rigid Victorians much indignation, which calmed down with the progress of her literary fame.

"Marriage, which has been the bourne of so many narratives, is still a great beginning, as it was to Adam and Eve, who kept their honeymoon in Eden, but had their first little one among the thorns and thistles of the wilderness. It is still the beginning of the home epic-the gradual conquest or irremediable loss of that complete union which makes the advancing years as a climax, and age the harvest of sweet memories in common."

Mary Ann Evans (George Eliot) was born in Chilvers Coton, Warwickshire. Her father was a carpenter who rose to be a land agent. When she was a few months old, the family moved to Griff, a 'cheerful red-brick, ivory-covered house', and there Eliot spent 21 years of his life among people that he later depicted in her novels.

She was educated at home and in several schools, and developed a strong evangelical piety at Mrs. Wallington's School at Neneaton. However, later Eliot rejected her dogmatic faith. When her mother died in 1836, she took charge of the family household. In 1841 she moved with her father to Coventry, where she lived with him until his death in 1849. During this time she met Charles Bray, a free-thinking Coventry manufacturer. His wife, Caroline (Cara) was the sister of Charles Hennel, the author of a work entitled An Inquiry Concerning the Origin of Christianity (1838).

The reading of this and other rationalistic works influenced deeply Eliot's thoughts. After her father's death, Eliot travelled around Europe. She settled in London and took up work as subeditor of Westminster Review. In Coventry she met Charles Bray and later Charles Hennell, who introduced her to many new religious and political ideas. Under Eliot's control the Westminster Review enjoyed success. She became the centre of a literary circle, one of whose members was George Henry Lewes, who would be her companion until his death in 1878.

Lewes's wife was mentally unbalanced and she had already had two children by another man. In 1854 Eliot went to Germany with Lewes. Their unconventional union caused some difficulties because Lewes was still married and he was unable to obtain divorce. Eliot did not inform her close friends Caroline and Sarah Hennell about her decision to live with Lewes-the both friends were shocked and angry because she had not trusted them.

Eliot's first collection of tales, Scenes of Clerical Life, appeared in 1858 under the pseudonym George Eliot-in those days writing was considered to be a male profession. It was followed by her first novel, Adam Bede, a tragic love story in which the model for the title character was Eliot's father. He was noted for his great physical strength, which enabled him to carry loads that three average men could barely handle. When impostors claimed authorship of Adam Bede, it was revealed that Marian Evans, the Westminster reviewer, was George Eliot. The book was a brilliant success. Her other major works include The Mill on the Floss (1860), a story of destructive family relations, and Silas Marner (1861). Silas Marner, a linen-weaver, has accumulated a goodly sum of gold. He was falsely judged guilty of theft 15 years before and left his community. Squire Cass' son Dunstan steals Marner's gold and disappears.

Marner takes care of an orphaned little girl, Eppie and she becomes for him more precious than the lost property. Sixteen years later the skeleton of Dunstan and Marner's gold is found. Godfrey Cass, Dunstal's brother, admits that he is the father of Eppie. He married the girl's mother, opium-ridden Molly Farren secretly before hear death. Eppie and Silas Marner don't wish to separate when Godfrey tries to adopt the girl. In the end Eppie marries Aaron Winthorp, who accepts Silas Marner as part of the household.

Middlemarch (1871-72), her greatest novel, was probably inspired by her life at Coventry. The story follows the sexual and intellectual frustrations of Dorothea Brooke. Eliot weaves into her story other narrative lines, which offer a sad comment upon human aspirations.

Among Eliot's translation works are D.F. Strauss's Das Leben Jesu kritisch bearbeitet (published anonymously in

1846), Ludwig Feuerbach's Das Wesen des Christentum, and Spinoza's Ethics (unpublished). Eliot's thoughts of religion were considered at that time advanced. When she visited Cambridge University in 1873 and discussed with F.W.H. Mayers of "the words of God, Immortality, and Duty", she pronounced "with terrible earnestness how inconceivable was the first, how unbelievable was the second, and yet how peremptory and absolute the third." Middlemarch is a novel of English provincial life in the early nineteenth century, just before the Reform Bill of 1832. The book was called by the famous American writer Henry James a 'treasure-house of detail.' It fuses several stories and characters, creating a a network of parallels and contrasts.

One of Eliot's main concerns is the way which the past moulds the present and the attempts of various characters to control the future. Harold Bloom has noted in The Western Canon (1994) the implicit but clear relation of the work to Dante's Comedy. Dorothea, an idealistic young woman, marries the pedantic Casaubon.

After his death she marries Will Ladislaw, Casaubon's young cousin, a vaguely artistic outsider. Doctor Tertius Lydgate is trapped with the egoistic Rosamond Vincy, the town's beauty. Lydgate becomes involved in a scandal, and he dies at 50, his ambitions frustrated. Other characters are Bulstrode, a banker and a religious hypocrite, Mary Garth, the practical daughter of a land agent, and Fred Vincy, the son of the mayor of Middlemarch. For modern feminist readers Middlemarch has been a disappointment: Dorothea was not prepared to give up marriage. "'I know that I must expect trials, uncle.

Marriage is a state of higher duties, I never thought of it as mere personal ease,' said poor Dorothea." However, Eliot's lament for Dorothea left no doubts about her views: "Some have felt that these blundering lives are due to the inconvenient indefiniteness with which the Supreme Power has fashioned the nature of women: if there were one level of feminine incompetence as strict as the ability to count three and no more, the social lot of women might be treated with scientific certitude. Meanwhile the indefiniteness remains, the limits of variation are really much wider than any one would imagine from the sameness of women's coiffure and the favourite love stories in prose and verse."-The book is required reading in university English courses. In 1860-61 Eliot spent some time in Italy collecting material for her historical romance Romola.

It was published serially first in the Cornhill Magazine and in book form in 1863. Henry James considered it the finest thing she wrote, "but its defects are almost on the scale of its beauties." In 1871 she mentioned to Alexander Main: "I have the conviction that excessive literary production is a social offence." When Harriet Beecher Stowe wrote admiringly of Silas Marner in 1869 Eliot began a correspondence with her.

In a letter from 1876 she wrote about Daniel Deronda (1876): "As to the Jewish element in 'Deronda', I expected from first to last in writing it, that it would create much stronger resistance and even repulsion than it has actually met with. But precisely because I felt that the usual attitude of Christians towards Jews is-I hardly know whether to say more impious or more stupid when viewed in the light of their professed principles, I therefore felt urged to treat Jews with such sympathy and understanding as my nature and knowledge could attain to.

Moreover, not only towards the Jews, but towards all oriental peoples with whom we English come in contact, a spirit of arrogance and contemptuous dictatorialness is observable which has become a national disgrace to us."

After Lewes's death Eliot married twenty years younger friend, John Cross, an American banker, on May 6, 1880. They made a trip to Italy and according to a story, he jumped in Venice from their hotel balcony into the Grand Canal. After honeymoon they returned to London, where she died of a kidney ailment on the same year on December 22. Cross never married again.

In her will she expressed her wish to be buried in Westminster Abbey, but Dean Stanley of Westminster Abbey rejected the idea and Eliot was buried in Highgate Cemetery.

Eliot's interest in the interior life of human beings, moral problems and strains, anticipated the narrative methods of modern literature.

D.H. Lawrence once wrote: "It was really George Eliot who started it all. It was she started putting action inside." The young Henry James described her "magnificently, awe-inspiringly ugly," but also studied her work carefully, critically, and acknowledged her greatness as a writer: "What is remarkable, extraordinary-and the process remains inscrutable and mysterious-is that this quiet, anxious, sedentary, serious, invalidical English lady, without animal spirits, without adventures, without extravagance, assumption, or bravado, should have made us believe that nothing in the world was alien to her; should have produced such rich, deep, masterly pictures of the multifold life of man." (Henry James in The Atlantic monthly, May 1885)

Chapter 3

George Eliot and Visual Arts

Landscape and landscape painting afforded George Eliot great visual pleasure and spiritual refreshment. Her enjoyment and careful study of natural appearances found full expression in her novels, impelled by personal feeling and summoned by a tradition of landscape description that had become established in British and American fiction in the time of Mrs. Radcliffe, Scott, and Fenimore Cooper.1 Eliot's responsiveness to landscape views in fiction may be seen in her appreciation of Charles Kingsley's "scene-painting" in Alton Locke, Yeast, and Westward Hoer own vision of landscape combined several important eighteenth- and nineteenth-century traditions. The cult of the picturesque and the English school of topographical painting, both of which had reached their prime in the eighteenth century, were second-nature to George Eliot in her perception and description of country scenes.

But she was also profoundly influenced by three nineteenth-century developments in landscape sensibility, each of which came to her in part through the work of Ruskin: the cult of detailed naturalism, which Ruskin advocated and the Pre-Raphaelites practiced; the nature poetry of Wordsworth, which Ruskin echoed in many parts of Modern Painters; and the moral critique of the cult of the picturesque, which finds its classic formulation in volume IV of Modern Painters To explore these five aspects of George Eliot's landscape vision is the purpose of the present chapter.

Several of the traditions just mentioned work together harmoniously in the following passage of Middlemarch:

The ride to Stone Court, which Fred and Rosamond took

the next morning, lay through a pretty bit of midland landscape almost all meadows and pastures, with hedgerows still allowed to grow in bushy beauty and to spread out coral fruit for the birds.

Little details gave each field a particular physiognomy, dear to the eyes that have looked on them from childhood: the pool in the corner where the grasses were dank and trees leaned whisperingly; the great oak shadowing a bare place in midpasture; the high bank where the ash-trees grew; the sudden slope of the old marl-pit making a red background for the burdock; the huddled roofs and ricks of the homestead without a traceable way of approach; the grey gate and fences against the depths of the bordering wood; and the stray hovel, its old thatch full of mossy hills and valleys with wondrous modulations of light and shadow such as we travel far to see in later life, and see larger, but not more beautiful.

These are the things that make the gamut of joy in landscape to midland-bred souls — the things they toddled among, or perhaps learned by heart standing between their father's knees while he drove leisurely. The narrator here is in part a Gilpinesque tourist, in search of the picturesque in all its roughness, variegation, chiaroscuro, and suggestive antiquity ("old, old thatch full of mossy hills and valleys with wondrous modulations of light and shadow such as we travel far to see in later life").

But there is also an element of Ruskinian naturalistic precision in the description of individual features in the landscape, the "little details" that give "each field a particular — physiognomy" such as "the great oak shadowing a bare place in mid-pasture." And finally there is a Wordsworthian emphasis upon the "joy" that such landscape brings in maturity to those who have grown up amidst it.

All these tones are characteristic of the George Eliot landscape, which we may now examine in greater detail. "The power of description, both of scenery and of character... may be very puissant in the hands of a fine writer, gifted with a real sense of the picturesque," G. H. Lewes argued in "The Novels of Jane Austen". The cult of the picturesque grew up in the late eighteenth century, making it fashionable to travel in search of landscape views that compose themselves pictorially. The models for such views derived in part from the neoclassical heroic landscapes of Claude Lorrain and the Poussins, in part from the wilder, more dramatic visions of Salvator Rosa, and in part from the leafy, aqueous, rock-strewn country scenes of Ruisdael, Hobbema, and other seventeenth-century Dutch painters.

William Gilpin's initial definition of the picturesque in 1768 as "that peculiar kind of beauty which is agreeable in a picture" was refined by a complex debate in the 1790s and early 1800s to mean a kind of aesthetic effect which is neither awesomely sublime nor smoothly beautiful but a blend of those two extremes distinguished by roughness, variety, sudden contrast, chiaroscuro, signs of age or decay, and a power to stimulate in the viewer a piquant mixture of painful and pleasurable impressions and associations.

The coming of Romanticism modified but did not extinguish the cult of the picturesque. Christopher Hussey is more right than not when he asserts that "the picturesque became the nineteenth century's mode of vision" (It was certainly a natural mode for George Eliot, whose letters and journals are full of descriptions in the Gilpin tradition. Italy in 1860 showed her "Claude-like scenes of mountains, trees, and meadows, with picturesque accidents of building, such as single round towers, on the heights" Biarritz in 1867 seemed to G. H. Lewes, and doubtless to Eliot as well, "so picturesque that it may be called a succession of Prouts".

Switzerland in 1860 was mediated through the novelist's prior experience of Alexandre Calame's landscape painting. Except for ruins, the valley of Bercka near Weimar in 1854 had all the necessary ingredients of the picturesque:

The hanging woods — the soft colouring and graceful outline of the uplands-the village with its roofs and spire of a reddish violet hue, muffled in luxuriant trees — the white Kurhaus glittering on a grassy slope — the avenue of poplars contrasting its pretty primness with the wild bushy outline of the wood-covered hill, which rises abruptly from the smooth, green meadows — the clear winding stream, now sparkling in the sun, now hiding itself under soft grey willows — all this makes an enchanting picture. Returning from Germany in 1855, the ardent tourist found a charming English landscape at Dover: "As I walked up the Castle hill this afternoon, the town, with its background of softly rounded hills shrouded in sleepy haze, its little lines of water looking golden in the sun, made a charming picture". Jersey in 1857 offered a feast for the wandering eye, and a stroll along the banks of the Trent near Newark in 1868 brought "some charming quiet pictures — Frith landscapes".

In 1879, less than two years before her death, Eliot sought to pass on her taste for the picturesque to young Blanche Southwood Lewes, who had just celebrated her seventh birthday with a visit to an exhibition and a boat ride on the Thames: "I am sure you must have liked being on the river in the steamboat for the first time. The wide river, and the bridges, and the great buildings that can be seen a long way by the waterside, are all very beautiful, are they not? It would seem to you like another and grander sort of picture, after seeing the small pictures on the wall at the Exhibition". Eliot wanted Blanche's vision to be shaped and enriched, as hers was, by the experience of pictures. Eliot's novels, from the start to the finish of her career, abound with picturesque descriptions in an eighteenth-century vein. She was especially fond of "pretty bits of midland landscape" like the one quoted above from Middlemarch. Here is another representative "bit," this time from Felix Holt.

The Rectory was on the other side of the river, close to the church of which it was the fitting companion: a fine old brick and-stone house, with a great bow-window opening from the library on to the deep-turfed lawn, one fat dog sleeping on the door-stone, another fat dog waddling on the gravel, the autumn leaves duly swept away, the lingering chrysanthemums cherished, tall trees stooping or soaring in the most picturesque variety, and a Virginian creeper turning a little rustic hut into a scarlet pavilion. After reading a similar description of a parsonage and farm in "Mr. Gilfil's Love-

Story," John Blackwood wrote to George Eliot: "The picture reminds me strongly of the genuine English rural landscapes with which we are all familiar on canvas or in nature". Blackwood's was precisely the sort of response Eliot wanted her language in such passages to elicit. The convention of the Gilpinesque tourist-guide may help to account for the anonymous observer who opens so many of George Eliot's stories, mediating between author, reader, and action.

The horseback traveller in Adam Bede, the armchair dreamer in The Mill on the Floss, the Florentine shade in Romola, and the stagecoach passenger in Felix Holt are visitors or revisitors on holiday, having no business in the scene except to appreciate it. They make a Gilpinesque discrimination of landscape and figures, and disappear as soon as they have drawn the reader into engagement with the prospect (though the traveller in Adam Bede does reappear later in the novel as the magistrate who helps Dinah gain admission to Hetty's prison cell). They are guides and tutors, demonstrating the quality of perception that the reader must learn to apply to the world within the novel.

Though it came so naturally to her, Eliot knew that the picturesque way of seeing has its dangers. For one thing, it can become facile and overgeneralized. She did not favour the Claudian technique, often imitated by Gilpin in his sketches of Wales and the Lake District, of reconstructing an actual landscape according to an ideal model; see Barbier, George Eliot's distaste for Claudian techniques1 may account for her inability to admire Karl Rottmann's Greek landscapes, which she saw at Munich in 1858. She preferred a sense of unique place and abundant local detail in landscape descriptions. From this preference stems her critique of Tom Tulliver's drawing lessons in The Mill on the Floss.

Tom found, to his disgust, that his new drawing-master gave him no dogs and donkeys to draw, but brooks and rustic bridges and ruins, all with a general softness of black-lead surface, indicating that nature, if anything, was rather satiny; and as Tom's feeling for the picturesque in landscape was at present quite latent, it is not surprising that Mr. Goodrich's productions seemed to him an uninteresting form of art... Tom learned to make an extremely fine point to his pencil, and to represent landscape with a "broad generality," which, doubtless from a narrow tendency in his mind to details, he thought extremely dull.

A broad generality in which no characteristic details can be discerned was not George Eliot's idea of a good landscape style. The picturesque must be tempered by the naturalistic. We shall see that in Adam Bede, as in Modern Painters, Claudian ideal landscape is something of a villain. George Eliot's taste for the representation of actual places shows itself in her imitation of eighteenth-century topographical painting, especially in her descriptions of English country houses and their grounds. John Steegman has shown how the bird's-eye perspective and diagrammatic cartography of early country-house portraits gave way in the eighteenth century to a lower viewpoint, a placing of the house itself in the middle or far distance, and a bringing forward of human and/or animal groups into the intervening space.

Engraved views of noblemen's and gentlemen's country seats were especially popular between 1760 and 1840. J. P. Neale's six-volume set, published between 1818 and 1823, had a standard pictorial format that can be characterized in the words of John Dixon Hunt: "The typical English landscape garden as generally visualized would consist of undulating grass that leads somewhere down to an irregularly shaped piece of water over which a bridge arches, of trees grouped casually, with cattle or deer, about the slopes, and of houses and other buildings glimpsed in the middle or far distance". When Phillipe Mercier, a transplanted imitator of Watteau, began around 1725 to make the figures in the foreground into portraits, he initiated a special and highly influential form of semitopographical English conversation piece which depicts "family groups in their proper setting, that is in their own park or garden, with a sight of the family home in the background."

Eliot's skill at country-house portraiture may be seen in her descriptions of Hall Farm and the Chase in Adam Bede, of

Transome Court in Felix Holt, and of Offendene, Brackenshaw Park, the Abbey, Diplow, and Gadsmere in Daniel Deronda. A favourite and recurring form of architecture in her novels is a plain red-brick structure built in the Queen Anne period, sometimes adjoining the ruins of a medieval abbey. The gables, windows, and doors are ornamented with limestone, but the contrast between the limestone and the brick is diminished by the growth of a powdery, greenish-grey lichen. A flowery lawn cut by graveled, often tree-lined walks or driveways runs from the house to a plantation of trees which nearly surround the house or screen it on the north.

The plantation frequently contains Scotch firs, while one or two large firs or cedars or beeches may stand immediately adjacent to the house. If the estate is landscaped, the garden is in the picturesque style, with rolling lawns, man-made lakes, serpentine paths, clumps of trees, and perhaps an occasional glimpse of a white temple. Eliot's affection for "grounds, which are laid out with a taste worthy of a first-rate landscape gardener" was expressed in her early descriptions of the Belvedere gardens at Weimar. Eliot's most elaborate country-house portrait is of the neo-Gothic Cheverel Manor in "Mr. Gilfil's Love-Story." Here the topographical element is very strong; for, as Margharita Laski has said, "Cheverel Manor is photographically Arbury Hall," the Newdigate family seat in Warwickshire near which George Eliot grew up.

Her description is also a full-fledged conversation piece, beginning with close-up portraits of Caterina Sarti and Lady Cheverel, and then placing the sitters in their habitat:

they sat down, making two bright patches of red and white and blue on the green background of the laurels and the lawn, which would look none the less pretty in a picture because one of the women's hearts was rather cold and the other rather sad. And a charming picture Cheverel Manor would have made that evening, if some English Watteau had been there to paint it: the castellated house of grey-tinted stone, with the flickering sunbeams sending dashes of golden light across the many-shaped panes in the mullioned windows, and a great beech leaning athwart one of the flanking towers, and breaking, with its dark flattened boughs, the too formal symmetry of the front; the broad gravel-walk winding on the right, by a row of tall pines, alongside the pool-on the left branching out among swelling grassy mounds, surmounted by clumps of trees, where the red trunk of the Scotch fir glows in the descending sunlight against the bright green of limes and acacias; the great pool, where a pair of swans are swimming lazily with one leg tucked under a wing, and where the open water-lilies lie calmly accepting the kisses of the fluttering light-sparkles; the lawn, with its smooth emerald greenness, sloping down to the rougher and browner herbage of the park, from which it is invisibly fenced by a little stream that winds away from the pool, and disappears under the wooden bridge in the distant pleasure-ground; and on this lawn our two ladies, whose part in the landscape the painter, standing at a favourable point of view in the park, would represent with a few little dabs of red and white and blue.

Eliot's sensitivity to colour is evident here, and the reference to an "English Watteau" is entirely apt since, as we have noted, Watteau's fêtes galantes were the immediate predecessors of Mercier's pioneering English conversation pieces.l4 Eliot even includes the artist in her scene, as Mercier did in his seminal Viscount Tyrconnel with His Family in the Grounds of Belton House. When the narrator moves inside Cheverel Manor to describe the dining-room and saloon, we seem to be observing two of Joseph Nash's views of The Mansions of England in the Olden Time (1839-49), staffed by figures in Georgian instead of Tudor or Restoration costume. What Neale had done for the exteriors of country houses, Nash did for their interiors, by publishing detailed engravings of their great halls, drawing-rooms, parlors, bay windows, galleries, bedchambers, staircases, porches, and chapels. Again, however, Eliot's description combines view-painting with portraiture, turning the picture into a conversation piece. She presents informal portraits of Sir Christopher Cheverel and Anthony Wybrow, surrounded by the architecture which is Sir Christopher's proudest domestic achievement.

George Eliot's penchant for topographical specificity in

landscape also took a form that was more characteristic of the nineteenth century than of the eighteenth. Her passion for precise naturalistic detail was kindled by the teachings of Ruskin, the practice of the Pre-Raphaelite painters, and the scientific researches of G. H. Lewes. After reading the third volume of Modern Painters in February of 1856 and reviewing it in April, Eliot spent May and June at llfracombe on the north coast of Devon, where Lewes was conducting the fieldwork in marine biology that eventually led to the publication of his Sea-Side Studies (1858).

Art and science were in perfect harmony during these happy months. The picturesque took on an ecological dimension:

From this end of the Capstone we have an admirable bit for a picture. In the background rises old Hillsborough jutting far into the sea-rugged and rocky as it fronts the waves, green and accessible landward; in front of this stands Lantern Hill, a picturesque mass of green and grey surmounted by an old bit of building that looks as if it were the habitation of some mollusk that had secreted its shell from the material of the rock; and quite in the foreground, contrasting finely in colour with the rest, are some lower perpendicular rocks, of dark brown tints patched here and there with vivid green. In hilly districts, where houses and clusters of houses look so tiny against the huge limbs of Mother Earth one cannot help thinking of man as a parasitic animal — an epizoon making his abode on the skin of the planetary organism.

It is difficult to know whether these words came originally from George Eliot or from Lewes, since they appear almost verbatim in Sea-Side Studies. But the ideas were in any case shared. Man, the figure in the landscape, becomes a mollusk or epizoon when viewed from a biological perspective. Ruskin's mixture of science and aesthetics was very much in Eliot's mind at llfracombe, as a letter sent from there to Barbara Leigh Smith suggests: "What books his last two are! I think he is the finest writer living".

She must have been thinking in part of Ruskin's defence of the naturalistic landscapes of the Pre-Raphaelite painters:

I have talked of the Ilfracombe lanes without describing them, for to describe them one ought to know the names of all the lovely wild flowers that cluster on their banks. Almost every yard of these banks is a "Hunt" picture — a delicious crowding of mosses and delicate trefoil, and wild strawberries, and ferns great and small. But the crowning beauty of the lanes is the springs, that gush out in little recesses by the side of the road — recesses glossy with liverwort and feathery with fern... I never before longed so much to know names of things as during this visit to llfracombe. The desire is part of the tendency that is now constantly growing in me to escape from all vagueness and inaccuracy into the daylight of distinct, vivid ideas. The mere fact of naming an object tends to give definiteness to our conception of it — we have then a sign that at once calls up in our minds the distinctive qualities which mark out for us that particular object from all others.

The "Hunt" mentioned here could be either William Henry ("Bird's Nest") Hunt, who had tutored Barbara Leigh Smith, or William Holman Hunt, whose landscape in The Hireling Shepherd Eliot had already praised for its "marvelous truthfulness". Both Hunts practiced a painstaking realism, and their treatment of vegetation made a lasting impression upon the novelist, who sought an equivalent precision in her own medium. She had been accustomed to think of "attention to vegetation as one of the most remarkable characteristics of the Pre-Raphaelite painters" by the essay on "Pre-Raphaelitism in Art and Literature" which she read and praised in the 1852 British Quarterly Review.

In his review of Modern Painters, volume IV, Lewes defined "the ideal of a pre-Raphaelite landscape" as "isolating one part of the landscape, and thus concentrating attention on it alone". This formulation was prompted by an experience he and George Eliot had in the Belvedere gardens at Weimar. Walking through the park, they came upon a set of "large glass globes of different colours" placed upon an artificial rock. "It is wonderful to see with what minute perfection the scenery around is painted in these globes," Eliot wrote. "Each is like a pre-Raffaelite picture, with every little detail of gravely walk, mossy bank, and delicately-leaved, interlacing boughs, presented in accurate miniature". The eighteenth-century connoisseur of the picturesque had composed his landscapes in a special mirror known as a Claude glass.

But George Eliot's equivalent of the Claude glass isolated "every little detail" for special attention, heightening what Mario Praz in Mnemosyne has called the "microscopic structure" of represented reality. Pre-Raphaelite attention to natural detail helped to shape George Eliot's technique of landscape description. The Huntian treatment of vegetation especially influenced her rendering of the hedgerows that she considered the most distinctive feature of the English midlands landscape.

In the following passage from Felix Holt, the precise botanical naming imitates the Hunts' leaf-by-leaf drawing:

But everywhere the bushy hedgerows wasted the land with their straggling beauty, shrouded the grassy borders of the pastures with catkined hazels, and tossed their long blackberry branches on the corn-fields. Perhaps they were white with May, or starred with palepink dog-roses; perhaps the urchins were already nutting amongst them, or gathering the plenteous crabs.

It was worth the journey only to see those hedgerows, the liberal homes of unremarkable beauty — of the purple-blossomed ruby-berried nightshade, of the wild convolvulus climbing and spreading in tendrilled strength till it made a great curtain of pale-green hearts and white trumpets, of the many-tubed honeysuckle which, in its most delicate fragrance, hid a charm more subtle and penetrating than beauty. Even if it were winter the hedgerows showed their coral, the scarlet haws, the deep-crimsoned hips, with lingering brown leaves to make a resting-place for the jewels of the hoar-frost.

These hedgerows reappear in Adam Bede and Middlemarch, where George Eliot's prose again follows the principle laid down at Ilfracombe: to describe them one ought to know the names of all the lovely wild flowers that cluster on their banks." Passages like these inspired Ruskinian praises from at least one of George Eliot's contemporaries: "Marian

Evans does really good landscape sketching, of an intensely truthful character"] Yet Eliot's strong local attachment to her native midlands scenery is due neither to the cult of the picturesque nor to the cult of outdoor naturalism. Rather it shows the Wordsworthian side of her landscape sensibility. "I am afraid you despise landscape painting," she wrote to an early correspondent, "but to me even the works of our own Stanfield and Roberts and Creswick bring a whole world of thought and bliss — 'a sense of something far more deeply interfused.'

The ocean and the sky and the everlasting hills are spirit to me, and they will never be robbed of their sublimity" This is the voice of a young person who has been reading the early volumes of Modern Painters in conjunction with "Tintern Abbey" and mediating her Wordsworthian responses to landscape through the vision of the landscape painter. The enthusiasm was by no means temporary, for in her maturity George Eliot continued to pair Ruskin with Wordsworth and to draw inspiration from the association. "The two last volumes of Modern Painters," she wrote in 1858, "contain, I think, some of the finest writing of this age. He is strongly akin to the sublimest part of Wordsworth, whom, by the bye, we are reading now with fresh admiration for his beauties and tolerance for his faults".

Eliot read Wordsworth often from 1839 till the end of her life. As she indicated in "Impressions of Theophrastus Such," she felt a considerable affinity of temperament with the great poet: "And I often smile at my consciousness that certain conservative prepossessions have mingled themselves for me with the influences of our midland scenery, from the tops of the elms down to the buttercups and the little wayside vetches". This vocabulary of influences, mingling, and prepossessions reflects the change Wordsworth had wrought in the literary representation of landscape. Wordsworth "began in the picturesque," as J. R. Watson has noted.The early poem, "An Evening Walk," continues a tradition of loco-descriptive poetry that descends from John Denham and James Thomson. But as early as "Descriptive Sketches), Wordsworth began to grow restless with the picturesque apprehension of nature, and to evolve a new sense of landscape which placed greater emphasis upon the affective and experiential interchange between the observer and the scene.

The Wordsworthian observer is in fl the landscape and part of it, rather than separated from it by an aesthetic distance. He is more concerned to render the emotional impact of the outdoor setting, the sense of its total presence, than to distinguish and analyse its constituent parts. The landscape affects him in a diffuse but profound and permanent manner, creating in his memory an "obscure sense/Of possible sublimity" which is a source of both joy and moral strength in later years.28 This complex sense of an environment that functions in many ways as a deity was immensely congenial to George Eliot. "I never before met with so many of my own feelings, expressed just as I could like them," she declared shortly after reading Wordsworth in 1839.

Having originated in a reaction against the picturesque tradition, the mature Wordsworthian mode is essentially nonpictorial. As Christopher Salvesen has noted Wordsworth is always much more aware of the presence of landscape, of its surrounding influence, than of any pictorial qualities it might have... the fundamental landscape of his best poetry is not at all detailed: the unifying force of nature is what creates it and holds it together, and this force is conveyed by Wordsworth's emotion rather than by his observation. He responds to a landscape rather than observes it: he feels it, almost, rather than sees.

The absence of pictorial qualities in Wordsworth's best poetry undermines most critical attempts to compare it with painting; see, for example, Kroeber and the critical review by E. D. H. Johnson. The distinction Salvesen is making could be illustrated by the well-known comparison between "I Wandered Lonely as a Cloud" and Dorothy Wordsworth's far more particularized journal description of the same field of daffodils (Nabholtz).

The distinction may also be illustrated by two passages from George Eliot:

Janet's way thither lay for a little while along the highroad, and then led her into a deep-rutted lane, which wound through a flat tract of meadow and pasture, while in front lay smoky Paddiford, and away to the left the mother-town of Milby. There was no line of silvery willows marking the course of a stream — no group of Scotch firs with their trunks reddening in the level sunbeams — nothing to break the flowerless monotony of grass and hedgerow but an occasional oak or elm, and a few cows sprinkled here and there. -

A very commonplace scene, indeed. But what scene was ever commonplace in the descending sunlight, when colour has awakened from its noonday sleep, and the long shadows awe us like a disclosed presence? Above all, what scene is commonplace to the eye that is filled with serene gladness, and brightens all things with its own joy? And Janet just now was very happy. And the mill with its booming — the great chestnut-tree under which they played at houses — their own little river, the Ripple, where the banks seemed like home, and Tom was always seeing the water-rats, while Maggie gathered the purple plumy tops of the reeds, which she forgot and dropped afterwards — above all, the great Floss, along which they wandered with a sense of travel, to see the rushing spring-tide, the awful Eagre, come up like a hungry monster, or to see the Great Ash which had once wailed and groaned like a man — these things would always be just the same to them.

The second of these passages is more truly Wordsworthian than the first, yet the first is more pictorial in the strict sense of the term. What makes it so is the addition of topographical and picturesque details to the basically nonpictorial Wordsworthian emphasis upon presences, awe, gladness, and joy. The second passage abounds with visual images, but they are not arranged pictorially. Their disposition is controlled rather by what Wordsworth might have called the inward eye of contemplation and memory, as opposed to the outward or bodily eye. It is not surprising, then, that Eliot's two most Wordsworthian novels — The Mill on the Floss and Silas

Marner — are her two least pictorial. Although both are full of visually memorable scenes, the construction of those scenes is seldom indebted to the visual arts.

To be sure, the panoramic landscape which opens The Mill on the Floss is pictorial, as Reva Stump has pointed out. The passage appeals to other senses than sight in an effort to create the illusion of a total environment, but the dominant mode of the description is picturesque.

The details constitute a virtual anthology of motifs from seventeenth-century Dutch landscape painting: a distant view of a town and river in a flat, wide, cultivated plain; a mill and cottage among trees by a stream; a covered wagon pulled by a team of horses across a bridge. It is tempting to connect this word-painting with Constable's Suffolk landscapes, especially in view of the many affinities between Constable and Wordsworth. But the motifs are commonplace, and since George Eliot never mentions Constable in any of her published writings, there is no independent evidence that his work was important to her. (Eliot did know Constable's biographer, C. R. Leslie, and she could have seen the six important Constable pictures in the Sheepshanks bequest, which came to the South Kensington Museum in 1857. But Ruskin's low estimate of Constable's art would hardly have escaped her notice.)

After its opening passage, the novel offers relatively little of a pictorial nature until Maggie emerges in Book 5 as a stately hamadryad among the Scotch firs in the Red Deeps.34 Pictures are used within the story to characterize the amusingly provincial taste of St. Ogg's, and to act as Hogarthian emblematic warnings of Maggie's fate, but the scenes and characters in the first four books of the novel are only rarely conceived as pictures. Likewise in Silas Marner, as Norma Jean Davis has pointed out, "there is a general absence of pictorial patterns". The principal exceptions to this rule are two contrasting scenes in Godfrey Cass's parlor at the Red House; the introduction of Nancy Lammeter; and the description of the churchgoers which opens part 2 and shows the main characters after a lapse of sixteen years. But the climacffc discovery of Eppie by Silas turns upon Silas's nearsightedness and is therefore not visualized pictorially, while the famous scene at the Rainbow Inn, as we have seen, is not visually indebted to Dutch genre painting. Silas Marner, too, works mainly by the Wordsworthian inner eye of memory and feeling.

In Daniel Deronda the English landscape has a Wordsworthian potential to heal and integrate the human personality, but that potential is largely unrealized by the English characters. Gwendolen's family has led a rootless and nomadic modern life, and therefore lacks the sense of selfhood that comes from full integration with a relatively permanent environment. Although their new home at Offendene affords "a glimpse of the wider world in the lofty curves of the chalk downs, grand steadfast forms played over by the changing days" the inhabitants are unable to incorporate that stability. Mrs. Davilow passes untouched through a landscape which combines picturesque and Wordsworthian elements in the most characteristic George Eliot manner.

It was a fine mid-harvest time, not too warm for a noonday ride of five miles to be delightful: the poppies glowed on the borders of the fields, there was enough breeze to move gently like a social spirit among the ears of uncut corn, and to wing the shadow of a cloud across the soft grey downs; here the sheaves were standing, there the horses were straining their muscles under the last load from a wide space of stubble, but everywhere the green pastures made a broader setting for the corn-fields, and the cattle took their rest under wide branches. The road lay through a bit of country where the dairy-farms looked much as they did in the days of our forefathers-where peace and permanence seemed to find a home away from the busy change that sent the railway train flying in the distance.

But the spirit of peace and permanence did not penetrate poor Mrs. Davilow's mind.. Only at the very end of the novel, after suffering has burned away her alienation, does Gwendolen have "a more wakeful vision of Offendene" and its landscape, accepting them at last as her home. She is finally able to hear what George Eliot, in the "Impressions of

Theophrastus Such," calls "the speech of the landscape". Just as the portraiture in the Jewish part of Daniel Deronda contrasts with the portraiture in the English part, so the landscapes of the two plots differ. The Jewish landscape belongs to Mordecai, and is not Wordsworthian but Turnerian and visionary, Its distinguishing features are a brilliant yellow sun near the horizon, a luminous hazy atmosphere, water, and indistinct shapes of boats and men.

Thus, for a long while, he habitually thought of the Being answering to his need as one distantly approaching or turning his back towards him, darkly painted against a golden sky. The reason of the golden sky lay in one of Mordecai's habits. He was keenly alive to some poetic aspects of London; and a favourite resort of his, when strength and leisure allowed, was to some one of the bridges, especially about sunrise or sunset.... Leaning on the parapet of Blackfriars Bridge, and gazing meditatively, the breadth and calm of the river, with its long vista half hazy, half luminous, the grand dim masses or tall forms of buildings which were the signs of world-commerce, the oncoming of boats and barges from the still distance into sound and colour, entered into his mood and blent themselves indistinguishably with his thinking.... Thus it happened that the figure representative of Mordecai's longing was mentally seen darkened by the excess of light in the aerial background.

When Daniel fulfills this vision, he is rowing downstream toward Blackfriars Bridge at the sunset hour of half-past four. He appears to Mordecai out of "a wide-spreading saffron clearness, which in the sky had a monumental calm, but on the river, with its changing objects, was reflected as a luminous movement". Eliot clearly has the work of Turner in mind here, as Edward Dowden rightly sensed when he referred in 1877 to "the Turneresque splendour" of the bridge scenes. The novelist had acquired a firsthand knowledge of Turner's pictures in 1851. She had spoken of "a Turnerian haze of network" in "Janet's Repentance" and of "a faery landscape in Turner's latest style" in "Brother Jacob". She also mentioned Turner in connection with a London sunset in a letter of

1868 to Barbara Bodichon Turner's visionary painting is well suited to the visionary temperament of Mordecai, in whom George Eliot boldly asserts the Romantic possibility of second sight and prophecy.

Turner, like Wordsworth, had gone beyond the picturesque mode; and so in a different way did Ruskin. In his discussion "Of the Turnerian Picturesque" in Modern Painters, Ruskin denied that the picturesque as traditionally defined is a valid aesthetic category, a tertium quid mediating between the sublime and the beautiful. Ruskin's preference was all for the sublime, and he argued that the qualities of roughness, variety, irregularity, and chiaroscuro are in fact qualities of the sublime which connoisseurs of the picturesque mistakenly transfer from mountains, trees, and other sublime natural growths to cottages, ruins, and other objects that are not inherently sublime. He thus defined conventional picturesqueness as a parasitical sublimity, and since it was in his view an entirely superficial effect, he called it also the "surface-picturesque."

The apprehension of the surface-picturesque involves a failure of the moral-aesthetic imagination, according to Ruskin, for the viewer not only fails to grasp the true nature of what he contemplates, but he also fails to sympathize with the human suffering which ruins and broken cottages so often imply. Ruskin declared that "the lower picturesque ideal is eminently a heartless one," and he characterized the lover of the lower picturesque as "kind-hearted, innocent, but not broad in thought; somewhat selfish, and incapable of acute sympathy with others". The only true form of the picturesque, Ruskin argued, is one in which the objects depicted express suffering, poverty, or decay in an unselfconscious manner. This mode of representation he called the noble, or Turnerian, picturesque, and attributed above all to Turner and Prout among contemporary painters.

A moral critique of the cult of the picturesque was not original with Ruskin. Gilpin was aware that banditti, though pictorially colorful, are morally reprehensible and socially undesirable. The moral question was also raised in the debates between Uvedale Price and Richard Payne Knight around 1800. By the mid-nineteenth century such reservations about the picturesque had become almost commonplace in England and America.But Ruskin's statement of the argument was classic for its eloquence, incisiveness, and passion; and it exercised a powerful influence upon contemporary readers such as George Eliot.

In the same volume of Modern Painters, in the famous chapter on "Mountain Gloom," Ruskin applies his critique compellingly. Here he is out to quash naive romantic notions of the beneficial effects of living close to nature. He undertakes to show that even the magnificent scenery of the Swiss Alps, created nature's nearest approximation to paradise, contains elements of suffering, poverty, and decay behind its picturesque surface. The landscape itself has a dark and ominous aspect, and its sublime influences do not protect its human inhabitants from squalor, misery, disease, ignorance, and Catholicism.

Ruskin vividly describes the dismal condition of the Swiss peasantry and then contrasts their reality with false and sentimentally picturesque representations of peasant life in contemporary opera nightly we give our gold, to fashion forth simulacra of peasants in gay ribands and white bodices, singing sweet songs, and bowing gracefully to the picturesque crosses: and all the while the veritable peasants are kneeling, songlessly, to veritable crosses, in another temper than the kind and fair audiences dream of, and assuredly with another kind of answer than is got out of the opera catastrophe.

The chapter effectively advances the argument made throughout Modern Painters that the fallen world contains both good and evil, that the greatest art represents both the beauties and the imperfections of nature, and that any art which does not acknowledge the existence of evil is likely to be false and sentimental. Ruskin's critique of the picturesque is an informing principle of George Eliot's great essay on Riehl's Natural History of German Life. Here the novelist-to-be transfers Ruskin's attack upon the opera to contemporary fiction and painting.

Opera peasants, whose unreality excites Mr. Ruskin's indignation, are surely too frank an idealization to be misleading; and since popular chorus is one of the most effective elements of the opera, we can hardly object to lyric rustics in elegant laced bodices and picturesque motley, unless we are prepared to advocate a chorus of colliers in their pit costume, or a ballet of char-women and stocking-weavers. But our social novels profess to represent the people as they are, and the unreality of their representation is a grave evil.

When she turns to contemporary English painting, the unreality of the peasants she finds represented there prompts Eliot to grumble about "cockney sentimentality" and to draw unfavorable comparisons between Holman Hunt and Teniers or Murillo. English painters display "a total absence of acquaintance and sympathy with our peasantry," she argues. They "treat their subjects under the influence of traditions and prepossessions rather than of direct observation....

The painter is still under the influence of idyllic literature, which has always expressed the imagination of the cultivated, and town-bred, rather than the truth of rustic life". She proceeds to contrast, in thoroughly Ruskinian manner, a/ sentimentalized view of hay makers seen from a safe aesthetic distance with a more realistic view from close up which does not shirk their coarseness and dependence upon drink. The artistic manifestoes of Ruskin and Eliot, both published in 1856, coincide historically with a general change in English rustic genre painting away from depictions of the countryside as a place of simple pleasures, pieties, and harmonies, toward depictions of "dreary landscapes" and scenes of rural poverty such as sickbeds, deathbeds, acts of charity, floods, evictions, redundancy, alcoholism, prostitution, workhouses, and emigration.

Social and moral concerns are reflected in the presentation of landscape throughout George Eliot's fiction. Felix Holt, for example, opens with a dioramic view of the midlands countryside circa 1832 as it passes before a hypothetical passenger on the outside box of a stagecoach. The reader is offered a rich description of such natural beauties as meadows, watercourses, ponds, lanes, willows, elders, yews, hedgerows, wildflowers, ricks, and cattle. But the landscape, as Arnold Kettle has pointed out, is sociological as well as pictorial; For an opposing view, see Conrad, Victorian Treasure-House,. It offers what Eliot, in the "Impressions of Theophrastus Such," calls "a piece of our social history in pictorial writing". The narrator of Felix Holt not only places a shepherd in the scene but pauses to characterize his mental horizons. She contrasts an impoverished, benighted cluster of laborers' cottages ("their little dingy windows telling, like thick-filmed eyes, of nothing but the darkness within") to a more prosperous, better-schooled village. Many of the visual details take on an emblematic moral significance, as they do so often in Ruskin's great set-piece descriptions.

Both Adam Bede and Middlemarch are deeply influenced by Ruskin's critique of the picturesque. The landscape of Adam Bede consistently reflects a Ruskinian awareness of the dark underside of an apparently Edenic setting. Loamshire at first seems the classic paysage riant, ideally fertile and perfectly suited to man's needs. But a close scrutiny of the opening prospect reveals some ominous tints. In the following passage the nameless Gilpinesque traveller begins and ends in the picturesque, but symbolic elements intervene. On the side of the Green that led towards the church, the broken line of thatched cottages was continued nearly to the church yard gate; but on the opposite, northwestern side, there was nothing to obstruct the view of gently-swelling meadow, and wooded valley, and dark masses of distant hill.

That rich undulating district of Loamshire to which Hayslope belonged, lies close to a grim outskirt of Stonyshire, overlooked by its barren hills as a pretty blooming sister may sometimes be linked in the arm of a rugged, tall, swarthy brother; and in two or three hours' ride the traveller might exchange a bleak treeless region, intersected by lines of cold grey stone, for one where his road wound under the shelter of woods, or up swelling hills, muffled with hedgerows and long meadow-grass and thick corn; and where at c very turn he came upon some fine old country-seat nestled in the valley or crowning the slope, some homestead with its long length of barn and its cluster of golden ricks, some grey steeple looking out from a pretty confusion of trees and thatch and dark-red tiles. The distant glimpse of Stonyshire introduces a touch of mountain gloom into the agreeable vista (Creeger). Bleakness and barrenness, according to Gilpin, are distinctly nonpicturesque; here they function as emblematic reminders of an alternate and far less pleasant state of nature.

The traveller proceeds to analyse the landscape in the approved Claudian terms of foreground, middle distance, and background. The prospect accommodates this conventional zoning, first by falling away from the viewer, who occupies a middle elevation, and then by rising in the distance to its maximum elevation in the form of large hills. But the description emphasizes that the zoning is nature's rather than man's; and the foreground, with its "level sunlight lying like transparent gold among the gently curving stems of the feathered grass and the tall red sorrel, and the white umbels of the hemlocks lining the bushy hedgerows," is far more Pre-Raphaelite than Claudian. Moreover, a strong consciousness of time invests the consideration of space. Although the moment is 18 June 1799, the description evokes the grand perennial cycle of nature, so that the reader seems to glimpse the same landscape under different seasonal aspects.

The passage of time brings renewal to nature, but has a different meaning for mortal man. The "keen and hungry winds of the north" and the "sound of the scythe being whetted [which] makes us cast more lingering looks at the flower-sprinkled tresses of the meadow" remind man of his finite term, as they often do in traditional pastoral literature. The description suggests that man will be swallowed up from view, much as the "tall mansion" and its landscaped park are swallowed up from view by the woods and meadows.

In his picture of Dinah Morris Preaching on Hayslope Green, E. H. Corbould neatly solves the problem posed by George Eliot's detailed and richly significant landscape description. He simply turns Dinah around, so that her backdrop is not the panoramic vista, as in the novel, but

Hayslope village and a piece of the intervening green, an altogether more manageable subject. The truly Ruskinian landscape always contains intimations of mortality as well as of immortality. The bay into which Romola's boat drifts is spectacularly beautiful and peaceful but contains a plague-stricken village. As Norma Jean Davis points out, "both Ruskin and Romola discover, in their exploration of Italian landscape, that behind the apparent picturesque beauty and green luxuriance are elements of death and decay". In Adam Bede Eliot twice introduces overt memento mori into apparently idyllic landscapes.

Early in the novel Adam and Seth carry a coffin through a scene of "Eden-like peace and loveliness," creating, as the narrator says, "a strangely-mingled picture". A moment later they come upon their drowned father's body. This effect of moral chiaroscuro is repeated in the setting through which the pregnant Hetty sets off in search of Arthur. The early February landscape is astir with signs of spring and hope, but the narrator thinks of the wayside crucifix one might encounter in a Continental countryside on such a day:

An image of a great agony — the agony of the Cross. It has stood perhaps by the clustering apple — blossoms, or in the broad sunshine by the cornfield, or at a turning by the wood where a clear brook was gurgling below; and surely, if there came a traveller to this world who knew nothing of the story of man's life upon it, this image of agony would seem to him strangely out of place in the midst of this joyous nature. He would not know that hidden behind the apple-blossoms, or among the golden com, or under the shrouding boughs of the wood, there might be a human heart beating heavily with anguish; perhaps a young blooming girl, not knowing where to turn for refuge from swift-advancing shame; understanding no more of this life of ours than a foolish lost lamb wandering farther and farther in the nightfall on the lonely heath; yet tasting the bitterest of life's bitterness.

This appeal for sympathy is a virtual reprise of the third and fourth paragraphs of Ruskin's "Mountain Gloom." There, too, a naive traveller comes upon "a cross of rough-hewn pine, iron-bound to its parapet" amidst an inspiring landscape. This cross is an emblem of the misery of the peasants who inhabit the landscape and who die contemplating images of the suffering Christ. Eliot's comparison of the incomprehending Hetty to a biblical lost lamb may have been prompted by Ruskin's comparison of the insensible Swiss peasants to the wild mountain goats which take no "passion of joy in all that fair work of God" surrounding them. The cross in the landscape is a reminder of unseen moral forces in nature.

The moral intrudes upon the picturesque again in the climactic recognition scene of Adam Bede. Adam, passing through the Fir-tree Grove, stops to contemplate a beech-tree as Gilpin himself might have done in his Remarks on Forest Scenery. The sensitive carpenter registers aesthetic detail as well as potential board-feet:

Adam delighted in a fine tree of all things; as the fisherman's sight is keenest on the sea, so Adam's perceptions were more at home with trees than with other objects. He kept them in his memory, as a painter does, with all the flecks and knots in their bark, all the curves and angles of their boughs; and had often calculated the height and contents of a trunk to a nicety, as he stood looking at it.

No wonder that, notwithstanding his desire to get on, he could not help pausing to look at a curious large beech which he had seen standing before him at a turning in the road, and convince himself that it was not two trees wedded together, but only one. For the rest of his life he remembered that moment when he was calmly examining the beech, as a man remembers his last glimpse of the home where his youth was passed, before the road turned, and he saw it no more. The beech stood at the last turning before the Grove ended in an archway of boughs that let in the eastern light; and as Adam stepped away from the tree to continue his walk, his eyes fell on two figures about twenty yards before him.

This is the moment of Adam's psychic fall from innocence to experience. His innocent perception of the picturesque variegation of tree-trunks and boughs gives way to a shattering recognition of Eve with her seducer. The recognition is still pictorial, since the "archway of boughs" makes a perfect frame; but the picture now admits the existence of treachery and evil in the idyllic scene. This episode may have been the model for the great recognition scene in Henry James's The Ambassadors, in which Lambert Strether, like Adam, sees two trusted friends in a compromised position amidst a landscape which only moments before had been a pleasant picture.

The Fir-tree Grove in Adam Bede is a delusory paradise for all who enter it. It is the regular trysting-place of Hetty and Arthur, and the scene of the seduction that has such tragic consequences. Michael Squires has rightly related the setting to the tradition of the locus amoenus in pastoral poetry, the erotic and magical pagan paradise which changes those who enter it the Red Deeps in The Mill on the Floss is a vestigial locus amoenus. Compare Ware Commons in chapter 12 of John Fowles's The French Lieutenant's Woman). But George Eliot treats the topos with a Protestant distrust that recalls Spenser's handling of the Bower of Blisse in The Faerie Queene. In pictorial terms, the grove is a Claudian mythological landscape, peopled with figures from Ovid. This ideal landscape is the symptomatic product of a mind that avoids reality to indulge in fantasies of self-gratification.

She thought nothing of the evening light that lay gently in the grassy alleys between the fern, and made the beauty of their living green more visible than it had been in the overpowering flood of noon: she thought of nothing that was present. She only saw something that was possible: Mr. Arthur Donnithorne coming to meet her again along the Fir-tree Grove. That was the foreground of Hetty's picture; behind it lay a bright hazy something — days that were not to be as the other days of her life had been. It was as if she had been wooed by a river-god, who might any time take her to his wondrous halls below a watery heaven.

In other words, Hetty prefers a Heroic Landscape with Poseidon and Tyro to a more realistic picture along the lines of, say, Millais's Waiting. Claude's presumed avoidance of the nature immediately surrounding him makes him the chief villain in the historical drama of landscape painting presented by Ruskin in Modern Painters. By the same token, Claudian landscape is something of a villain in Adam Bede. The aesthetic and the moral remain compatible in Adam Bede. Ruskin's critique of the surface-picturesque opens the way to a true landscape which intimates the possibility of salvation through moral struggle. The same is true in Middlemarch, but in the later novel the vision of true landscape is much more problematic. George Eliot explores more deeply than ever before the disturbing possibility that the aesthetic and the moral are incompatible, that art itself has no worthy human use. As Barbara Hardy has said: "The art/life antithesis is a very important subject in Middlemarch.... Many characters are defined and even tested by their response to art, and art itself is defined and even tested by its relevance and meaning for human beings of different kinds".

These issues are crystallized in chapter 39, which narrates Mr. Brooke's visit to the farm of his tenant, Dagley. Here the lower picturesque is precisely what Ruskin called it: an eminently heartless ideal. It is true that an observer, under that softening influence of the fine arts which makes other people's hardships picturesque, might have been delighted with this homestead called Freeman's End: the old house had dormer-windows in the dark-red roof, two of the chimneys were choked with ivy, the large porch was blocked up with bundles of sticks, and half the windows were closed with grey worm-eaten shutters about which the jasmine boughs grew in wild luxuriance; the mouldering garden wall with hollyhocks peeping over it was a perfect study of highlymingled subdued colour, and there was an aged goat (kept doubtless on interesting superstitious grounds) lying against the open back-kitchen door.

The mossy thatch of the cow-shed, the broken grey barn-doors, the pauper labourers in raggedbreeches who had nearly finished unloading a wagon of corn into the barn ready for early thrashing [sic]; the scanty dairy of cows being tethered for milking and leaving one half of the shed in brown emptiness; the very pigs and white ducks seemed to wander about the uneven neglected yard as if in low spirits from feeding on a too meagre quality of rinsings, — all these objects under the quiet light of a sky marbled with high clouds would have made a sort of picture which we have all paused over as a "charming bit," touching other sensibilities than those which are stirred by the depression of the agricultural interest, with the sad lack of farming capital, as seen constantly in the newspapers of that time. But these troublesome associations were just now strongly present to Mr. Brooke, and spoiled the scene for him.

At Freeman's End, picturesque unevenness betokens neglect and brown emptiness signifies want. As Eliot says in Daniel Deronda, again echoing Ruskin: "What horrors of damp huts, where human beings languish, may not become picturesque through aerial distance!" the narrator of Middlemarch will not indulge the nostalgia for "dear, old, brown, crumbling, picturesque inefficiency" which gives pleasure to the narrator of "Amos Barton". Even Mr. Brooke's connoisseurship gives way to a true perception of his tenant's misery.

The aestheticist view of life is questioned throughout Middlemarch. We have seen that Will Ladislaw accuses Naumann of looking at the world "entirely from the studio point of view". By the same token Dorothea's conscience is troubled by aesthetic apprehension as such. She is unable to bring the "severe classical nudities and smirking Renaissance-Correggiosities" in her uncle's art collection at Tipton Grange into "any sort of relevance with her life".

Her trip to Rome helps her better to understand what Will calls the "old language" of classical and Renaissance art, but it does not bridge the gap between that art and her own sense of purpose. As Richard S. Lyons has pointed out in "The Method of Middlemarch, Dorothea renews her attack upon Mr. Brooke's collection after her return from Rome: "I used to come from the village with that dirt and coarse ugliness like a pain within me, and the simpering pictures in the drawing room seemed to me like a wicked attempt to find delight in what is false, while we don't mind how hard the truth is for the neighbours outside our walls". As the novel progresses, Ladislaw becomes less the aesthete, but Dorothea does not become more the connoiseuse.

Dorothea can find relevance in simple portraiture, which she values more for iconic than for aesthetic reasons. The miniature of Ladislaw's grandmother sustains her through some bad times because it reminds her of Will himself and of his great regard for her. Dorothea is also sustained by a hard-won vision of the English landscape, a vision that is partly pictorial but not sentimentally picturesque. She tends from the first to envision her own destiny as somehow involved with the midlands countryside.

Even in the sculpture gallery of the Vatican Museum her first thoughts are of the English landscape: "She did not really see the streak of sunlight on the floor more than she saw the statues: she was inwardly seeing the light of years to come in her own home and over the English fields and elms and hedge-bordered highroads; and feeling that the way in which they might be filled with joyful devotedness was not so clear to her as it had been". Dorothea values nature and duty more highly than art, and her priorities reflect certain moments in George Eliot's own museum-going.

The landscape that matters most to Dorothea upon her return from Rome lies immediately outside the west window of her boudoir at Lowick. The window gives onto an avenue of lime-trees leading to an entrance-gate, beyond which may be seen a bit of road and a large expanse of open, flat field. Dorothea views this prospect under several different diurnal, seasonal, and emotional aspects, so that it affords a series of landscape images in which objective and subjective elements strive to achieve a stable balance. E. D. H. Johnson has pointed out in "The Truer Message" that the sequence of views from Dorothea's boudoir window provides an index to her growth toward self-knowledge (p. 200).

The most important views occur in chapters 28, 54, and 80; and they form a progression from despair through indifference to affirmation which corresponds roughly with the progression outlined by Carlyle in Sartor Resartus from the Everlasting Nay through theCentre of Indifference to the Everlasting Yea.

In chapter 28 Dorothea is at an ebb, having suffered the disappointment of virtually all her marital hopes. The landscape outside her boudoir reflects her mood of cold constriction and drab imprisonment:

She saw the long avenue of limes lifting their trunks from a white earth, and spreading white branches against the dun and motionless sky. The distant flat shrank in uniform whiteness and low hanging uniformity of cloud.... Her blooming full-pulsed youth stood there in a moral imprisonment which made itself one with the chill, colourless, narrowed landscape....

Dorothea's subjectivity dominates this landscape of despair. The description borders on the pathetic fallacy, a concept which George Eliot noted with interest in "Arts and Belles Lettres," her review of the third volume of Modern Painters. The novelist here displays what John Stuart Mill called "the power of creating scenery, in keeping with some state of human feeling; so fitted to it as to be the embodied symbol of it, and to summon up the state of feeling itself, with a force not to be surpassed by anything but reality". Mill was speaking of Tennyson's earliest poems, especially of "Mariana"; and indeed it is of "Mariana" and Millais's splendid painting of Tennyson's heroine that one is reminded most strongly by chapter 28 of Middlemarch Dorothea's duty is no clearer to her in chapter 54, but as a widow she suffers less acutely than she did as a wife. She has recuperated from the worst of her bereavement, and her condition is now comfortable but neutral and aimless.

Again the landscape reflects her spiritual state:

She had not yet applied herself to her work, but was seated with her hands folded on her lap, looking out along the avenue of limes to the distant fields. Every leaf was at rest in the sunshine, the familiar scene was changeless, and seemed to represent the prospect of her life, full of motiveless ease — motiveless, if her own energy could not seek out reasons for ardent action. The prospect is no longer jaundiced by Dorothea's despair, but it is still dominated by her subjectivity.

There is no fruitful interchange between objective and subjective, between nature and the perceiving mind. The possibility of a more balanced relationship with the landscape is adumbrated in chapter 37 and realized in chapter 80. "She had been so used to struggle for and to find resolve in looking along the avenue towards the arch of western light," we are told in the earlier instance, "that the vision itself had gained a communicating power". Once the vision itself communicates, it can offer the joy and moral strength that work through time and memory to make up Wordsworthian maturity. Dorothea attains such maturity in chapter 80, after suffering through a night of dark despair brought on by Will Ladislaw's apparent rejection of her love. Her psychic resurrection is assisted by her recognition of an independent life in the landscape outside her boudoir window.

She opened her curtains, and looked out towards the bit of road that lay in view, with fields beyond outside the entrance-gates. On the road there was a man with a bundle on his back and a woman carrying her baby; in the field she could see figures moving — perhaps the shepherd with his dog. Far off in the bending sky was the pearly light; and she felt the largeness of the world and the manifold wakings of men to labour and endurance. She was a part of that involuntary, palpitating life, and could neither look out on it from her luxurious shelter as a mere spectator, nor hide her eyes in selfish complaining.

The landscape is no longer problematic; its objective reality affords Dorothea an alternative to self-pity, and makes possible a creative interaction between her mind and the world outside it. Though faith is gone, the world remains; and work still has meaning, as it does for Carlyle's Teufelsdrockh in the phase of the Everlasting Yea. The perception of otherness is not sickening, as in Sartre's La Nausée, but healing. The recuperation of Rex Gascoigne in Daniel Deronda begins with a similar act of attention to a landscape peopled by working figures immediately outside his own window.

The vista in chapter 80 of Middlemarch holds its Wordsworthian and Carlylean elements within a highly pictorialized structure. The window provides a frame, and the prospect is divided into foreground, middle distance, and background. The lighting is specified and the figures in the scene are precisely located. Critics have sought analogues for the description in the paintings of Rubens and Millet, but the details given by Eliot are so minimal and generic as to defy identification with the work of any particular artist. They are at any rate not conventionally picturesque; they manifest no roughness, irregularity, vivid chiaroscuro, or ruin. Eliot is evoking not the surface-picturesque but the noble picturesque, which consists, according to Ruskin, in the unconscious expression of human suffering "nobly endured by unpretending strength of heart... the world's hard work being gone through all the while, and no pity asked for, nor contempt feared".

The best pictorial analogue for the window-scenes in Middlemarch is not to be found in landscape painting at all but in a popular motif of nineteenth-century Romantic genre painting: the figure looking out a window who presents his or her back to a viewer located inside the room. The motif is operative in European painting from the seventeenth century well into the twentieth; its classic nineteenth-century embodiment is in the work of Caspar David Friedrich, especially the Frau am Fenster of about 1822.

Millais's Mariana belongs to this tradition, as does Moritz von Schwind's Morgenstunde, a picture George Eliot might have seen at Munich in 1858. The real subject of such paintings, at least in the nineteenth century, is usually the spiritual interaction between the spectator and the prospect. Romantic Fensterbilder are an appropriate analogue to the window-scenes in Middlemarch because Dorothea's presence in those scenes is always visualized as carefully as the landscape itself, and because the quality of her apprehension is the true centre of the audience's interest.

In natural description, then, no less than in characterization and domestic scenes, George Eliot was deeply influenced by pictorial conventions. Her vision of nature was shaped by eighteenth-century traditions of the picturesque and topographical, and by nineteenth-century modes of landscape sensibility which came to her through Wordsworth, Ruskin, and the Pre-Raphaelites She was well aware that the beholder's share of perception may be conditioned by the experience of art.

She lends this awareness to Daniel Deronda as he contemplates a Gothic capital at the Abbey:

'I wonder whether one oftener learns to love real objects through their representations, or the representations through the real objects,' he said, after pointing out a lovely capital made by the curled leaves of greens, showing their reticulated underside with the firm gradual swell of its central rib. 'When I was a little fellow these capitals taught me to observe, and delight in, the structure of leaves.'

These remarks are in the spirit of Ruskin, as Henry Auster has pointed out, but they must also reflect many of George Eliot's own encounters with the natural world. She knew that art can help one see and feel, and indeed she valued art chiefly because it can. But what happened to Eliot's descriptive art when it became, in turn, subject to someone else's imagination — when, in short, an illustrator set about to render it into visual forms? Inevitably the pictures were modified from what the author had conceived. The next chapter will examine Frederic Leighton's illustrations of Romola, both for the light they throw upon the text and for the questions they raise concerning literary illustration in general.

Chapter 4

George Eliot's 'Philosophical Power' and usage of 'Humor'

After all that has been written about George Eliot's place as an artist, it may be doubted if attention has been properly directed to her one unique quality. Whatever be her rank amongst the creators of romance (and perhaps the tendency now is to place it too high rather than too low), there can be no doubt that she stands entirely apart and above all writers of fiction, at any rate in England, by her philosophic power and general mental calibre. No other English novelist has ever stood in the foremost rank of the thinkers of his time.

Or to put it the other way, no English thinker of the higher quality has ever used romance as an instrument of thought. Our greatest novelists could not be named beside her off the field of novel-writing. Though some of them have been men of wide reading, and even of special learning, they had none of them pretensions to the best philosophy and science of their age. Fielding and Goldsmith, Scott and Thackeray, with all their inexhaustible fertility of mind, were never in the higher philosophy compeers of Hume, Adam Smith, Burke, and Bentham. But George Eliot, before she wrote a tale at all, in mental equipment stood side by side with Mill, Spencer, Lewes, and Carlyle.

If she produced nothing in philosophy, moral or mental, quite equal to theirs, she was of their kith and kin, of the same intellectual quality. Her conception of Sociology was quite as profound as that of Mill, and in some ways keener in insight; if Lewes knew more of psychology or biology, she could teach him much in history and in morals. There are in "Silas Marner," "Adam Bede," and the "Spanish Gypsy," volcanic bursts of prophetic teaching which Teufelsdröckh never surpassed. That is to say, George Eliot, who at her death left no living novelist to be mentioned beside her, was all her life in intellectual fellowship with the first philosophic minds of her day. Turn it the other way. None of our English thinkers of the first, second, or even third rank, have resorted to romance as a vehicle of thought. The only possible exceptions that occur to me are Swift, Dr. Johnson, and Miss Martineau; but "Gulliver," "Rasselas," and "Deerbrook" are romances only by courtesy for their authors.

Abroad there have been examples of men of foremost intellectual force who have written novels. Of these one only—Goethe—has written a true novel in a vein worthy of himself. And it is to "Wilhelm Meister" that we may most aptly go for analogues to the George Eliot cycle of novels. Of course, as poet, as a secular force of European rank, Goethe himself stands apart. But in his "Wilhelm Meister" we have those meditations upon life, human nature, and society, that supreme culture, and a certain Shakespearean way of looking down upon the world as from a vantage-ground afar, which again and again recur in George Eliot and give her the unique impression of tragic mystery amongst modern novelists.

Then again Voltaire, Rousseau, and Diderot wrote prose fictions which may by a stretch of language be called novels. But the wit of "Candide," the pathos of "The Religieuse," the passion of "Héloïse" do not make up a tale fit to be placed beside "Silas Marner," as a complete gem of art in the true field of romance. Voltaire, Rousseau, Diderot, Goethe, Victor Hugo, Carlyle may take rank above George Eliot in the sum of the intellectual impulse they gave to their time. But none of them, unless it be the author of the "Misérables," can be said to be her equal in the painting of real life and actual manners.

And here we may find at once the strength and the weakness of George Eliot. With a mental equipment of the first order, her principal instrument was art. And so she played a double part—as the most philosophic artist, or the most artistic philosopher in recent literature. It has been well said that there are flashes of hers which recall Pascal, Dante, Tacitus. There are certainly some which are worthy of Burke, Condorcet, or Vauvenargues. There are single passages which Bacon might have conceived, and others which Montaigne might have written.

And again there are thoughts which Coleridge and De Maistre have never surpassed. One need not compare her in the sum with any of these famous thinkers. It is plain that in philosophy she has not produced work that can weight with theirs. But it is the sustained commerce with men like these, the continually recurring sense that we are in contact with a mind of their order, of the same intellectual family, which rouses in us so intense a delight in her novels that we are apt to indulge in hyperbolic language.

But the question comes in, and it must be answered, "Could she play the double part perfectly?" Did her philosophy, culture, moral earnestness, overweight her art? or was her art the complete and easy instrument for interpreting all that her brain and her soul contained? Few are now convinced that her art was always equal to so great a demand. For that reason it may be doubted whether it will ultimately take the very first rank. A few of the greatest sons of men have combined all that their age had attained with supreme creative ease.

Milton, Shakespeare, Dante, and Virgil seem to use their vast intellectual power as if poetry were their mother tongue, their natural organ of thought. Alone of the moderns, Goethe wields his panoply of learning with perfect ease, bounding in his full suit of mail on to his charger like some paladin, and careering in it over the field as if it were a robe of tissue. But it is given only to the one or two of the greatest to interpret the profoundest thought, to embody the ripest knowledge, in the inimitable mystery of art.

And thus it comes about we so often feel the art of George Eliot to be short of perfect. The canvas of laborious culture is too often visible through the colouring of the picture. We find so much to think about that we crave a little rest for simple enjoyment. The chorus is very majestic; we are amazed by forked flashes of wisdom, sonorous gnomes, prophetic strains worthy of the immortal Trilogy; but the Chorus is often a little slow; and sometimes slightly senile, goody, prolix. We have come to a tragedy, we know; but we crave more business, incident, light and air....

Let us who love the art of George Eliot abstain, if only in obedience to her teaching, from all extravagance of eulogy. Certain that she belongs to the foremost intellectual forces of our time, and seeing that she is a novelist (for neither poems nor essays express her genius truly), some are apt to decide that she stands in the very front rank of the artists of the modern world. That is surely to claim a great deal too much. Cervantes, Fielding, Scott, of course, stand immeasurably apart and above, by virtue of their wealth of imagination, their range of insight into manners, and sympathy with character of every type. Goldsmith, Defoe, Richardson, I think too Sterne and Lesage, stand again in another class by virtue of their consummate art in producing, in some more limited field, images of pathos, humour, naïveté, or vitality, worthy in their own sphere of the mightiest master's hand.

The place of George Eliot will doubtless ultimately be found in the group where we set George Sand, Balzac, Jane Austen, Dickens, Thackeray, the Brontés. Judging her purely as artist, we can hardly hope that her ultimate popularity will quite equal theirs. That she is immeasurably superior to them all as thinker, teacher, inspirer of thought and purifier of soul will perhaps be little disputed. As facile creator of types, painter of varied character, veracious chronicler of manners, she has not their range, vivacity, irrepressible energy. In art very much must be given to mass of impression, vividness of enjoyment, fertility of creation.

The inexhaustible charm of George Sand, the microscopic vivacity of Jane Austen, the pathetic oddities of Charles Dickens, the terrible Hogarthian pencil of Balzac and Thackeray were all deliberately foregone by a novelist who read so deeply, who looked on life so profoundly, and who meditated so conscientiously as George Eliot.—From a review of Cross's "Life of George Eliot," in the "Fortnightly Review" (March, 1885).

George Eliot's humour allies itself with her intellect on the one hand, and with her sympathies and moral perceptions on the other. The grotesque in human character is reclaimed from the province of the humorous by her affections, when that is possible, and is shown to be a pathetic form of beauty. The pale, brown-eyed weaver, gazing out from his cottage with blurred vision, or poring with miserly devotion over his golden hoard, touches us, but does not make us smile. The comedy of incident, the farcical, lies outside her province; once or twice, for reasons that appear hardly adequate, the comedy of incident was attempted, and the result was not successful.

The humour of George Eliot usually belongs to her entire conception of a character, and cannot be separated from it. Her humorous effects are secured by letting her mind drop sympathetically into a level of lower intelligence, or duller moral perception, and by the conscious presence at the same time of the higher self. The humorous impression exists only in the qualified organs of perception which remain at the higher, the normal point of view. What had been merely an undulation of matter, when it touches the prepared surface of the retina, breaks into light.

By the fire of the "Rainbow Inn," the butcher and the farrier, the parish clerk and the deputy clerk puff their pipes with an air of severity, "starting at one another as if a bet were depending on the first man who winked," while the humbler beer drinkers "keep their eyelids down, and rub their hands across their mouths as if the draughts of beer were a funeral duty, attended with embarrassing sadness." The slow talk about the red Durham is conducted with a sense of grave responsibility on both sides. It is we who are looking on unobserved who experience a rippling over of our moral nature with manifold laughter; it is to our lips the smile rises—a smile which is expressive not of any acute access of risibility, but of a voluminous enjoyment, a mass of mingled feeling, partly tender, partly pathetic, partly humorous.

The dramatic appropriateness of the humorous utterances of George Eliot's characters renders them unpresentable by way of extract. Each is like the expression of a face which cannot be detached from the face itself. The unresentful complacency with which Dolly Winthrop speaks of the frailties of masculine human creatures is part of the general absence of severity and of high views with respect to others which belongs to her character, and receives illustration from her like complacent forbearance with the natural infirmities of the pups. "They will worry and gnaw—worry and gnaw they will, if it was one's Sunday cap as hung anywhere so they could drag it. They know no difference, God help 'em; it's the pushing o' the teeth as sets them on, that's what it is."

Contrast Dolly's indulgent allowances in men's favour, tempered by undeniable experiences of their scarcely excusable failings, with the keen and hostile perceptions of Denner, Mrs. Transome's waiting-woman, with mind as sharp as a needle, whose neat, clean-cut, small personality is jarred by the rude power, and coarse, incoherent manners of men. "It mayn't be good luck to be a woman," Denner said, "but one begins with it from a baby: one gets used to it.

And I shouldn't like to be a man—to cough so loud, and stand straddling about on a wet day, and be so wasteful with meat and drink. They're a coarse lot, I think." We turn for a kindlier judgment to Dolly. "Eh, to be sure," said Dolly, gently (while instructing Silas in the mysteries of Eppie's wardrobe), "I've seen men as are wonderful handy wi' children. The men are awk'ard and contrairy mostly, God help 'em; but when the drink's out of 'em, they aren't unsensible, though they're bad for leeching and bandaging—so fiery and unpatient."—From "George Eliot" in "Studies in Literature"(1906).

Chapter 5

Critical Analysis of Maggie's Relation with her Brother

It is by her nature, complex, passionate, sensuous, by her sex, intellectualized and spiritualized, that Maggie Tulliver is most important to the reader. In her relations to her brother, which are apparently the chief interest of the book, she is interestingly and novelly studied; but these, though they involve the catastrophe, do not involve the climax. That is reached, as it seems to me, not when she and Tom are drowned together in the flood of the Floss, but when her reason and her conscience are provisionally overborne by her love for Stephen Guest, and she floats with him down a tide and out upon a sea more perilous than any inundation, and saves herself only by a powerful impulse of her will, which is almost a convulsion.

The fruition of her love would have been a double treason, treason to her cousin Lucy, who was Guest's betrothed, and treason to Philip Wakem, to whom she was herself pledged; and the sense of this blackened it with guilt, and turned it to despair, even while she yielded and yielded to the love of being loved.

Never has an unhappy passion been more faithfully studied in a character with strength enough finally to forbid it; or more subtly felt from that first moment when Maggie begins to rejoice in her beauty because of her love for the man who loves it, till that last moment when she refuses to marry him, and goes back to suffer shame rather than to merit shame. Every step of the way is accurately and firmly traced up to that passage where Stephen Guest comes to ask her to row with him on the river, and from which there seems no retreat.... It does not seem to me that the true logic of the late is Maggie's death with Tom Tulliver, or Stephen's marriage with Lucy.

It is a forced touch where the husband and wife stand together beside the grave of the brother and sister; but in the novels, the best of the novels, fifty years ago, they forced their touches rather more than they do now. To kill people or to marry them is to beg the question; but into some corner the novelist is commonly driven who deals with a problem.

It is only life that can deal masterfully with problems, and life does not solve them by referring them to another life or by stifling them with happiness. How life would have solved the problem of Maggie Tulliver I am not quite prepared to say; but I have my revolt against George Eliot's solution. All the more I must own that the heroine's character, from the sort of undisciplined, imaginative, fascinating little girl we see her at first, into the impassioned, bewildered, self-disciplined woman we see her at last, is masterly.

Having given my opinion that her supreme expression is in her relation to her lover, I have my doubts, or at least my compunctions in behalf of her relation to her brother. Unquestionably the greatest pathos of the story appeals to us from her relation to her brother.

The adoring dependence, the grieving indignation, the devotion, the revolt, the submission, and the reunion which make up her love for him is such a study of sisterly affection as I should not know where to match. The very conditions of her intellectual and emotional superiority involve a moral inferiority to the brute simplicity, the narrow integrity, the heroic truth of the more singly natured man. Maggie saw life more whole than Tom, but that part of it which he saw he discerned with a clearness denied to her large but cloudy vision. It is a great and beautiful story, which one reads with a helpless wonder that such a book should ever be in any wise superseded, or should not constantly keep the attention at least of those fitted to feel its deep and lasting significance.—

From George Eliot's "Maggie Tulliver and Hetty Sorrel," in "Heroines of Fiction" (1901).

GENDER ROLES IN THE MILL ON THE FLOSS

Mary Ann Evans, born in Warwickshire, England, wrote the novel The Mill on the Floss during the Victorian era of 1859 under the pseudonym George Eliot. In keeping the Victorian mindset, the novel encompasses many stereotypes of gender roles for its main characters. Evans received criticism during her lifetime for not following the expected gender roles of the time period.

She may have written The Mill on the Floss as a subtle outcry against society's expectations (or lack thereof) of men and especially of women. The gender roles of the Victorian period are clearly seen in The Mill on the Floss and mostly followed; however, sometimes the roles are reversed or contrary to what the reader would expect. The characters of Tom, Phillip, Lucy and Maggie all demonstrate how Evans defines gender roles throughout the novel.

Tom Tulliver, a central character in the novel, is first introduced to the reader as a lively and adventurous thirteen year old boy. Tom clearly enjoys traditionally manly activities such as fishing, riding big horses and thinking about owning a gun one day. He does not seem to worry much about his future and quite enjoys the fact that his younger sister Maggie looks up to him as a friend and "protector". The reader has every reason to suspect that Tom will enjoy a life laden with adventures and few responsibilities until it is his time to take over the family business and become a man.

Mr. Tulliver, Tom's father, has different plans for his boy, though. Mr. Tulliver expects Tom to go to school and receive an education and be "a bit nimble with his tongue and his pen, and [become] a smart chap". It is at the point in Tom's life when he goes to live with Mr. Stelling, a clergyman/tutor, to be taught in the ways of Latin, arithmetic and history that Tom is most lost in terms of gender roles. All of his previous experiences seem to be of no use to him in this new environment. With no other boys under Mr. Stelling's charge,

Tom cannot fight physically for his place in the world. He also has a very hard time with the new subjects he is being taught because he has had no previous exposure to them.

Therefore, he cannot even prove himself through his studies. During this time, Tom is described as, "more like a girl than he had ever been in his life before". He had become quite aware of his difficulties in grasping the new concepts that were thrown at him every day made him appear "stupid" and this knowledge gave him a "girl's susceptibility" Toward the middle of the novel and the end of Tom's school days, Tom learns of the terrible accident his father has been in and he must return home.

It is during this period that Tom shakes off all womanly and even childish expressions. Tom is pressed too quickly into manhood and soon becomes ultra-masculinized. He trudges off to work everyday and upon returning, refuses to talk to anyone while he eats his dinner. This mindset rules the rest of Tom's life until the end of the novel, and subsequently his life, when he is again put into the position of a woman as his sister rescues him during the flooding of the Floss.

Phillip Wakem, a character who becomes increasingly important as the novel comes to an end, stands in stark contrast to the character of Tom Tulliver. Phillip, born with a deformity of the spine, is considered weak throughout the entire novel. When Tom and Phillip become schoolmates at King's Lorton with Mr. Stelling, Phillip is always depicted in a gentler light with finer features and more refined talents. Phillip is a master of the arts, such as drawing and music. And where Tom would go out and experience adventures, Phillip would only read about them and retell the quests of others. As Phillip becomes older, he befriends Maggie Tulliver, Tom's sister, and falls in love with her.

However, Maggie in the beginning does not see Phillip as a potential lover, a sign that she does not see Phillip as a "real" man. He is repeatedly described as womanly or feminine when pledging his love for Maggie. Maggie does enjoy Phillip's beautiful singing voice, although it is mentioned many times to the reader that it is a tenor and not a manlier bass. Phillip does show more manly traits as he becomes older and even opposes his father's opinion of Maggie Tulliver when Phillip informs his of the plan to marry her. However, Phillip cannot hold Maggie's attention forever. He ends up losing her to another gentleman who exhibits a more traditional male gender role.

Lucy Deane, a relative to the Tullivers, is not a main character in the novel. However, it is important to note that she is one of the characters who followed gender roles almost perfectly as an adult. As a child, Lucy was brought up to portray the role of a perfectly feminine girl. She had "the neatest little rosebud mouth to be kissed: everything about her was neat-her little round neck with the row of coral beads, her little straight nose...her clear eyebrows...to match her hazel eyes". As a result of her upbringing, Lucy longed to play with her cousins, Maggie and Tom.

On one occasion in particular, the reader is shown Lucy's delight in going on an "adventure" with Tom to forbidden parts of Aunt Pullet's garden, "a rare treat to do something naughty". The reader does not hear very much about Lucy once Tom has left for school and the next time Lucy is brought into the plot, she is a young woman.

As a young woman, Lucy upholds the Victorian gender role of a female and is very petite and demure. She is even described as becoming physically sick when Maggie runs off with her would-be fiancÃe. Lucy's behaviour proves that even though she had a desire, albeit a small one, to break free of the mold, society pushed her back into a pattern of "appropriate" behaviour as she matured.

Maggie Tulliver, the heroine of the story, is first shown to the reader as a spitfire of a child with quite an active imagination. Maggie, against every wish of her mother, plays out doors with Tom, won't keep her bonnet over her hair, and refuses to wear the gorgeous and expensive clothes her relatives send her. Her father affectionately refers to her as a "little wench" throughout the novel and Maggie continually defies society's expectation for her actions. Maggie reads every book she can get her hands on and gives herself a sort of "self-education". Maggie proves herself so smart that she is almost as good at Latin as Tom is and she had never taken a lesson.

As a child, Maggie does not understand why people expect her to act in such a way that would make her physically uncomfortable and deny her the right to express all of her vibrant feelings. As she ages and comes to deal with her father's illness, Maggie begins to let herself be pushed into a more traditional mold.

She reads the writings of Thomas A Kempis and decides to live a life of piety and self-denial. She believes that in doing this she will becomes less bound to the desires of "this" world and more attuned to the rewards in the "next life". This decision is clearly motivated by the desire she feels to fit into her society, now that she must take on more responsibilities at home due to her father's illness.

Out of Maggie's mindset of piety comes a love for Phillip Wakem. However, at first it is not a true love for Phillip. Maggie feels more completed by the sense that it is a selfless love because Phillip needs to have the love of Maggie to fill the void of physical affection in his life.

These actions are merely Maggie trying to fit into the more traditional role that is expected of her. However, after a few years away spent being a Governess, Maggie returns to her old self. When she stays with her cousin Lucy upon her return, Maggie meets Lucy's soon to be fiance Stephen. Maggie starts to have feelings for Stephen and against her better judgment, runs away with him.

Her actions show that she has begun to embrace her true self and not just act in a way to please the "society" in Garum Firs. In the end of the novel, Maggie stays true to herself and becomes Tom's rescuer when the flooding of the Floss destroys the mill.

Evans, in her never ending quest for true realism, portrays each character as behaving in varied ways due to varied external and internal forces. No one character can be said to be the epitome of one gender role or the other. The seamless blending of masculine and feminine traits gives each character a depth not seen in many other authors' works, while also proving a very powerful point.

Evans is trying to tell the reader that being true to one's inner self is the most important part of life. She shows through each character that living life inside a social construction is not rewarding and in fact mostly causes pain for the character. Evans' lesson, although not the easiest to follow, should be applied everyday in "real" life.

Chapter 6

Virginia Woolf and George Eliot

Writing of the life of Percy Bysshe Shelley in 1927, Virginia Woolf observed that "there are some stories which have to be retold by each generation, not that we have anything new to add to them, but because of some queer quality in them which makes them not only Shelley's story but our own." This has proved true for the lives of any number of great men and women over the past few centuries: it has been true for no one, perhaps, as much as for Virginia Woolf herself. In the opening of her comprehensive new biography of Woolf, British scholar Hermione Lee lists a few first sentences of other Woolf biographies: " 'Virginia Woolf was a Miss Stephen' 'Virginia Woolf was a sexually abused child: she was an incest survivor' 'Was Virginia Woolf "insane"?' 'Was Virginia Woolf mad?'" Etcetera, etcetera. "What no longer seems possible," Lee writes, "is to start: 'Adeline Virginia Stephen was born on 25 January 1882.'"

Why not? Evidently because her life has come to stand for a great deal; it has become a heavily loaded symbol in the current dialogues over gender, class, madness, and marriage. The famously gifted, original, neurotic, courageous, difficult, and very imperfect human being she once was has disappeared, and in its place is a secular saint.

Ms. Lee points out that "all readers of Virginia Woolf's diaries (even those who have decided to dislike her) will feel an extraordinary sense of intimacy with the voice that is talking there. They will want to call her Virginia, and speak proprietorially about her life." This has proven to be so, to an extent that would have appalled the fastidious and publicity-shy novelist. Woolf's literary style, and the chatty, confidential skill with which she charmingly feminized the belletrist tradition of the previous generation, has long made readers feel they know her, while her beauty and vulnerability have made them feel protective toward her. It is possible to see similarities between the apotheosis of Woolf and the process of canonization that is currently taking place over Princess Diana, another beautiful and vulnerable, but not exactly saintly, woman.

Feminist critics and readers—and the cult of St. Virginia is due, above all, to the feminist revolution—have chosen to see in Woolf the kind of martyr-heroine that substantiates present-day dogmas about male and female relations. This version of Woolf portrays her as a frail woman who invited domination. She was a victim of sexual abuse—incest, even; she was oppressed by a patriarchal system personified by a devouring and controlling father; her unfortunate mental illness caused her to be further oppressed by "male" medicine and by a husband who jealously guarded her every move. To add insult to injury, this version has it, she continued to be victimized even after her death by her nephew and biographer, Quentin Bell.

There are such layers of nonsense in this picture that it is difficult to know how to begin to scrape them away. First of all, to see Woolf as having been victimized by these men is to deny her the very considerable triumphs, both material and psychological, that her life represents. Woolf proved herself to be no victim but a tough and resourceful person who overcame the handicaps of her sex and her mental illness to a remarkable degree and carved out for herself a life of freedom, work, and friendship which would have been inconceivable to women a generation earlier.

The sexual abuse so lovingly dwelt upon by today's critics, a shameful catalogue of offensive groping and fondling by her older half-brother, George Duckworth, was an unsavory fact which she confronted with unusual honesty; she was even able to joke about it with her sister Vanessa (also an object of George's ungoverned lust). The "male" medical treatment which Woolf received during her bouts of manic-depression was a failure not, surely, because of its gender but because the miracle of lithium had yet to be discovered. Yet the picture of Woolf as a defenseless woman imprisoned by a cabal of wicked, conniving, and incurably masculine doctors, Mariana in her moated grange, has appealed to those who seek metaphors for male domination and female oppression (or who have read a little too much Foucault). That Woolf herself did not see the situation in this light is testified to by the fact that when she fictionalized her experience in Mrs. Dalloway she made the sufferer a man.

The aspersions that have been cast by a generation of Woolf critics on Sir Leslie Stephen, Leonard Woolf, and Quentin Bell would have surprised and horrified Virginia Woolf, and rightly so. At their most extreme and destructive, commentators have agreed with Louise de Salvo's position, in Virginia Woolf: The Impact of Childhood Sexual Abuse on Her Life and Work, that "Virginia Stephen was raised in a household in which incest, sexual violence, and abusive behaviour were a common, rather than a singular or rare occurrence, a family in which there is evidence that virtually all were involved in incest or violence or both." Others, while not expressing themselves quite so forcefully, have deplored the influence on the delicate Virginia of the possessive and repressive men in her life.

It is true that Woolf was repelled by heterosexual sex and frequently preferred women to men as companions. Vita Sackville-West described her, interestingly, as "curiously feminist: she dislikes possessiveness and love of domination in men. In fact she dislikes the quality of masculinity." Yet she was deeply attached to the men in her life, attached to them, and in many ways— whether her worshipers like it or not—dependent upon them.

There can be no doubt that Sir Leslie Stephen was a difficult father, but he was also a loving one. His relationship with his daughter—like the relationships of most parents and most children, it should be emphasized—was simultaneously destructive and enriching, and Virginia Woolf responded to his egotism with a combination of love and rage. As Hermione Lee intelligently observes, "Virginia wrote and rewrote her father all her life.

She was in love with him, she was furious with him, she was like him, she never stopped arguing with him; and when she finally read Freud in 1939 she recognized exactly what he meant by 'ambivalence.' Stephen was emotionally voracious, demanding the attention, adoration, and servitude of all the women in his household: first his wife Julia, and then, after Julia's death, his stepdaughter Stella Duckworth and, to a rather lesser degree, his young daughters Vanessa and Virginia. If he had lived to ninety-six, Virginia Woolf wrote, "like other people one has known," she felt that "his life would have entirely ended mine.... No writing, no books;—inconceivable."

This projection is probably true: not because her father wished her ill, or begrudged her success, but because an ego so powerful tends to allow room for no other such in its immediate vicinity. Had he lived longer, Stephen would probably have been very happy for his talented younger daughter to have had a nice literary career in his style and in his shadow, ending up, ideally, as his biographer. A bossy paterfamilias, no better or worse than most. Yet Stephen has been portrayed in recent years as a veritable Mr. Barrett of Wimpole Street, a pattern of oppressive Victorian patriarchy. His detached and rather unsympathetic treatment of Virginia's retarded half-sister, Laura Stephen—a treatment normal, alas, for the period and never challenged by Virginia, either during her childhood or later—is used to add colour and menace to the devilish picture.

Even Hermione Lee, a fine critic and meticulous biographer, feels compelled to apologize for his excesses of "patriarchal" behaviour. Indeed, one grows thoroughly sick of the word "patriarchy" before many pages of Virginia Woolf have gone by: Lee is by no means immune to the glamour of academic jargon, and she even resorts to the disgusting affectation of using parentheses between words, as in "(en)treaties." To reduce Stephen to a catalogue of oppressive and patriarchal values is to paint a figure that would have been unrecognizable to his contemporaries or even to his family.

Although he had settled into a crusty and pessimistic middle age by the time his youngest daughter knew him, he had been in his time a highly influential radical, a supporter of Irish independence, Church disestablishment, and parliamentary reform. "For some young men," writes Lee, "he paved the way (like his beloved Meredith, like Gissing or Samuel Butler...) for the intellectual revolutions of the next century." Perhaps if we are to settle on any definitive portrait of Sir Leslie Stephen—at least insofar as he figures in the life of his daughter Virginia—it should be Virginia's own portrait of him as Mr. Ramsay in To the Lighthouse.

Only the most unresponsive reader could feel the self-indulgence and bombast of Mr. Ramsay without also feeling the softness and the dependence, could respond to the anger in the portrait without divining the helpless love. Mr. Ramsay is a critical and mocking comment on Sir Leslie Stephen, but he is also a deeply affectionate one, and anyone who fails to recognize the fact must be so patently dense that he, or she, should not be allowed to claim the title of literary critic. The late Quentin Bell, Virginia Woolf's much-loved nephew, enjoyed a privileged relationship with his aunt throughout his youth; after Leonard Woolf's death he probably remembered her better than any person still living. His Virginia Woolf (1972), intelligent and humane, affectionate but unsparing, is one of the great masterpieces of the genre; it was also considered the definitive Woolf biography until the appearance of Ms. Lee's.

As such it inevitably came under fire as a phallocentric document from the feminist critics who seek to deliver their heroine from male hands. Hostile critics like Jane Marcus have railed against Bell, the obsolete 'sexist who, they contend, sought to define and misrepresent "their" Virginia. Bell was attacked for every even slightly unflattering thing he said about his aunt. He was attacked for the crime of being a man attempting to write about a woman. He committed the ultimate sin, though, when he stated that Virginia Woolf was not a feminist. Well of course, that depends on just what your definition of feminism is, as any idiot should be able to figure out. Bell, coming from a different generation and tradition from his younger, largely American critics, probably adhered to the rather narrow notion that feminists are overtly political, strident, often mannish. Virginia Woolf did not attach her name to political causes; she was ambivalent about votes for women, and did not join the suffragist struggle; she was, in spite of her unconventional sex life, an intensely feminine person.

A more catholic definition of feminism, one that would accept as both "feminist" and beneficial the great revolution that over the course of the last hundred and fifty years has allowed women the fundamental right to control their own lives and income, would have to classify Virginia Woolf not only as a feminist but as one of the most important feminists of our era: as the author of A Room of One's Own alone, she has exerted an unparalleled imaginative influence on feminist thought.

It is all a question of definition, and if the question were put to him, Quentin Bell would surely have agreed that if his aunt were not the first sort of feminist, she was most undoubtedly the second. However he might define "feminist," Bell wrote of his aunt with extraordinary grace and insight. He wrote with love, yet accepted that his aunt did not always behave in a lovable fashion. He included every wart, while painting a complete portrait in which the overwhelming impression was of singular beauty. Yet Woolf's self-proclaimed defenders cannot forgive Bell for having included any unattractive features at all. What could he know about her, anyway? He was only a man. How dare he claim to define, to "own," to criticize, their exalted Virginia? Even Hermione Lee goes along with this school of thought.

As they grew up, the [Bell] children conspired with their parents to create a family image of Virginia Woolf as the batty, playful, malicious, untrustworthy, eccentric genius. The letters between the children about Virginia always strike this note; it lingers on into Quentin Bell's biography, and has greatly influenced the British reading of her life. There is a great deal of truth in this image, however, and nowhere in her 760-page biography does Lee really succeed in dislodging it. Virginia Woolf was playful, untrustworthy, and eccentric; it is what makes her impossible to define and pin down, as current feminist critics would so much like to do. She was also, beyond any doubt, snobbish and malicious. Were she by some magic able to come back to life, there can be no doubt that among the first victims of her snobbery and her malice would be the earnest and political academics who claim her for their own.

The third perceived maleficent male in Virginia Woolf's life was the one she cared for the most: her husband. It is my opinion after reading both Bell and Lee that Leonard Woolf was one of the most devoted and long-suffering husbands in history. Romantically in love with his wife, he agreed, shortly after marriage, with her decision that they forego sexual relations, which were intolerable to her. His assiduous care undoubtedly kept her out of mental institutions and allowed her to have a productive and creative life. He took pride in her talent and intellect and encouraged her to exercise them to the utmost; he suppressed his own ego, judging her work to be more important than his own.

It is true that he pushed for a quiet life in the country when she would have preferred the excitement of London, and that he made clear his opinion that they had better not have children. But on balance Leonard must be seen as having been tremendously beneficial to his wife, a fact that her final letter to him bears out: "I want to tell you that you have given me complete happiness.... No one could have been so good as you have been." Of course, it is possible to go overboard in praising this unconventional marriage. Lee pooh-poohs the idea that the Woolfs' marriage might have been lacking in some essential element, blaming "standard assumptions about what a full-blooded sexual life needed to consist of."

Are these "standard assumptions" so very wrong, then? I don't think so. And I find the Woolfs' pseudo-sexual fantasy life, in which they took on the personae of cuddly animals, revolting. ("In their secret play Leonard was often the little stringy creature, the mongoose, the 'Servant,' and she was the big mandril, goddess or mistress." Ugh! These, like so many revelations about the sex lives of the Bloomsburyites, are details that posterity could well have lived without.)

Still, whatever their initial motivations might have been, Leonard and Virginia chose each other and stood by their choice unwaveringly. They tried, as Lee points out, to reshape the possibilities of marriage, and to a large extent they succeeded. For Leonard to be calumniated as a parasite feeding on his wife's genius, a domestic tyrant who controlled her every move and kept her in an emotional prison, is a libelous disgrace.

The truth is that critics like Jane Marcus and Elaine Showalter seem unable to accept the fact that Virginia Woolf decided to marry and to place herself in a position of considerable emotional dependency upon a man. The fact that a woman who so passionately sought independence on one level while shrinking from it on another seems too hard for the literal-minded, who expect their heroes never to behave unheroically, to stretch their imaginations around.

The process of canonization of St. Virginia has turned Woolf into an untouchable figure she was not and could never be, and has obscured the imperfect and vastly more interesting reality. She was a powerful, important, and revolutionary writer but not, in my opinion, one of the very greatest. Her dislike for the vulgarity she perceived on first reading the manuscript of Ulysses indicates her own great failing, for an artist who is afraid of being vulgar will always be handicapped. Her avoidance of vulgarity led her too often to vulgarity's opposite, and far more serious, sins: preciosity and fancy. Her recognition, however, of Joyce's "show- offishness" indicates one of her own strengths: she did not use her work for ostentation; she undertook her literary experiments with a sincere desire to achieve new effects, to translate the immediacy of experience to the page more exactly than had ever been done before.

She was the author of a masterpiece of art, To the Lighthouse, and a masterpiece of polemic, A Room of One's Own; an excellent but not whol- ly successful novel, Mrs. Dalloway; and a number of interesting but not immortal experimental novels. She was also indisputably one of the greatest literary critics of the last two centuries. Her essays are as fresh and as pertinent as they were when she wrote them, although some of her judgments—as, for example, those on Arnold Bennett and H. G. Wells—are accepted too religiously. As a critic, she was always far wiser than her own critics have been about her.

In her literary criticism, Virginia Woolf was one of the first, and most important, to take full measure of a writer whose posthumous career bears curious similarities to Woolf's own: George Eliot. Many critics before Woolf, of course, had taken the measure of George Eliot, but Woolf looked at her from the point of view of a woman experiencing the feminine essence of the work, and in that sense she broke new ground.

Woolf saw in Eliot's heroines the story of Eliot herself:

Thus we behold her, a memorable figure, inordinately praised and shrinking from her fame, despondent, reserved, shuddering back into the arms of love as if there alone were satisfaction and, it might be, justification, at the same time reaching out with "a fastidious yet hungry ambition" for all that life could offer the free and inquiring mind and confronting her feminine aspirations with the real world of men. Triumphant was the issue for her, whatever it may have been for her creations.

"Shrinking back into the arms of love": an odd phrase to apply a spirit as independent as George Eliot's is perceived to have been, but a true one nevertheless. Eliot, like Woolf, was a woman unusually dependent on her male partner in life, and, as with Woolf, feminist scholars have found it hard to forgive her for it. Rosemary Ashton's new biography of Eliot gives an intelligent and balanced account of a life rife with contradiction:

The distinctiveness of George Eliot's life—the particular turns it took, the successive milieus she inhabited, the shock waves caused in respectable, orthodox social circles by some of her actions—needs to be stressed. Nowadays few bat an eyelid at young people, and young women in particular, professing no religious faith, pursuing studies and careers in bedsits, living with men to whom they are not legally married. Marian Evans did all these things, yet as others observed of her, and as she herself recognized, her temperament was at bottom one which sought approval and desired to conform. Herbert Spencer saw that though intellectually she threw off her early beliefs, religious and political, "her natural feeling was a longing to agree as far as possible."

Every circumstance of Eliot's life bears out this interpretation of her character. When her father turned her out of the house after she rejected Church of England Christianity, she grieved, but gave not an inch. When she and George Henry Lewes, who was still married to another woman, set up house together, she faced the defection of her brother, Isaac, with sad resignation (the couple's frustrated love is movingly echoed in the troubled relationship of Tom and Maggie Tulliver in The Mill on the Floss), and she stoically endured a social ostracism she never sought.

This ostracism was a sorrow to her for many years; in the end, however, she decided to interpret it as a blessing:

For myself I prefer excommunication. I have no earthly thing that I care for, to gain by having been brought within the pale of people's personal attention, and I have many things to care for that I should lose—my freedom from petty worldly torments, commonly called pleasures, and that isolation which really keeps my charity warm instead of chilling it, as much contact with frivolous women would do.

Eliot, much like Virginia Woolf, dissociated herself from party politics; though she consistently allied herself with progressivism and reform, she was no radical, strongly disapproving of sudden or violent change. Again like Woolf, she was ambivalent about women's suffrage but passionate about women's education: she made a donation, for example, to the newly founded Girton College, but did not wish for her name to be linked with any cause —fearing, perhaps, that her scandalous reputation might do such causes more harm than good. If one had to sum up George Eliot, one would have to conclude that she was not by nature unconventional—that is, she had no wish to flout convention—but that she was possessed of a personal honesty so fundamental and uncompromising that it forced her into an unconventional life whether she wanted one or not. Her refusal to pay lip service to organized religion (unconsciously hitting on the same phrase as her contemporary, Karl Marx, she stated that for herself it was best "to do without opium") or received morality (she considered her relationship with Lewes, whether or not it was ratified by law, to be a marriage) placed this upright, firmly moralistic woman in the absurd position of social renegade. A more unlikely renegade never lived.

"I think she is a highly feminine and attractive character," Virginia Woolf wrote to Lady Robert Cecil while researching the life of George Eliot for an essay in 1919, "—most impulsive and ill-balanced... and I only wish she had lived nowadays, and so been saved all that nonsense. I mean, being so serious, and digging up fossils, and all the rest of it."

One might likewise wish that Woolf herself had been saved the obsessions of her own time—Freud and significant form and doctrinaire pacifism and obligatory sexual frankness—but the truth is that every age has its hobbyhorses. Woolf saw herself and her circle as having created something finer and better than Victorian society, and when Lytton Strachey, for example, called The Voyage Out "very, very unvictorian," he meant it as the ultimate compliment. Woolf's statement that "On or about December, 1910, human character changed," is perhaps her most frequently quoted mot.

It is also the most ridiculous, for when has human nature ever changed? After a comparison of the lives and mores of Woolf's circle with that of Eliot, the only possible response is "plus ça change...."

Woolf did not see it that way: pondering the unlikely friendship between Clive Bell and Duncan Grant, she felt that her own generation, "with the truthtelling mechanism at hand," dealt with love and marriage far better than their

Victorian parents had done. But one wonders! Take Virginia's sister, Vanessa Bell. Her marriage to Clive Bell was for years what we would nowadays call "open," and eventually they went their more or less separate ways, Vanessa setting up house with the painter Duncan Grant. Though Grant gave her a child, Angelica (who was told that Clive Bell was in fact her father), he remained a homosexual, retaining his lover, "Bunny" Garnett, as a part of the household. Standing by the bassinet of the newborn Angelica, Bunny Garnett said that he would probably end up marrying the little girl, as indeed he eventually did. Anyone inclined to celebrate the unconventional freedom of the Bell/Grant/Garnett household is invited to read Angelica Garnett's memoir, Deceived by Kindness, which paints a grim picture of her childhood and its perpetual aura of lies and secrets.

Vanessa Bell rejected her own mother's scenario of domestic slavery, the "angel in the house" image, only to repeat the pattern in an even more self-destructive guise. And what about those staid Victorians, anyway? George Eliot's own life should serve as an antidote to that stale cliché. Estranged from her pious father, the agnostic Marian Evans moved to London and began work on the Westminster Review, taking lodgings with John Chapman, the Review's twenty-nine-year-old editor. Chapman's menage consisted of himself; his wife Susanna, fourteen years older than himself; their children; and the children's governess, Elisabeth Tilley, Chapman's mistress and accepted as such by his wife. It was not long before the energetic Chapman began paying attentions to his brilliant young lodger; this proved too much for wife and mistress, who successfully joined forces and booted the intruder out. Chapman's journal records the scene.

M. departed today, I accompanied her to the railway. She was very sad, and hence made me feel so. She pressed me for some intimation of the state of my feelings,—(I told her that I felt great affection for her, but that I loved E. and S. also, though each in a different way.) At this avowal she burst into tears. I tried to comfort her, and reminded her of the dear friends and pleasant home she was returning to,—but the train whirled her away very sad. This was pure farce, though not, perhaps, appreciated as such by Marian Evans/George Eliot herself until she was safely embarked on her relationship with Lewes.

Although Lewes and Eliot were never legally married, the relationship was a marriage and more than a marriage, distinguished by daily routine, mutual fidelity, and each partner's infinite pleasure and comfort in the other's company. But again, how very unusual were the circumstances of the "marriage," and how roundly they contradict twentieth-century stereotypes about the Victorians—stereotypes largely invented and propagated by Woolf and her circle.

Lewes was not free to marry Marian Evans because he was already married, to Agnes Jervis. Lewes and Agnes had for some time agreed to conduct independent sex lives, and Agnes had by the time of Marian's appearance on the scene two children by the impecunious publisher Thornton Hunt; they were eventually to produce a total of four. The generous Lewes, almost as a matter of course, supported these four children as well as his own three throughout his life, and paid a regular stipend to the errant Agnes as well, an obligation that George Eliot would take on after Lewes's death. It became such an accepted arrangement that when one month Agnes overspent her allowance and Lewes remonstrated, Hunt sent him a challenge. "There is something ludicrous in the extravagance of this," Lewes wrote; "A challenge from him to me, and on such grounds!" As we examine the life of George Eliot, it becomes clear how lucky and wise she was in her choice of a life partner. Lewes was an extraordinarily kind, capable, and affectionate man, "a man of heart and conscience," as Eliot described him, "wearing a mask of flippancy." Without being a genius in any one field, he was wonderfully facile at many, and wrote on history, science, philosophy, literature, psychology, and the theater with almost equal ease; he was a first-rate editor, and a popularizer of any number of subjects. At the time he and Eliot became lovers he was, unlike her, emotionally sophisticated and sexually experienced.

He shared her philosophy without having come by it in

the same tortuous fashion: "There is no evidence," writes Ashton, "that he had ever held a religious belief." He was vigorous, affectionate, easily amused: the depressive Eliot could not have hit on a husband who could better complement and enliven her habitually low spirits. The woman who had always believed herself to be "a negation of all that finds love and esteem" found herself loved unconditionally; the writer who had an exaggerated fear of criticism and bad reviews was shielded from them for the rest of Lewes's life.

Lewes, needless to say, has earned a good deal of posthumous criticism for his habit of hiding unpleasant reviews from Eliot. Perhaps, it is said, she might have profited from these reviews to have become an even greater artist. But it is safe to say that Lewes, who over and above all his other qualities was possessed of unusual common sense, knew his companion better than we, and that his course of action was designed to encourage the consistently high quality of her work rather than to let her settle for mediocrity.

Eliot then, like Virginia Woolf, was a women of remarkable intellectual dependence who lived in a state of intense emotional dependence upon a man. As such she has always been a troubling figure to feminist critics, and her work is as troubling as her life. It is felt that Eliot's heroines are not rebellious enough; they do not challenge patriarchal society sufficiently. In truth, the gap between what Eliot was and what these critics would like her to be lies in her larger intelligence, her superior ability to grasp complexities and contradictions. Victorian culture was more than a mere "patriarchal society", its power structure less rigidly hierarchical than appearances might indicate.

Eliot was a realist, not a fantasist; if her heroines often fail to liberate themselves from the nets they fall into, it is because so many of the real women she observed also failed, and Eliot had no wish to substitute doctrine, or wishful thinking, for truth. Great novels tend to be too slippery to squeeze into any preconceived political mold, and for over a century now George Eliot, like Virginia Woolf, has consistently proved greater than the critics who seek to define her.

Chapter 7

Virginia Woolf on George Eliot

George Eliot was the pseudonym of novelist, translator, and religious writer Mary Ann Evans (1819-1880). This article by Virginia Woolf was first published in The Times Literary Supplement, 20th November, 1919. To read George Eliot attentively is to become aware how little one knows about her. It is also to become aware of the credulity, not very creditable to one's insight, with which, half consciously and partly maliciously, one had accepted the late Victorian version of a deluded woman who held phantom sway over subjects even more deluded than herself.

At what moment and by what means her spell was broken it is difficult to ascertain. Some people attribute it to the publication of her Life. Perhaps George Meredith, with his phrase about the 'mercurial little showman' and the 'errant woman' on the dais, gave point and poison to the arrows of thousands incapable of aiming them so accurately, but delighted to let fly.

She became one of the butts for youth to laugh at, the convenient symbol of a group of serious people who were all guilty of the same idolatry and could be dismissed with the same scorn. Lord Acton had said that she was greater than Dante; Herbert Spencer exempted he novels, as if they were not novels, when he banned all fiction from the London library. She was the pride and paragon of all her sex. Moreover, her private record was not more alluring than her public. Asked to describe an afternoon at the Priory, the story-teller always intimated that the memory of those serious Sunday afternoons had come to tickle his sense of humour.

He had been so much alarmed by the grave lady in her low chair; her had been so anxious to say the intelligent thing. Certainly, the talk had been very serious, as a note in the fine clear hand of the novelist bore witness. It was dated on the Monday morning, and she accused herself of having spoken with due forethought of Marivaux when she meant another; but not doubt, she said, her listener had already supplied the correction. Still, the memory of talking about Marivaux to George Eliot on a Sunday afternoon was not a romantic memory. It had faded with the passage of years. It had not become picturesque.

Indeed, one cannot escape the conviction that the long, heavy face with its expression of serious and sullen and almost equine power has stamped itself depressingly upon the minds of people who remember George Eliot, so that it looks out upon them from her pages. Mr Gosse has lately described her as he saw her driving through London in a victoria:

A large, thick-set sybil, dreamy and immobile, whose massive features, somewhat grim when seen in profile, were incongruously bordered by a hat, always in the height of Paris fashion, which in those days commonly included an immense ostrich feather.

Lady Ritchie, with equal skill, has left a more intimate indoor portrait:

She sat by the fire in a beautiful black satin gown, with a green shaded lamp on the table beside her, where I saw German books lying and pamphlets and ivory paper-cutters. She was very quiet and noble, with two steady little eyes and a sweet voice. As I looked I felt her to be a friend, not exactly a personal friend, but a good and benevolent impulse.

A scrap of her talk is preserved. 'We ought to respect our influence,' she said. 'We know by our own experience how very much others affect our lives, and we must remember that we in turn must have the same effect on others.' Jealously treasured, committed to memory, one can imagine recalling the scene, repeating the words, thirty years later, and suddenly, for the first time, bursting into laughter. In all these records one feels that the recorder, even when he was in the actual presence, kept his distance and kept his head, and never read the novels in later years with the light of a vivid, or puzzling, or beautiful personality dazzling his eyes. In fiction, where so much of personality is revealed, the absence of charm is a great lack; and her critics, who have been, of course, mostly of the opposite sex, have resented, half consciously perhaps, her deficiency in a quality which is held to be supremely desirable in women.

George Eliot was not charming; she was not strongly feminine; she had none of those eccentricities and inequalities of temper which give to so many artists the endearing simplicity of children.

One feels that to most people, as to Lady Ritchie, she was 'not exactly a personal friend, but a good and benevolent impulse'. But if we consider these portraits more closely, we find that they are all the portraits of an elderly celebrated woman, dressed in black satin, driving in her victoria, a woman who has been through her struggle and issued from it with a profound desire to be of use to others, but with no wish for intimacy, save with the little circle who had known her in the days of her youth. We know very little about the days of her youth; but we do know that the culture, the philosophy, the fame, and the influence were all built upon a very humble foundation-she was the granddaughter of a carpenter.

The first volume of her life is a singularly depressing record. In it we see her rising herself with groans and struggles from the intolerable boredom of petty provincial society (her father had risen in the world and become more middle class, but less picturesque) to be the assistant editor of a highly intellectual London review, and the esteemed companion of Herbert Spencer. The stages are painful as she reveals them in the sad soliloquy in which Mr Cross condemned her to tell the story of her life.

Marked in early youth as one 'sure to get something up very soon in the way of a clothing club', she proceeded to raise funds for restoring a church by making a chart of ecclesiastical history; and that was followed by a loss of faith which so disturbed her father that he refused to live with her. Next came the struggle with the translation of Strauss, which, dismal and 'soul-stupefying' in itself, can scarcely have been made less so by the usual feminine tasks of ordering a household and nursing a dying father, and the distressing conviction, to one so dependent upon affection, that by becoming a bluestocking she was forfeiting her brother's respect.

'I used to go about like an owl', she said, 'to the great disgust of my brother'. 'Poor thing', wrote a friend who saw her toiling through Strauss with a statue of the risen Christ in front of her, 'I do pity her sometimes, with her pale sickly face and dreadful headaches, and anxiety, too, about her father.' Yet, though we cannot read the story without a strong desire that the stages of her pilgrimage might have been made, if not more easy, at least more beautiful, there is a dogged determination in her advance upon the citadel of culture which raises it above our pity. Her development was very slow and very awkward, but it had the irresistible impetus behind it of a deep-seated and noble ambition.

Every obstacle at length was thrust from her path. She knew everyone. She read everything. Her astonishing intellectual vitality had triumphed. Youth was over, but youth had been full of suffering. Then, at the age of thirty-five, at the height of her powers, and in the fulness of her freedom, she made the which was of such profound moment to her and still matters even to us, and went to Weimar, alone with George Henry Lewes.

The books which followed so soon after her union testify in the fullest manner to the great liberation which had come to her with personal happiness. In themselves they provide us with a plentiful feast. Yet at the threshold of her literary career one may find in some of the circumstances of her life influences that turned her mind to the past, to the country village, to the quiet and beauty and simplicity of childish memories and away from herself and the present.

We understand how it was that her first book was Scenes of Clerical Life and not Middlemarch. Her union with Lewes had surrounded her with affection, but in view of the circumstances and of the conventions it has also isolated her. 'I wish it to be understood', she wrote in 1857, 'that I should never invite anyone to come and see me who did not ask for the invitation.' She had been 'cut off from what is called the world', she said later, but she did not regret it.

By becoming thus marked, first by circumstances and later, inevitably, by her fame, she lost the power to move on equal terms unnoted among her kind; and the loss for a novelist was serious. Still, basking in the light and sunshine of Scenes of Clerical Life, feeling the large mature mind spreading itself with a luxurious sense of freedom in the world of her 'remotest past', to speak of loss seems inappropriate. Everything to such a mind was gain. All experience filtered down through layer after layer of perception and reflection, enriching and nourishing.

The utmost we can say, in qualifying her attitude towards fiction by what we know of her life, is that she had taken to heart certain lessons learnt early, if learnt at all, among which, perhaps, the most branded upon her was the melancholy virtue of tolerance; her sympathies are with the everyday lot, and play most happily in dwelling upon the homespun of ordinary joys and sorrows.

She has none of that romantic intensity which is connected with a sense of one's own individuality, unsated and unsubdued, cutting its shape sharply upon the background of the world. What were the loves and sorrows of a snuffy old clergyman, dreaming over his whisky, to the fiery egotism of Jane Eyre? The beauty of those first books, Scenes of Clerical Life, Adam Bede, The Mill on the Floss, is very great. It is impossible to estimate the merit of the Poysers, the Dodsons, the Gilfils, the Bartons, and the rest with all their surroundings and dependencies, because they have put on flesh and blood and we move among them, now bored, now sympathetic, but always with that unquestioning acceptance of all that they say and do, which we accord to the great originals only.

The flood of memory and humour which she pours so

spontaneously into one figure, one scene after another, until the whole fabric of ancient rural England is revived, has so much in common with a natural process that it leaves us with little consciousness that there is anything to criticize. We accept; we feel the delicious warmth and release of spirit which the great creative writers alone procure for us. As one comes back to the books after years of absence they pour out, even against our expectation, the same store of energy and heat, so that we want more than anything to idle in the warmth as in the sun beating down from the red orchard wall.

If there is an element of unthinking abandonment in thus submitting to the humours of Midland farmers and their wives, that, too, is right in the circumstances. We scarcely wish to analyse what we feel to be so large and deeply human. And when we consider how distant in time the world of Shepperton and Hayslope is, and how remote the minds of farmer and agricultural labourers from those of most of George Eliot's readers, we can only attribute the ease and pleasure with which we ramble from house to smithy, from cottage parlour to rectory garden, to the fact that George Eliot makes us share their lives, not in a spirit of condescension or of curiosity, but in a spirit of sympathy. She is no satirist.

The movement of her mind was too slow and cumbersome to lend itself to comedy. But she gathers in her large grasp a great bunch of the main elements of human nature and groups them loosely together with a tolerant and wholesome understanding which, as one finds upon rereading, has not only kept her figures fresh and free, but has given them an unexpected hold upon our laughter and tears.

There is the famous Mrs Poyser. It would have been easy to work her idiosyncrasies to death, and, as it is, perhaps, George Eliot gets her laugh in the same place a little too often. But memory, after the book is shut, brings out, as sometimes in real life, the details and subtleties which some more salient characteristic has prevented us from noticing at the time. We recollect that her health was not good.

There were occasions upon which she said nothing at

all. She was patience itself with sick child. She doted upon Totty. Thus one can muse and speculate about the greater number of George Eliot's characters and find, even in the least important, a roominess and margin where those qualities lurk which she has no call to bring from their obscurity. But in the midst of all this tolerance and sympathy there are, even in the early books, moments of greater stress. Her humour has shown itself broad enough to cover a wide range of fools and failures, mothers and children, dogs and flourishing midland fields, farmers, sagacious or fuddled over their ale, horse-dealers, inn-keepers, curates, and carpenters. Over them all broods a certain romance, the only romance that George Eliot allowed herself- the romance of the past. The books are astonishingly readable and have no trace of pomposity or pretence.

But to the reader who holds a large stretch of her early work in view it will become obvious that the mist of recollection gradually withdraws. It is not that her power diminishes, for, to our thinking, it is at its highest in the mature Middlemarch, the magnificent book which with all its imperfections is one of the few English novels written for grown-up people. But the world of fields and farms no longer contents her. In real life she had sought her fortunes elsewhere; and though to look back into the past was calming and consoling, there are, even in the early works, traces of that troubled spirit, that exacting and questioning and baffled presence who was George Eliot herself. In Adam Bede there is a hint of her in Dinah. She shows herself far more openly and completely in Maggie in The Mill on the Floss.

She is Janet in Janet's Repentance, and Romola, and Dorothea seeking wisdom and finding one scarcely knows what in marriage with Ladislaw. Those who fall foul of George Eliot do so, we incline to think, on account of her heroines; and with good reason; for there is no doubt that they bring out the worst of her, lead her into difficult places, make her self-conscious, didactic, and occasionally vulgar.

Yet if you could delete the whole sisterhood you would leave a much smaller and a much inferior world, albeit a world of greater artistic perfection and far superior jollity and comfort. In accounting for her failure, in so far as it was a failure, one recollects that she never wrote a story until she was thirty-seven, and that by the time she was thirty-seven she had come to think of herself with a mixture of pain and something like resentment. For long she preferred not to think of herself at all. Then, when the first flush of creative energy was exhausted and self-confidence had come to her, she wrote more and more from the personal standpoint, but she did so without the unhesitating abandonment of the young. Her self-consciousness is always marked when her heroines say what she herself would have said. She disguised them in every possible way. She granted them beauty and wealth into the bargain; she invented, more improbably, a taste for brandy. But the disconcerting and stimulating fact remained that she was compelled by the very power of her genius to step forth in person upon the quiet bucolic scene.

The noble and beautiful girl who insisted upon being born into the Mill on the Floss is the most obvious example of the ruin which a heroine can strew about her. Humour controls her and keeps her lovable so long as she is small and can be satisfied by eloping with the gipsies or hammering nails into her doll; but she develops; and before George Eliot knows what has happened she has a full-grown woman on her hands demanding what neither gipsies, nor dolls, nor St Ogg's itself is capable of giving her. First Philip Wakem is produced, and later Stephen Guest. The weakness of the one and the coarseness of the other have often been pointed out; but both, in their weakness and coarseness, illustrate not so much George Eliot's inability to draw the portrait of a man, as the uncertainty, the infirmity, and the fumbling which shook her hand when she had to conceive a fit mate for a heroine. She is in the first place driven beyond the home world she knew and loved, and forced to set foot in middle-class drawing-rooms where young men sing all the summer morning and young women sit embroidering smoking-caps for bazaars.

She feels herself out of her element, as her clumsy satire

of what she calls 'good society' proves. Good society has its claret and its velvet carpets, its dinner engagements six weeks deep, its opera, and its faery ball rooms... gets its science done by Faraday and its religion by the superior clergy who are to be met in the best houses; how should it have need of belief and emphasis? There is no trace of humour or insight there, but only the vindictiveness of a grudge which we feel to be personal it its origin. But terrible as the complexity of our social system is in its demands upon the sympathy and discernment of a novelist straying across the boundaries, Maggie Tulliver did worse than drag George Eliot from her natural surroundings.

She insisted upon the introduction of the great emotional scene. She must love; she must despair; she must be drowned clasping her brother in her arms. The more one examines the great emotional scenes the more nervously one anticipates the brewing and gathering and thickening of the cloud which will burst upon our heads at the moment of crisis in a shower of disillusionment and verbosity.

It is partly that her hold upon dialogue, when it is not dialect, is slack; and partly that she seems to shrink with an elderly dread of fatigue from the effort of emotional concentration. She allows her heroines to talk too much. She has little verbal felicity.

She lacks the unerring taste which chooses one sentence and compresses the heart of the scene within that. 'Whom are you doing to dance with?' asked Mr Knightley, at the Weston's ball. 'With you, if you will ask me,' said Emma; and she has said enough. Mrs Casaubon would have talked for an hour and we should have looked out of the window. Yet, dismiss the heroines without sympathy, confine George Eliot to the agricultural world of her 'remotest past', and you not only diminish her greatness but lose her true flavour. That greatness is here we can have no doubt.

The width of the prospect, the large strong outlines of the principal features, the ruddy light of her early books, the searching power and reflective richness of the later tempt us to linger and expatiate beyond our limits. But is it upon the heroines that we would cast a final glance. 'I have always been finding out my religion since I was a little girl,' says Dorothea Casaubon. I used to pray so much-now I hardly ever pray.

I try not to have desires merely for myself...' She is speaking for them all. That is their problem. They cannot live without religion, and they start out on the search for one when they are little girls. Each has the deep feminine passion for goodness, which makes the place where she stands in aspiration and agony the heart of the book-still and cloistered like a place of worship, but that she no longer knows to whom to pray.

In learning they seek their goal; in the ordinary tasks of womanhood; in the wider service of their kind. They do not find what they seek, and we cannot wonder. The ancient consciousness of woman, charged with suffering and sensibility, and for so many ages dumb, seems in them to have brimmed and overflowed and uttered a demand for something-they scarcely know what-for something that is perhaps incompatible with the facts of human existence.

George Eliot had far too strong an intelligence to tamper with those facts, and too broad a humour to mitigate the truth because it was a stern one. Save for the supreme courage of their endeavour, the struggle ends, for her heroines, in tragedy, or in a compromise that is even more melancholy. But their story is the incomplete version of the story that is George Eliot herself.

For her, too, the burden and the complexity of womanhood were not enough; she must reach beyond the sanctuary and pluck for herself the strange bright fruits of art and knowledge. Clasping them as few women have ever clasped them, she would not renounce her own inheritance-the difference of view, the difference of standard-nor accept an inappropriate reward.

Thus we behold her, a memorable figure, inordinately praised and shrinking from her fame, despondent, reserved, shuddering back into the arms of love as if there alone were satisfaction and, it might be, justification, at the same time reaching out with 'a fastidious yet hungry ambition' for all that life could offer the free and inquiring mind and confronting her feminine aspirations with the real world of men.

Triumphant was the issue for her, whatever it may have been for her creations, and as we recollect all that she dared and achieved, how with every obstacle against her-sex and health and convention-she sought more knowledge and more freedom till the body, weighted with its double burden, sank worn out, we must lay upon her grave whatever we have it in our power to bestow of laurel and rose.

Chapter 8

Martyrdom and the Unjust Society

George Sand wrote of Stowe's style in Uncle Tom's Cabin, "We should feel that genius is heart, that power is faith, that talent is sincerity, and finally, success is sympathy". Faith, sincerity, and sympathy are indeed the overarching narrative tones Stowe strikes in the novel and are the feelings she wishes to awaken in her readers. Sympathy is likewise what Eliot wishes to stir in her readers in relating Maggie Tulliver's tragic life. Both Uncle Tom's Cabin and The Mill on the Floss utilize religious themes to accomplish these aims.

Each points out the hypocrisy of conventional religious sentiments, highlights sincere religious sentiments within a few select individuals, and compares its suffering hero/heroine to Christ the martyr. By casting their narratives in familiar religious paradigms, the authors ably strike deepest into the hearts of their readers, impressing them with the tragedy of the situations they describe.

Religious authority and traditional Christian themes play a significant role in Uncle Tom's Cabin. As part of the nineteenth century tide of American Protestantism in which social behaviour and spiritual regeneration were seen as interdependent, Stowe felt the novel was an "errand of mercy," by calling for an improvement in human welfare and humanitarian reform. She contrasted the social system of slavery, which corrupted the owners, oppressed the innocent, and undermined American democratic ideals, with a theological system based on compassion, mercy, and "brotherly" love. And this theological viewpoint is presented as the higher moral authority, one that any true believer cannot fail to recognize and obey. The novel is both an appeal for righteous moral action on the part of white northerners against slavery and a confirmation of Christian life as spiritually sublime in the rendering of characters like little Eva and Uncle Tom.

George Eliot also deals with themes of morality and religious sensibility in The Mill on the Floss. Narrow and unimaginative morality is contrasted with wide-ranging fellow-feelings of sympathy and compassion, the latter being the truer expression of Christian teaching. Eliot believed that a "large sympathy" beyond egoism was indispensible to moral growth, therefore the individual must develop within the confines of duty to his/her community. Through her choices, Maggie Tulliver, like Uncle Tom, represents an ideal of Christian suffering and passive transcendence. And, like Uncle Tom's Cabin, Eliot's novel is both an indictment of moral hypocrisy and inaction and an affirmation of the redemptive power of patient endurance.

Religious authority is presented in many guises in Uncle Tom's Cabin in order to contrast real religious feeling with the hypocritical forms of religious sentiment. Mrs. Shelby evinces real Christian virtue and understanding when she exclaims upon learning of her husband's intention to sell Tom and Eliza's son, "I was a fool to think that I could make anything good out of such a deadly evil. It is a sin to hold a slave under laws like ours...I never thought that slavery was right". Yet she is impotent in changing the system or even affecting her husband's actions. She is subject to the system herself despite her efforts at alleviating her slaves' hardships; her moral authority is relegated to the theoretical in no small part because she is a woman.

Likewise, Augustine St. Clair recognizes the evils of slavery and also tries to alleviate its effects by treating his slaves well. And one might think being a wealthy man, St. Clare could more easily put his ideas into practice, but when his brother asks him why he doesn't free his slaves he replies, "One man can do nothing against the whole action of a community. Education, to do anything, must be a state education; or there must be enough agreed in it to make a current". Thus, St. Clare conveniently renders himself ineffective.

Yet, Stowe makes these characters' actions understandable, if pathetic, whereas she absolutely condemns those who distort Christian teaching to justify slavery. Stowe expresses her contempt when St. Clare exclaims to his wife, Marie, "Religion! Is that what you hear at church religion? Is that which can bend and turn, and descend and ascend, to fit every crooked phase of selfish, worldly society, religion? Is that religion which is less scrupulous, less generous, less just, less considerate for man, than even my own ungodly, worldly, blinded nature?". Of course, St. Clare's answer, and Stowe's, is no. True religion must not submit to and be used by the wealthy and powerful to justify injustice, but must flow from the spring of sincere spiritual feeling.

The contrast between true religious feeling and the outer form of it is also a theme of The Mill on the Floss. Most of the characters who claim to live their lives according to a religious standard, or exhort others to, are usually disguising their adherence to a narrow, puritanical notion of morality that is based as much on public opinion as on Christian teaching. Distant from the great social issue of slavery, this novel is able to explore the finer distinction between those who uphold the letter of Christian teaching and those who adhere to the spirit of it. Eliot writes of the Dodsons, "Their religion was of a simple, semi-pagan kind, but there was no heresy in it...[consisting of adherence] to traditional duty and propriety". A surplus of passionate piety, such as Maggie temporarily finds comfort in as an adolescent, whould horrify them.

Unlike Simon Legree, no one is branded as being outright evil in St. Oggs, yet Eliot shows how narrow morality disguised as religious sentiment can still be selfishly used to maintain the status quo and to stifle sympathy for one's fellows. This happens not only when the town condemns Maggie after she returns from her escapade with Stephen Guest, but is most particularly examined in Tom's character and his treatment of Maggie. Tom, like his aunts, lacks imagination and that flexibility of mind which enables one to empathize with another's plight. He is "the man of maxims...the popular representative of the minds that are guided in their moral judgment solely by general rules...without the trouble of exerting patience, discrimination, impartiality". As Maggie tells him, "You have no pity-you have no sense of your own imperfections and your own sins". Even Dr. Kenn, who represents actual religious authority and who is presented as a sincerely compassionate man attempting to aid Maggie with support, acceptance and sympathy, has eventually to bow to social pressure.

The aforementioned characters in both novels actually highlight the ineffectiveness of the teachings and exhortations of the traditional religious authorities to affect society for the better. Even characters who have their hearts in the right place, like Mrs. Shelby and Dr. Kenn, are helpless when their viewpoints contradict those of the larger society and, combined with the lukewarm indifference and spiritual apathy of most people who are like St. Clare or Tom, it is no wonder the overall power of religiously motivated understanding and reform is limited. Yet each author does present an alternative role for those with genuine spiritual feelings to play in affecting society for the better.

Stowe holds up the Quakers, or the Society of Friends, as a group possibly to be emulated, but at the very least to be admired, for acting directly and forthrightly from their consciences and beliefs. More specifically, both little Eva and Uncle Tom are presented as models of Christian sincerity and virtue. Contrasted with her father, Eva is shown to have true religion when she says of the cruelties of slavery, "I'm not nervous, but these things sink into my heart." No matter the hardship, Tom refuses to be swayed from his faith. And the power of true Christian love is shown in the reform and conversion of Topsy. If only in the traditional Protestant sense, the idealized examples of Tom and Eva serve to reawaken the majority of Protestant readers to the original force and depth of their own religious beliefs.

Unlike Stowe, Eliot herself abandoned the Protestant evangelical tradition and sought for a more humanistic philosophy that transcended doctrine. Gleaning ideas from the philosophers Comte, Feuerbach, and Spinoza, Eliot portrayed her many of her characters, like Maggie, who rely on intuitional knowledge, or "feeling" as a basis and guide to moral duty. Newton writes of Eliot, "Instead of submitting feeling to an external authority separate from it, which had been the main difficulty during her Christian period, she discovers that in feeling itself she can find the basis for the larger moral vision she has been seeking".

Yet, this "feeling" is not selfish but is based on one's duty to one's fellows. Maggie tells Stephen she cannot do anything that would "rend me away from all that my past life has made dear and holy to me. I can't set out on a fresh life, and forget that". This view is part of Eliot's conception of society as a slowly evolving organsim, an idea articulated by the philospher Auguste Comte. Society and the individual progress together and when these forces conflict, as in Maggie's case, it is tragic. Eliot argued, "Tragedy consists in the terrible difficulty of the adjustment of our individual needs to the dire necessities of our lot"). Therefore Maggie's story, in a less traditional and more humanistic sense, also serves to awaken in the reader a feeling of sympathy which Eliot thought was the starting point of moral development. Tom's absolute faith and obedience, Eva's innocently indiscriminate love, and Maggie's recurring committment to be "good," are all intended to be examples of true religious sensiblity that we should admire and emulate.

Yet, neither author advocates revolutionary change but rather glorifies patient suffering and passive endurance. Implicitly and explicitly, both Eliot and Stowe compare Maggie and Tom respectively to Christ the martyr. Like Christ in the Garden of Gethsemene, Maggie prays, "I have received the Cross, I have received it form thy hand; I will bear it, and bear it till death, as thou hast laid it upon me". Tom not only meets Legree's hatred and ill treatment with "Christian love" but lays down his life for his friends Cassy and Emmeline. As

Tom tells George Shelby moments before his death, "Heaven has come! I've got the victory!" echoing Christ's acceptance of death on the Cross.

Also like Christ, Maggie's and Tom's suffering and death promote the "salvation" of those around them. Tom's sacrifice helps Cassy rediscover her faith, enables her to become reunited with her daughter Eliza and to indirectly participate in the founding of the new African homeland of Liberia, and convinces young Shelby to free all his slaves which includes Tom's wife and children.

Maggie's suffering and sacrifice is an example to Philip Wakem, Lucy, Stephen, and at the end, Tom, of someone who values her love of others over her own happiness regardless of whether that love is returned. Her choice to return to St. Oggs and remain there is due not to outer influences but rather to her desire to remain true to her own moral ideals. Eliot tells the reader this choice is indispensible for Maggie's spiritual growth when she writes, "That is the path we all like when we set out on our abandonment of egoism-the path of martyrdom and endurance".

By casting Tom and Maggie in the ultimate spiritual and cultural mold of Christ the martyr, Stowe and Eliot wrench this powerful symbol away from conventional religion and recast it to bring attention to the plight of the powerless and downtrodden of the time, namely black people and women. Christianity, traditionally a religion of the oppressed had, by mid-nineteenth century and especially in traditional Protestant denominations, come to function as a genteel veneer of piety for the middle class.

In appropriating this symbol, these authors are communicating to their readers in the most vivid way possible that the Christian work of alleviating oppression, injustice, and suffering is not done. Gifted women like Maggie cannot develop themselves because the societal structure will not provide them with a proper education and an opportunity to use it. Women in general in both novels have few choices beyond choosing a husband and raising a family.

Maggie is treated the way she is simply because she's

female, not because she lacks ability or intelligence. And Tom, the "perfect" slave in that he is loyal, hardworking, and gentle, is murdered out of spite by a degenerate plantation holder. For those who claimed that the problems of slavery are due to the inferiority of the slave, Stowe shows that the slave owner is more corrupt than the slave.

In fact, Tom has internalized the true Christian faith to a greater extent than the pious northerners. Not only are the authors trying to shame the reader by illustrating the needless suffering of good and innocent people, but they are showing the evil of the systems themselves since Maggie and Tom are exceptional; if they cannot escape or overcome the strictures of the systems they live under, then who can? And ironically, Maggie and Tom are squashed because of voluntary submission to the system that oppresses them, thereby mirroring the ideal of patient suffering back at the "Christian" societies they live in. In other words, they "died so that we may live" and understand.

Despite Stowe's and Eliot's reluctance to advocate revolutionary change by directly calling for an abolition to slavery and a granting of equal rights for the former slaves, or appealling for political and economic rights for women equal to those of men under the law, by utilizing the symbol of Christ, a truly revolutionary figure if one studies his story in any depth at all, they challenge their readers all the same but in a uniquely subversive way. By mirroring the symbol of Christ back at the reader in the stories of Maggie Tulliver and Uncle Tom, the authors challenge the reader to follow Christ's dictums of treating the lowly, the oppressed, and the suffering as you would him, and to love all others as one love's oneself.

COLONIALISM IN VICTORIAN ENGLISH LITERATURE

The Victorian period in British history marks the high point of British imperialism. Though the British policy of colonial expansion had begun earlier, during the nineteenth century Britain not only consolidated its existing empire, but also experienced an unprecedented expansion in its colonial possessions. This process began after the 1857 Mutiny in India, when India was placed under the direct control of the Crown, and continued through the scramble for Africa in the late 1800s, so that by the end of the century it could be proudly proclaimed that "the sun never sets on the British Empire."

The tremendous upsurge of imperial activity during the nineteenth century, though physically taking place in areas distant from British shores, had a broad and pervasive impact on British culture. The literature of the period is thus inextricably embroiled in the imperialist project. In the view of many critics, irrespective of the direct involvement of individual literary works with the colonial enterprise, the overall contours of Victorian literature are consistently shaped by the influence of colonial ideology, which informed the collective unconscious of the British public during the entire period.

The most obvious influence of colonialism on Victorian literature is evident in the colonial novels of writers like H. Rider Haggard, Rudyard Kipling, and Joseph Conrad. These novels, which include works like Haggard's She (1889) and Kipling's Kim (1901), are usually set in the distant lands that Britain colonized and attempt to expose the insular domestic public to the exotic strangeness of their country's colonial possessions. The reality of colonialism enters these texts as the necessary background that makes possible their narratives of adventure and romance.

The linking of colonialism with the genre of the romantic adventure story is also evident in the abundant children's fiction of the time, which includes works by Robert Louis Stevenson and R. M. Ballantyne. While using Britain's colonial enterprise as the setting of their narratives, such novels also participate in the construction and propagation of colonial ideology by providing an implicit justification for British imperialism.

Colonialism, therefore, appears in these colonial novels not only as the literal backdrop for their narrative action, but also as the ideological framework that provides the raison d'être of the action. The impact of colonialism, however, is not restricted to the so-called colonial novels. The nineteenth century's dominant genre of domestic fiction is also implicitly informed by colonial ideology.

Though the novels of writers like Jane Austen, Charlotte Brönte, Charles Dickens, and George Eliot focus on domestic British society, Britain's overseas possessions frequently play an important role in the action. Thus, Sir Thomas Bertram's estate in Mansfield Park is maintained by his possessions in Antigua while David Copperfield's Mr. Micawber achieves success in Australia and St. John Rivers in Jane Eyre leaves for India to fulfill his missionary aspirations.

Colonialism thus provides an expanded canvas even to the domestic novels, which reveal the inextricable involvement of domestic British society in the colonial enterprise. At the same time, the implicit presence in these novels of ideas such as the savage nature of natives and the white man's burden of bringing civilization to them also involves these texts in the dissemination of racial and colonial ideologies that provided the conceptual framework for colonialism.

Though an awareness of the colonial presence in Victorian literature is evident in critical studies during the first half of the twentieth century, such criticism is usually restricted to an examination of colonial novels and an evaluation of the authors' differing attitudes to the colonial enterprise as reflected in their writings.

It is only in the latter half of the twentieth century, in the so-called postcolonial period, that critics have explored the pervasive influence of colonial ideology throughout nineteenth-century British culture and society. Edward Said's Orientalism (1978) is a seminal work in this respect, providing an exhaustive analysis of the West's construction of the Orient as its "other." Such a construction, Said argues, is not motivated by any desire to represent faithfully the reality of the colonized cultures and their people.

Instead, it works as a form of ideological control, allowing the West to create a series of Manichean oppositions between the colonizer and the colonized that make the latter manageable and provide a moral justification for the colonial enterprise. Even literary works like Conrad's Heart of Darkness (1902) that overtly question the validity of colonialism are informed by this Manichean aesthetic, which problematizes their critique of imperialism. In such cases, while the colonized "other" functions as a vantage point for a self-critique of Western civilization, it is still not allowed to articulate a distinct subject-position of its own. The use of the "other" for self-critique and the construction of alternative subject-positions within the British context is also explored by feminist postcolonial critics like Gayatri Spivak and Jenny Sharpe.

These critics analyse the relationship between colonial ideology and the growth of British feminism in Victorian England evident in the works of writers like Jane Austen and Charlotte Brönte. Similarly, colonial ideology is also seen to have an impact on the representation of domestic class relations, whereby the lower classes are frequently portrayed as internal "others" who share the characteristics of the colonized and hence require similar strategies of control.

By thus exploring the class, gender, and racial politics that inform colonial ideology, postcolonial critics reveal the complexities of colonialism and its multi-faceted influence on Victorian society and literature. At the same time, such criticism reveals a contemporary relevance to the literary output of the nineteenth century. The exploration of the ideological complicities and resistances that characterize Victorian literature provides an insight into the complex ideological configurations of neo-colonialism that are an inescapable reality of late-twentieth-century culture and politics.

Chapter 9

Themes, Motifs, and Symbols in Mill on the Floss

Both characters and places in The Mill on the Floss are presented as the current products of multi-generational gestation. The very architecture of St. Ogg's bears its hundreds of years of history within it. Similarly, Maggie and Tom are the hereditary products of two competing family lines—the Tullivers and the Dodsons—that have long histories and tendencies.In the novel, the past holds a cumulative presence and has a determining effect upon characters who are open to its influence.

The first, carefully sketched out book about Maggie and Tom's childhood becomes the past of the rest of the novel. Maggie holds the memory of her childhood sacred and her connection to that time comes to affects her future behaviour. Here, the past is not something to be escaped nor is it something that will rise again to threaten, but it is instead an inherent part of Maggie's (and her father's) character, making fidelity to it a necessity.

Book First clearly demonstrates the painfulness of life without a past—the depths of Maggie's childhood emotions are nearly unbearable to her because she has no past of conquered troubles to look back upon with which to put her present situation in perspective. Stephen is held up as an example of the dangers of neglecting the past.

Dr. Kenn, a sort of moral yardstick within the novel, complains of this neglect of the past of which Stephen is a part and Maggie has worked against: "At present everything seems tending toward the relaxation of ties—toward the substitution of wayward choice for the adherence to obligation which has its roots in the past." Thus, without a recognition of the past with which to form one's character, one is left only to the whims of the moment and subject to emotional extremes and eventual loneliness.

THE IMPORTANCE OF SYMPATHY

The Mill on the Floss is not a religious novel, but it is highly concerned with a morality that should function among all people and should aspire to a compassionate connection with others through sympathy. The parable of St. Ogg rewards the ferryman's unquestioning sympathy with another, and Maggie, in her final recreation of the St. Ogg scene during the flood, is vindicated on the grounds of her deep sympathy with others.

The opposite of this sympathy within the novel finds the form of variations of egoism. Tom has not the capability of sympathizing with Maggie. He is aligned with the narrow, self-serving ethic of the rising entrepreneur: Tom explains to Mr. Deane that he cares about his own standing, and Mr. Deane compliments him, "That's the right spirit, and I never refuse to help anybody if they've a mind to do themselves justice." Stephen, too, is seen as a figure that puts himself before others. His arguments in favour of his and Maggie's elopement all revolve around the privileging of his own emotion over that of others', even Maggie's.

In contrast, Maggie's, Philip's, and Lucy's mutual sympathy is upheld as the moral triumph within the tragedy of the last book. Eliot herself believed that the purpose of art is to present the reader with realistic circumstances and characters that will ultimately enlarge the reader's capacity for sympathy with others.

We can see this logic working against Maggie's young asceticism. Maggie's self-denial becomes morally injurious to her because she is denying herself the very intellectual and artistic experiences that would help her understand her own plight and have pity for the plight of others.

PRACTICAL KNOWLEDGE VERSUS BOOKISH KNOWLEDGE

The Mill on the Floss, especially in the first half of the novel, is quite concerned about education and types of knowledge. Much of the early chapters are devoted to laying out the differences between Tom's and Maggie's modes of knowledge. Tom's knowledge is practical: "He knew all about worms, and fish, and those things; and what birds were mischievous, and how padlocks opened, and which way the handles of the gates were to be lifted." This knowledge is tangible and natural—it brings Tom in closer association to the world around him.

Meanwhile, Maggie's knowledge is slightly more complicated. Other characters refer to it as "uncanny," and her imagination and love of books are often depicted as a way for her to escape the world around her or to rise above it—"The world outside the books was not a happy one, Maggie felt."

Part of the tragedy of Maggie and Tom Tulliver is that Tom received the education that Maggie should have had. Instead of Maggie blossoming, Tom is trapped. When Tom must make a living in the world, he discovers that his bookish education will win him nothing: Mr. Deane tells Tom, "The world isn't made of pen, ink, and paper, and if you're to get on in the world, young man, you must know what the world's made of."

Tom soon returns and takes advantage of his skills for practical knowledge, making good in the newly entrepreneurial world. Tom's practical knowledge is always depicted as a source of superiority for Tom. From his childhood on, Tom has no patience for Maggie's intellectual curiosity. The narrowness of Tom's miseducation under Mr. Stelling seems somewhat related to the narrowness of Tom's tolerance for others' modes of knowledge. Yet Eliot remains clear that Maggie's intellectualism makes her Tom's superior in this case—"the responsibility of tolerance lies with those who have the wider vision."

THE EFFECT OF SOCIETY UPON THE INDIVIDUAL

Society is never revealed to be a completely determining factor in the destiny of Eliot's main characters—for example, Maggie's tragedy originates in her internal competing impulses, not in her public disgrace. Yet, Eliot remains concerned with the workings of a community—both social and economic—and tracks their interrelations, as well as their effect upon character, as part of her realism.

The Mill on the Floss sets up a geography of towns and land holdings—St. Ogg's, Basset, Garum Firs, Dorlcote Mill—and describes the tone of each community (such as the run-down population of Basset).

The novel tracks the growth of the particular society of St. Ogg's, referencing the new force of economic trends like entrepreneurial capitalism or innovations like the steam engine.

A wide cast of characters aims to outline different strata in the society—such as the Dodsons, or the Miss Guests—through their common values, economic standing, and social circles. In the first part of the novel, Eliot alludes to the effect these communal forces have on Maggie's and Tom's formation. Toward the end of the novel, the detailed background of St. Ogg's society functions as a contrast against which Maggie seems freshly simple and genuine.

MOTIFS: THE DISPARITY BETWEEN THE DODSONS AND THE TULLIVERS

Early on in the novel a distinction between the two families from which Tom and Maggie are descended is drawn out. The Dodsons are socially respectable, concerned with codes of behaviour, and materialistic. The Tullivers are less socially respectable and have a depth of emotion and affection. The constant repetition of the characteristics of the two clans serves to create a division along which Maggie's and Tom's growth can be tracked. Tom is associated with the Dodsons, even more so when an adult, and Maggie is associated with the Tullivers.

MUSIC

We often see Maggie nearly lose consciousness when listening to music; she is so overcome with emotion and forgetful of any punitive or self-denying impulses. As a motif, music works the opposite way too: when Maggie experiences moments of profound, unconscious discovery or understanding, these moments are accompanied by a sense of music, as when she reads Thomas a Kempis for the first time and feels as though she hears, "a strain of solemn music." The vulnerability that Maggie experiences in relation to music can also put her in danger.

Stephen Guest woos Maggie with music, not with words, and we see that his singing creates an "emotion that seemed to make her at once strong and weak: strong for all enjoyment, weak for all resistence." Music in The Mill on the Floss is not meant to indicate moments when Maggie is either succumbing to evil or experiencing good, but rather it indicates her generally heightened sensibilities—Maggie seems to experience everything with more emotion than others, and music is used throughout the novel to underscore this effect.

ANIMAL IMAGERY

Especially in the early books of The Mill on the Floss, Tom, and especially Maggie, are associated with animal imagery. The imagery is usually of farm-type animals—ponies, dogs, ducks—and usually points to the character's capacity for affection or non-adherence to social convention.

Following Darwin, Eliot uses this imagery also to gesture toward the wider relation between humans and animals that can be especially seen in young children. Thus, when Maggie and Tom reconcile in Chapter IV of Book First, the narrator points out, "We [adults] no longer approximate in our behaviour to the mere impulsiveness of the lower animals, but conduct ourselves in every respect like members of a highly civilized society.

Maggie and Tom were still very much like young animals."

DARK AND LIGHT WOMEN

The motif of darkness and lightness of women—meaning their eyes, hair, or skin—is often used to emphasize the uniqueness of Maggie's appearance. The motif of darkness and lightness connects to the motif of the distinctions between the Dodsons and the Tullivers—the Tullivers have darker skin, while the Dodsons have lighter skin.

The Dodsons, and indeed, all of St. Ogg's, respect or covet Lucy Deane's fair appearance. Her lightness is also prized in a larger cultural arena, and, in Book Fourth, Maggie becomes frustrated by the traditional plot lines in which the light, blond women live happily ever after in love. Maggie's family views her darkness as ugly and unnatural, yet by the end of the novel, it has made men perceive Maggie as more beautiful because her darkness is a rarity.

SYMBOLS: THE FLOSS

The Floss is a somewhat difficult symbol to track, as it also exists for realistic effect in the workings of the novel. On the symbolic level, the Floss is related most often to Maggie, and the river, with its depth and potential to flood, symbolizes Maggie's deeply running and unpredictable emotions. The river's path, nonexistent on maps, is also used to symbolize the unforseeable path of Maggie's destiny.

ST. OGG

St. Ogg, the legendary patron saint of the town, was a Floss ferryman. One night a woman with a child asked to be taken across the river, but the winds were high and no other boaters would take her. Only Ogg felt pity for her in her need and took her. When they reached the other side, her rags turned into robes, and she revealed herself to be the Blessed Virgin. The Virgin pronounced Ogg's boat safe to all who rode in it, and she sat always in the prow.

The parable of Ogg rewards the human feeling of pity or sympathy. Maggie has a dream during her night on the boat with Stephen, wherein Tom and Lucy row past them, and Tom is St. Ogg, while Lucy is the Virgin. The dream makes explicit Maggie's fear of having neglected to sympathize with those whom she hurts during her night with Stephen (and also, perhaps, her fear that they will not sympathize with her in the future). But it is Maggie, finally, who stands for St. Ogg, as she rows down river thinking only of Tom's safety during the flood in a feat of "almost miraculous, divinely-protected effort."

MAGGIE'S EYES

Eliot depicts Maggie's eyes as her most striking feature. All men (including Philip, Bob Jakin, and Stephen) notice her eyes first and become entranced. Maggie's eyes are a symbol of the power of emotion she contains—the depth of feeling and hunger for love that make her a tragic character. This unique force of character seems to give her power over others, for better or for worse. In Book First, Maggie is associated with Medusa, the monster who turns men to stone by looking at them. Maggie's eyes compel people, and different characters' reactions to them often reflect the character's relationship with Maggie.

Thus, Philip, who will become Maggie's teacher, in a sense, and first love, notices that her eyes "were full of unsatisfied intelligence, and unsatisfied, beseeching affection." Bob Jakin, who views Maggie as superior to him and a figure of whom to be in awe, reports that Maggie has "such uncommon eyes, they looked somehow as they made him feel nohow." Finally, Stephen, who will exploit the inner struggle that Maggie has felt for the entire novel, notices that Maggie's eyes are "full of delicious opposites."

THE MYSTERY OF AMOS BARTON

An anonymous short story, written 150 years ago, about a real-life country clergyman caused suspicion and intrigue in literary circles. Kathryn Hughes celebrates the arrival of George Eliot. January is always a headache for the editors of literary newspapers and magazines. January 1857 was no different. John Blackwood, editor of Blackwood's magazine, was faced with the seasonal nightmare of empty pages and dwindling inspiration. The magazine, an Edinburgh-based monthly, had presented work by everyone from Thomas de Quincey to Elizabeth Barrett Browning. Its associated publishing house was also currently home to Bulwer-Lytton and Margaret Oliphant. Nonetheless, 150 years ago this month, the cupboard was feeling distinctly bare.

Blackwood was too cautious and competent an editor not to have a fall-back plan. He had in hand one long short story that had been sent to him the previous November by GH Lewes, a journalist who contributed regular pieces on natural history. In a covering letter Lewes explained that he was not himself the author of "The Sad Fortunes of the Rev Amos Barton", but was acting on behalf of a friend who preferred to stay anonymous. With customary hyperbole Lewes had described the story as better than anything that had been written since Jane Austen 50 years earlier. Blackwood was not about to go that far but, having read through the story a couple of times, he agreed that "If the author is a new writer I beg to congratulate him on being worthy of the honours of print and pay. I shall be very glad to hear from you or him soon."

Although delighted that so discerning a judge as John Blackwood was prepared to publish his friend's first fiction, Lewes was still not going to break any confidences: "I am not at liberty to reveal the veil of anonymity-even as regards social position. Be pleased, therefore, to keep the whole secret." While the gentlemanly Blackwood doubtless tried his best not to speculate about the identity of his new author, there was no stopping his employees. By the end of January, the firm's London manager, Joseph Langford, was writing anxiously to his boss: "Who wrote Amos Barton? Can you tell me? I have heard a hint that I dare not entertain."

Langford's question was being asked increasingly loudly all over literary London and Edinburgh, with the result that, just a week later, Lewes's shy friend broke cover and reached out to Blackwood's directly. On February 5 the firm received a letter from its newest author declaring: "Whatever may be the success of my stories, I shall be resolute in preserving my incognito... and accordingly I subscribe myself, best and most sympathising of editors, Yours very truly George Eliot." Whatever he may have guessed privately, it would be nearly another year before Blackwood was formally told that "George Eliot" was in fact none other than Marian Evans, the woman journalist who was notoriously living "in sin" with Lewes. Even though Lewes's split from his wife and children several years earlier was amicable, a formal divorce had proved impossible.

And so, in the summer of 1854, Marian Evans and George Henry Lewes-both clever, plain, middle-aged and hard-up-had settled down to unwedded bliss in Wandsworth, the obscure location chosen in order to minimise any social awkwardness. That no respectable woman, even of the most liberal stripe, would deign to visit the Leweses (Evans insisted on taking the title "Mrs Lewes" even though most people could not say it without a smirk) was made less painful if the long journey out to south-west London could be used as an excuse.

So the decision of Evans and Lewes that her very first fiction should be submitted anonymously was a shrewd one. Langford's shocked "I have heard a hint that I dare not entertain" gives a sense of just how sensitive even the most liberal publishers were to the slightest bit of scandal adhering to their publications. And Blackwood was no liberal: in fact, here was a man who christened each of his successive pet dogs "Tory". What made things even more ticklish was that the subject of George Eliot's first fiction was the church. "Amos Barton" was one of three stories that aimed to examine "the actual life of our country clergy about a quarter of a century ago", and would be published collectively as Scenes of Clerical Life.

Not only was it bad that Evans lived without benefit of clergy, but she also happened to be a well-known religious free-thinker who had translated from the German two of the books that had done most to dismantle belief in the literal truth of the Bible among intellectual Anglicans. Had she chosen to write about tinkers, tailors, soldiers or even sailors, it would be difficult enough. But one of the most famous agnostics in the country had decided to write, of all things, about Christianity in action. No wonder she wanted to use another name. As if that weren't enough for Blackwood to worry about, there was the style in which "Amos Barton" was written.

As a literary critic on the Westminster Review, Evans had poured scorn on the dopey religious fiction churned out for middle-class women. In one particularly cutting essay, "Silly Novels by Lady Novelists", she had run through the daft kinds of things on offer-curates who turn out to be Dukes in disguise, beautiful heroines who can dispute theology at the drop of a lace handkerchief.

Evans, who as a teenager living near Nuneaton had gone through an intensely evangelical phase, was determined that her fiction would be of a far more realistic kind, rooted in the actual experiences of the church and chapel-going lower-middle classes. To this end, her main character, Amos Barton, is wilfully lacking the kind of qualities that the readers of Blackwood's magazine might normally have hoped to find in a literary hero. With a bad sniff, pock-marked skin and uncertain grammar, "it was not in his nature to be superlative in anything; unless, indeed, he was superlatively middling, the quintessential extract of mediocrity".

An evangelical killjoy who forbids workhouse inmates to take snuff or the choir to sing the wedding psalm, Barton is nonetheless hugely flattered by the attentions of an apparently glamorous parishioner, Countess Caroline Czerlaski, who promises to put in a good word for him with the Dean. Barton's infatuation with the Countess means that he overlooks the needs of his long-suffering wife. It is only when Milly Barton gives birth prematurely and dies shortly afterwards that Amos comes to realise just how thoughtless his behaviour has been.

If Amos Barton has none of the brooding charisma that lady readers might expect of their clerical heroes, then the minor characters have none of the picturesque charm usually demanded of rustics. The local farmer and his wife, Mr and

Mrs Hackit, the doctor, Mr Pilgrim, and Mrs Patten, "a childless old lady who had got rich chiefly by the negative process of spending nothing", gather in the evening to chew the fat over Barton's odd modernising ideas and his poor wife Milly. In what would be the first of many choric scenes in Eliot's novels written in broad Midlands dialect, Mrs Patten gets indignant at Barton's quizziness about the state of her soul: "I've never been a sinner." Meanwhile, Mrs Hackit, who some critics have suggested is based on Evans's mother, declares: "How nice... [Mrs Barton] keeps her children!... six children and another a-coming. I don't know how they make both ends meet."

Conventional church-going Christianity, then, is not sufficient to bind up a community. Rather, suggests Eliot, developing what will become one of the key doctrines in her mature fiction, it is "sympathy" that brings people together. Once Amos's life goes horribly wrong, the villagers forget how much they dislike their curate's pedantic evangelical ways and start to respond to him as a human being in need. "Cold faces looked kind again, and parishioners turned over in their minds what they could best do to help their pastor." The squire tucks a £20 note into his letter of condolence and offers to find a place at school for the two eldest girls. "Amos failed to touch the spring of goodness by his sermons, but he touched it effectually by his sorrows; and there was now a real bond between him and his flock."

Although Evans had secretly always wanted to write fiction, it was not until she was almost 40 that she plucked up the courage to try her hand with "Amos Barton". She knew she could do descriptive and expository writing-journalism had taught her that-but she worried that she lacked the imaginative spark necessary for a novel. Even the normally loyal Lewes had commented that he was not sure if she had "dramatic power". In such insecure circumstances Evans did what many first-time writers do, and ransacked her own family history for plot and character. As a result, nearly all the events described in Scenes of Clerical Life are taken from recollections of her own church-going Midlands childhood of the 1820s. Oddly, it never seems to have crossed Evans's mind that the real-life protagonists of her fiction might still be living 35 years later, nor that they would be surprised to find themselves served up as entertainment.

One of these was John Gwyther, who had been the local curate during Evans's childhood and recognised his own story in that of the sniffing, pock-marked Amos Barton. In June 1859 Gwyther wrote with a kind of bewildered pain to Blackwood wondering why anyone would want to put him in a story.

Blackwood, alarmed at the way his new signing was turning out to be not so much an original literary artist as a hack who cobbled together events from real life, insisted that Eliot send the following-if grudging-letter to the unhappy churchman: "For any annoyance, even though it may have been brief and not well founded, which the appearance of the story may have caused Mr Gwyther, the writer is sincerely sorry."

This, as it turned out, was just the beginning of Evans's and Blackwood's troubles. As more and more people in Warwickshire read Scenes, the gossip intensified as to who the author-someone who had clearly once walked among them-could be. The most likely contender emerged as a down-and-out called Joseph Liggins who, so the rumours went, had not been paid a penny for his work by the dastardly Blackwood's. A group of well-meaning local gentlemen even started a fund to compensate the poor man for his hard-handling. It was not before Evans and Lewes wrote a couple of stern letters to the Times (neither of which, confusingly, revealed the true identity of George Eliot) that the theory finally started to splutter out.

The critical reaction to "Amos Barton" was mixed. Right from the start Blackwood was not certain about the story's merit and canvassed opinion among his own circle. One close friend, WG Hamley, with whom he usually found himself agreeing, came out "dead against Amos", finding the true-to-life style depressing. Thackeray was diplomatically noncommital, while the urbane Albert Smith reported that members of the Garrick "generally seem to have mingled their tears with their tumblers over the death bed of Milly".

A year later, when "Amos", together with two companion pieces, was released in book form as Scenes of Clerical Life, critical response had drifted in a more positive direction. The Times' critic was "highly favourable" and lauded Eliot's "pathos in depicting ordinary situations", seeming not the least put out by the sniffy noses. Even more gratifying was the response of Charles Dickens, to whom Evans had requested that Blackwood should send a copy of the book.

The great man immediately guessed that, whatever it said on the dust-jacket, this book was clearly written by a woman or, if not, "I believe that no man ever before had the art of making himself, mentally, so like a woman, since the world began."

This was all the encouragement that Evans needed. Next time she would try a full-length novel, quite possibly entitled Adam Bede. George Eliot had been born. Kathryn Hughes's George Eliot: The Last Victorian is published by Fourth Estate.

Chapter 10

Realism, the Masses, and Nationalism in Felix Holt

The industrial novel occupies a unique place in the context of debates about realism. As Erich Auerbach suggests, the subject matter of the realist novel-the masses or "the common people"-comes into being as a serious subject for literature as part of realism's inexorable logic:

Realism had to embrace the whole reality of contemporary civilization, in which to be sure the bourgeoisie played a dominant role, but in which the masses were beginning to press threateningly ahead as they became ever more conscious of their own function and power. The common people in all its ramifications had to be taken into the subject matter of serious realism.

Within realism's impulse or dynamic toward the representation of the masses lies the search for the ever more novel or strange, the desire for the discovery of new aesthetic material with which to work. Citing the Goncourts as exemplary of this driven fascination with the common people, Auerbach quotes Edmond de Goncourt himself, who articulates this appeal in terms that strongly echo those of the imperial or colonizing impulse, seeking adventure in foreign places: "the people, the mob, if you will, has for me the attraction of unknown and undiscovered populations, something of the exoticism which travelers go to seek".

For our purposes here what is important are the textual and aesthetic determinants of such an attitude. Auerbach argues that this attitude necessarily excludes from its representation "everything functionally essential, the people's work, its position within modern society, the political, social, and moral ferments which are alive in it and which point to the future". Given this, one may well ask, what then can or does the so-called industrial novel do? If, indeed, the impetus motivating its representational concerns functionally precludes the representation of its supposed subject matter-the working people and their work-what does the industrial novel in fact represent?

Raymond Williams, in his ground-breaking work Culture and Society, reads the industrial novel as a genre defined by its conflicting concerns. On the one hand, these novels embody a critical response to industrialism, with, in some cases, genuine sympathy for the plight of the working class. On the other hand, in the face of the actual conditions of the working class, they back down from any serious involvement out of fear, opting instead for a backdoor exit of sorts involving either the death or the emigration-to a new world, often the New World-of their politically engaged and potentially militant protagonists.

Williams identifies this ultimate withdrawal, fueled as it is initially out of sympathy, as the determining "structure of feeling" of the industrial novel. This conflict between concern on the one hand and fear on the other not only determines the internal structure of these novels, but constitutes as well their failure realistically to represent the social conditions of their time.

The fear of violence, according to Williams, distorts even the best of intentions: Elizabeth Gaskell's Mary Barton, which comes closest for Williams to identifying imaginatively with and hence representing the "lived experience" of the working class, is finally unable to sustain its sympathy for that experience once the threat of violence arises and with it, the potential for that violence to be organized through collective solidarity and struggle.

This inability is marked in Gaskell's text by the recourse to conventional sentimental fiction, as the novel's centre moves from John Barton and his participation in the workers' union to the love trials of Mary Barton and her journey to exonerate her lover, falsely accused of murder. In other cases, such as that of Dickens's Hard Times, withdrawal takes the form of confused passivity amidst the tangle of complex social forces: Blackpool's "Aw a muddle!" becomes synonymous with Dickens's treatment of the working class in general; a typically adolescent posture in its claim to have "seen through" society while simultaneously rejecting any real engagement in that society, Dickens's work thus figures for Williams more as a symptom than an assessment, realistic or otherwise, of the very confusions of industrial society that it purports to represent.

Whatever the actual specifics of each individual novel's resolution-be it that of Alton Locke, North and South, or Felix Holt-the strategy, one of containment, remains essentially the same.' Moreover, as Williams notes in conclusion, it is a strategy or structure of feeling whose provenance is by no means limited to the nineteenth century, but whose legacy remains with us today. While Williams's argument has great explanatory power, most notably in its identification of the structure motivating the oft-noted murky politics of these novels, Williams's own interpretive politics themselves bear further investigation.

In the midst of his critique of Mary Barton we find Williams bemoaning what he sees as Gaskell's shift towards sentimental fiction as a fall of sorts: "[Mary's] indecision between Jem Wilson and 'her gay lover, Harry Carson'; her agony in Wilson's trial; her pursuit and last-minute rescue of the vital witness; the realization of her love for Wilson: all this, the familiar and orthodox plot of the Victorian novel of sentiment, but of little lasting interest".

Implicit in this diagnosis is a strict delineation of "industrial" novels as separate from and superior to (if done authentically) merely sentimental fiction which for Williams can be of "little lasting interest." Such a view is problematic for a number of reasons, not the least of which is the fact that Williams's model has served as an exemplar for subsequent interpretations of the industrial novel. Hence, once categorized as "industrial," a novel is subject to interpretation based on its politics, politics here meaning that which deals with broad social issues properly circumscribed in the public sphere.

Within such a framework, a novel such as Mary Barton (or Felix Holt, Sybil, and so on) is either judged a good book by critics sympathetic to its liberal or humanitarian politics or a bad book by those who condemn this self-same liberalism. In either case, the so-called industrial novel is relegated to the "political" camp of literature in contrast to the homier domain of "domestic" or sentimental fiction. And should a novel stray out of the factory and into the home, within a Marxist framework it spells political doom.

All this is not to say that we should relish the sentimental strains of Mary Barton or any other industrial novel. Instead, it is to point out the particular representational quandary in which many critics, following the lead of Williams, have placed the industrial novel. On the one hand, these novels cannot be "great" literature if and when they stray from their mission of authenticity, which, needless to say, they always do. And, when they do stray into the realm of properly domestic fiction, they certainly cannot be considered great because sentimental fiction (obviously?) is of no "lasting interest." On the face of it, such a division falsely implies that domestic fiction deals exclusively with the domestic sphere whereas industrial fiction has as its singular domain the public sphere.

In addition to this sort of exclusion of the domestic from the public sphere, there is another exclusion which operates with a certain specificity to the industrial novel, given its project, broadly defined, of representing industrialization and its social effects. This exclusion is one in which the notion of "culture" (here inclusive of more than simply literary culture) is used as an ideological weapon to exclude the realm of production from the bourgeois public sphere.3 That is, culture becomes part of the bourgeois public sphere's arsenal of exclusions and disavowals; through the ideology of culture, the producers of England's wealth are barred from participation and inclusion in the public sphere because they are deemed deficient in cultural capital.

Culture becomes a litmus test for workers being admitted into the public sphere. Thus, the same notion of Arnoldian culture which has worked to situate the industrial novel outside of the literary canon, also serves to exclude the sphere of production from the public sphereboth in the industrial novel and in Victorian society itself. Paradoxically, while Williams's body of work emphasizes the need to theorize culture not, as Arnold does, as something discrete and autonomous but rather as integral to all social practices, for the most part he leaves out the cultural formation of imperialism and its determining effects upon England and English culture.

As I will argue, however, the crisis of industrialism, the industrial novel's raison d'etre, and its connected attempt to understand the newly-emerging experience and processes of modernity, cannot be understood outside the context of English nationalism and Empire. It is here that the exoticism of the Goncourts is more generally applicable. If we read the industrial novel as a narrative of "internal" travel, with its respective authors operating as adventure-seeking travelers of sorts, the masses, through metaphoric displacement, are situated much like the exotic, colonial Other, but with the added thrust that their threat to England is if anything greater than that of the colonial, existing as it does within the internal, domestic boundaries of England.

Faced with the cultural anxiety wrought by the possibility of internal disruption and division, the industrial novel emplots a paradigmatic structure wherein the attempt to represent the fearfully internal Other-the working class-necessitates its eventual absorption into a new community, one whose membership admits an identification beyond that of class interest, in place of class distinctions; that is, the unifying ideology of the national body. The cementing of this national ideology is predicated on the erasure of class and gender inequalities. Or, as Benedict Anderson has formulated it, "regardless of the actual inequality and exploitation that may prevail in the imagined community of 'nation,' the nation is always conceived as a deep, horizontal comradeship."

In the following reading of George Eliot's Felix Holt, I will argue that this process occurs through a series of displacements involving ever-wider spheres: from production to the domestic sphere of consumption, from the domestic sphere to the national sphere, and finally from the national to the imperial sphere, with each move entailing a symbolic resolution of conflict. A central precondition for this symbolic resolution of conflict is the exclusion of work and working-class struggle from representation; an exclusion prompted, on the one hand, by the very real demands being made by the English working class for political representation and, on the other hand, naturalized almost seamlessly by a politics of culture which shifts the terms of political representation away from the productive sphere altogether.

In order to mute class conflict and the disparities of wealth which divide the productive sphere, the working class is represented in the pub or the home thereby allowing it to be defined in terms of its pleasures as opposed to its productive activity. A "crime" committed by an individual member of the working class-be it theft, murder, or some act of violence-functions initially to rob working-class voices of their political legitimacy. This shift in narrative focus provides the space necessary for the construction of a "moral community," independent of industrial production. In the end, a sense of community united under the concept of "nation" is cemented against what are perceived of as both the external and internal forces threatening its dissolution.

George Eliot's Felix Holt promises perhaps too much. Beginning in the memorable year 1832, it immodestly sets as its task the tracing of changc in the English industrial landscape and the effects of this change on the fictional town of Treby Magna. The opening passage takes us back in time to the period immediately preceding the novel's setting, when "the glory had not yet departed from the old coach-roads". Eliot compares the sights, sounds, and fullness of immediately apprehensible experience offered by the long, slow journey by coach to a future where travel will more likely resemble a "bullet" being "shot... through a tube." Speed becomes the new determining force; that which will alter not only the landscape but our ability to relate to it as well. For Eliot, the high-speed "tube journey's" limitations are twofold. First, it is disruptive to memory.

Second, and perhaps most importantly for the task at hand, it defies representation: "The tube-journey can never lend much to picture and narrative; it is as barren as an exclamatory O!"). Such a crisis of representation would seem to put Eliot's own role as writer in danger, if indeed she is to relate to us the changes in Treby Magna effected by industrialization. By setting the novel in 1832, however (although it was written in 1866), Eliot seems to want to avoid this representational impasse. By returning to this earlier period she will describe the process of this change, but not the experiences of it which are yet to come, foreseeable yet unrepresentable some time in the still indefinite future (which was actually Eliot's own present).

Eliot does, however, in a sense flesh out the barren O! of this future, of how it might be experienced, by telling us what it will not be, by showing us what the coach journey is and what it offers. Taking us alone with her on a hypothetical trip from Avon to Kent, Eliot gives us a vision of the English countryside verdant with over-blossoming nature and a pace of life consonant with the rhythms of rural existence; the shepherd here moves in sync with the slow pace of his grazing cattle. Twined and tendrilled with wild convolvulus, many-tubed honeysuckle, scarlet haws, deep-crimson hips, blackberry branches, pale pink dogroses, and ruby-berried nightshade, it is a landscape demarcated by the "unmarketable beauty" of traditional English hedgerows.

Were we to catch a glimpse of the people contentedly ensconced behind these hedgerows, we would see faces begrimed with dirt; yet, lest we mistakenly confer upon this dirt a lack of moral uprightness, of wanton uncleanliness, Eliot is quick to inform us that this is not your ordinary dirt but Protestant dirt, the kind of dirt that makes its possessors clean. And these Protestants in particular are doubly scrubbed, saved as they are "from the excesses of Protestantism by not knowing how to read". These are the glory days: the days before the rick-burners, the riots, and the encroachment of handlooms and mines-and with them Dissenters-on this pastoral cornucopia.

As the coach continues on its way, however, this scene passes, and we near the villages and hamlets with their coal-pits and manufacture. At this juncture, a schism is registered. Whereas those inhabitants peopling the rural countryside are "sure that old England was the best of all possible countries" this manufacturing midlands' population is not so easily convinced. Indeed, the connection between the town and the country becomes hard if not impossible to discern; the traveller has literally passed from "one phase of English life to another" where dirt is no longer imbued with any great moral rectitude but is simply dirty. In this new landscape, it becomes difficult to read the signs so transparent in the agricultural regions.

Whereas rural life apparently hides nothing valuable beneath its tendrils-"If there were any facts which had not fallen under their own observation, they were facts not worth observing" -such transparency between vision and object becomes unsettled and disrupted once we enter the new landscape of the town. Representation itself becomes indeterminate, precariously and dangerously up for grabs by a variety of different and contradictory interpretations.

Here the parson preaches a sermon invoking his parishioners to "plough up the fallow-ground of your hearts" and its meaning is so opaque, so susceptible to being divergently interpreted that one group sees in it an argument for fallows and yet another sees it, au contraire, as an argument against them. Shaken by this highly unstable state of affairs, the parson simply expires in a fit of apoplexy. Within Felix Holt one is hard-pressed to find any direct representation of work.

The way in which we learn what little we do about the workers in the novel is through negation: by looking at what the workers do when they are not on the job, we are presumably to glean some sense of who they are and what they do when they are. Thus Eliot takes us not to the mine or the factory but to the pub. It is here that we are to get our sense of the workers' lives and their "miseries," and the relationship between the two: "One way of getting an idea of our fellow countrymen's miseries is to go and look at their pleasures". The scene is the Cross-Keys, the local pub where the working class enjoys its leisure-time.

Upon entrance we are presented with a "fungous-featured landlord" and a "yellow sickly landlady" in an establishment pouring "doctored ale," and reeking of "an odour of bad tobacco, and remarkably strong cheese". Surely, if this dank, fetid atmosphere-by all accounts more suitable for the cultivation of mushrooms and mold than people's pleasures-provides the space for the workers' leisure, we are meant to be impressed with the fact that their miseries must be dreadful indeed. To drive home this point the narrator impresses upon us that in comparison to other watering-holes the Cross-Keys actually presented a "high standard of pleasure".

Talk in the pub revolves around the political issues occupying the minds of Trebians, specifically the impending election and more generally the question of representation upon which it centers. Not surprisingly, there are plenty of political opportunists enlisted by each side ready to bend the ears of these working men in order to gain support for their particular candidate. One such man is Mr. Johnson, who visits the Sproxton pub with the express purpose of rallying the workers to the Radical cause of Harold Transome.

In the course of buying rounds and sponging for Radical support, Mr. Johnson informs the workers of their no less than national role and importance in the upcoming elections:

"No, no: say, as this country prospers it has more and more need of you, sirs. It can do without a pack of lazy lords and ladies, but it can never do without brave colliers. And the country will prosper. I pledge you my word, sirs, this country will rise to the tip-top of everything, and there isn't a man in it but what shall have his joint in the pot, and his spare money jingling in his pocket, if we only exert ourselves to send the right men to parliament-men who will speak up for the collier, and the stone-cutter, and the navvy, (Mr.

Johnson waved his hand liberally), "and will stand no nonsense. This is a crisis, and we must exert ourselves. We've got Reform, gentlemen, but now the thing is to make Reform work. It's a crisis-I pledge you my word it's a crisis."

From the venerable Mr. Johnson's speech it would appear that the interests of working men occupy a central role in the election. But as with all political prevarications it is but another example of how words do not necessarily speak the truth. The levels of deception are numerous. To begin with, Mr. Johnson delivers himself in the service of Harold Transome, a landowning aristocrat who has taken on the false mantle of a Radical simply by calling himself one. Moreover, the colliers and miners themselves do not yet have the vote; their role therefore, according to Mr. Johnson, is rather to amass themselves for Harold Transome by making their presence felt on election day and when the opportunity arises, attacking Transome's opponents.

This appeal falls on willing ears. One worker, aptly named Dredge, overzealously takes up the pugilistic aspects of the cause and has to be rebuked, gently reminded that actual hard knocks are out of the question-although the slinging of soft muddy things would be well within bounds. In contrast to the enthusiasm the workers as a whole show for Johnson's slick speech and reasoning, our hero Felix Holt, witnessing this bravado performance, leaves the pub in disgust, loathe to hear his own heartfelt convictions (about the importance of the working man, not their enlistment as potential disrupters of the election process) travestied by such a political charlatan.

One might read this scene as a straightforward condemnation of men like Johnson who play willy-nilly with the sympathies of the working class. Certainly opportunists are one focus of the narrative's critique. But it is a double-edged critique: the ease with which Johnson can manipulate the miners' sentiments is equally if not more biting about the marked absence of political acuity in the working class. Their sympathies are to be played with so cavalierly because they lack a proper education in political know-how. They hang on the last word of Johnson's speech (crisis), for instance, not because they understand what this word means-they most surely do not, we are told-but precisely because they do not know its meaning and for this reason (or lack of reason) are thoroughly persuaded. His words convince by their very incomprehensibility.

This caricature of working-class sensibility is crucial to explaining the effect the absence of industrial work has on the structure of the novel as a whole. By parodying the workers, the narrative provocatively casts suspicion on their political abilities. In the process, the question of their representation moves from the issue of their natural right to self-representation as working members of English society to an evaluation of whether, given their political immaturity, they are in a position to be able to represent themselves." At stake becomes a valuation of political knowledge, a valuation in which the collier and miner come up woefully short. From the issue of knowledge it is then but a small step to the question of culture itself.

As Eliot makes explicit in the "Address to Working Men" (a speech appended to the end of the novel and delivered in the fictive voice of Felix Holt), "degrading, barbarous pleasures" such as those of the working class are nothing less than a sign of cultural privation, of the lack of those "precious benefits" which she calls the "common estate of society." And this "common estate," which Eliot, via the pub, shows no mere expansion of the franchise can provide, is "that treasure of knowledge, science, poetry, refinement of thought, feeling, and manners, great memories and the interpretation of great records, which is carried on from the minds of one generation to the minds of another" (. The literary quandary of how to represent modern labour has been translated into an issue of political representation, which in turn rests on who the rightful heirs of such a conveyed tradition of culture can and should be.

Such a shift is integrally connected to the actual debates about reform in England beginning in the 1830s and continuing into the 1860s with the passing of the Second

Reform Bill in 1867, just one year after Eliot wrote Felix Holt. The nature of this period of reform has been characterized by critics such as Williams and Patrick Brantlinger as one involving two distinct phases: the first, the middle-class reform of the 1830s through the mid-1850s in which political reformist action was believed to be the mechanism through which to alleviate social problems (grouped under the umbrella term the "Condition of England") and the second, in which the optimism and energy of this earlier period of reform is replaced by the "cult of progress," i.e. the belief in the inevitability of historical progress, of "laws" of evolution and organic growth that displace human agency as the motor of change.

These two phases are divided along class lines. Whereas the first Reform Bill centered on the issue of enfranchising the middle class, with the 1867 Bill the middle class found itself in a decidedly different position, possibly having to cede rather than gain power through the extension of the franchise to the working class. With the middle class in a position potentially to lose power, the political ground of reform radically shifted; the hegemony of the middle class was threatened. At this point broad issues of culture began to play a significantly larger part in English political life.

Culture and its related terms-education, responsibility, moral and intellectual fitness, obligation, trust and so on-slowly came to displace questions of natural right; these cultural criteria took precedence over what properly constituted an individual's right to representation. Or, as Brantlinger notes, "one stood for or against a new reform bill, depending partly on one's definition of culture and on one's belief as to whether those who were to be enfranchised had enough of it or not". Curiously enough, it is this latter phase of reform that Felix Holt narrates.

As the pub scenes illustrate, what is of central concern is whether the workers have the cultural capital to warrant a political right to representation. And if the caricature of their political and intellectual ineptitude were not evidence enough, the depiction of their mob violence on election day resulting, as it does, in an anarchic, seemingly politically unmotivated riot, definitively answers this concern with a resounding no. Thus, while Felix Holt is set in the period of crisis of the first Reform Bill of 1832, ideationally the crisis it confronts and attempts to reconcile is that of the second Reform Bill, contemporaneous with the actual period in which Eliot was writing the novel. In the narrative's own practice, then, the present is not written as a continuation of the past but rather is projected back onto the past. The collapse of present into past conflates two distinct historical moments into one moment, a moment, moreover, that as the result of the fusion must always remain an ideal.

This metaleptic return has direct consequences for Eliot's representations of work. Since the ultimate basis for political judgment rests on cultural capital, neither work nor the workplace are necessary sites for political claims to representation. Production is repressed, excluded from the status of reality. In a sense, then, it becomes not so much a question of being unable to represent work but of its seeming irrelevance to the "present" 1860s politics of culture. In the process, thirty-odd years of history are conflated, years that include, significantly, the working-class militancy of the 1840s when, from a middle-class British perspective, workers' struggle in the political form of Chartism reared its ugly head and threatened to divide the nation along class lines. The active forgetting of that which has not yet happened-given the historical setting of Felix Holt-eliminates with it the memory of class conflict.

It is precisely this attempt to purge the past of its fractious discontinuities that is necessary to constitute the nation. It is the absent space of work which will be filled by the concept of "nation," which, unlike work, serves to unite the heterogeneous workers and middle-class citizens populating Felix Holt. In essence, the "Condition of England" question is "answered" through its supersession by culture: the nation becomes synonymous with culture, English culture, which in turn provides the ideological cement necessary to symbolically unite worker and capitalist in their mutual national identification as English.' Much like our coachman, whose narrative was temporarily derailed by the penetration of urban capital (manifest in the railroad) into the countryside, the narrative of Felix Holt, faced with the presence of industrial labour, shifts gears, moving into a prophetic register which foretells the steady, progressive realization of a national destiny.

A second look at Mr. Johnson's speech bears out this shift in political terrain. Framed by an unquestioned belief in history as progress-"as this country prospers," he begins-Johnson's speech mirrors the movement of reform just described, and diverts attention from labour politics per se to a national politics: "the country will prosper... will rise to the tip-top of everything." As the future tense of his discourse appropriately emphasizes, he moves here into the prophetic mode, virtually prophesying the nation and its fortunes. This prophetic mode, as with the coachman, leaves the realm of descriptive, realistic narrative, and indeed must: the prophetic therefore constructs a political space divorced from political action and devoid of those very real conflicts which would hamper national unity.

The only form of action entertained is the workers' rioting which results from a misguided and wholly unpolitical mob mentality, a mentality, it is underscored, "animated by no real political passion" To the extent that the workers are thus reduced to a "mad crowd", their collective subjectivity is limited to passive receivership (possibly) of England's great cultural heritage. In Arnoldian fashion, culture and its expression in the "nation" come to stand virtually in opposition to history: like Arnold understands of "anarchy," History within Felix Holt is too embedded in the thick of things, too susceptible to divisions of class and ideology. Reaching across this divide, culture functions as a protective enclosure, a space where the social practices of labour are suspended. Within the weave of culture, the fabric of social relations in modern society and the abstract form of social domination intrinsic to them are severed from their socio-historical constitution in determinate, structured forms of practice.

The politics of culture in which Felix Holt is engaged, as discussed above, more properly represent the period of reform of the 1860s following the Chartist struggles of the 1840s, a period which contains within it the defeat of the first wave of working-class militancy: action on the workers' part has already been effectively quelled and overcome. When attempting to confront industrial labour, then, the narrative shifts into a register that already precludes it from social consideration. Within the text, Chartism and the alternative vision of work it carries with it is represented as an historical impossibility-though ostensibly the novel is fictively situated in 1832.

Yet Eliot does attempt to narrate a form of labour complementary to her mobilization of culture. To do so she must turn back to the past. In an attempt to reconnect figuratively the brain and the hands, to offer an alternative to the nonrepresentability of the hands alone, Eliot leaves the domain of the industrialized working class and returns to the residual socio-economic mode of artisanal production. Mental and manual labour are combined in the figure of Felix Holt as artisan and organic intellectual. This return can be read generally as a desire to maintain social positions that are the creation of obsolete modes of production. And, within the context of the novel, it serves to carve out an extra-economic realm seemingly independent of industrial production.

The strangeness of Felix's socio-economic markings are acknowledged in the text: "Felix was known personally, and vaguely believed to be a man who meant many queer things, not at all of an every-day kind". Part of this "queerness" results from Felix's marginal position outside the economy of exchange: "He had put a stop to the making of saleable drugs, contrary to the nature of buying and selling". From his newly created role as lower-middleclass artisan, Felix putatively escapes the snares of modernization-market relations and the instrumentality they express.

On the one hand, there is a utopian element in Eliot's move back to quasi-artisanal production; a desire somehow to reestablish the fast-disappearing connection between manual and mental labour, to slow down the pace of change and resist the fragmentation threatening the cohesiveness of the rural community. Herein lies the creative performative capacity utterly denied the industrial worker. On the other hand, caught as he is in an historically outmoded economic structure and cultural form, Felix represents a regressive resistance to "modernity" itself. Like Eliot's disembodied notion of culture, he is literally "not at all of an every-day kind".

In essence, the narrative's investment in him lies in the contrast he provides to the modern worker. As the fictive author of the "Address to Working Men" he advises the workers to recognize the organic, evolutionary nature of things, and therefore to "take the world as it is"; to accept the superiority of the "masters" who hold the keys to this cultural treasure, which is "the life of the nation" (. In this sense, Felix Holt hovers didactically over the text as a model-of resistance to the penetration of capital and of acquiescence to a politics of class conciliation premised on a unifying vision of cultural nationalism. To expose the ideologies and discourses of modern nationalism and its construction within bourgeois culture is to discover the traces of the repressed history contained in (the absence of) industrial labour.

Just as the division between work and culture presupposed a reconfiguration of the relation between external and internal (the workers, potentially external forces of disruption, are "internalized" within the boundaries of English culture), the relation of England to its other "Others"-the Orientalized East-operates through the construction of internal/external boundaries of mutual exclusivity. The Orient enters Felix Holt in the guise of Harold Transome, who arrives back on England's shores at the beginning of the novel. We learn little about Harold's exploits while he has been away in Greece save for the fact that he has accumulated large sums of money and an heir. While the actual source of Harold's money is left unspecified, we do know that his experience abroad has reshaped his views on the processes of modernization at home.

The apparent (and grossly stereotypical) slothfulness of the Easterner serves to justify conveniently the selfinterested practices of competitive English commerce: If you had lived in the East, as I have, you would be more tolerant. More tolerant, for example, of an active industrious selfishness, such as we have here, though it may not always be quite scrupulous: you would see how much better it is than an idle selfishness.

This selfish industriousness which Harold espouses is sharply contrasted to Felix's resistance to market forces. Indeed the dichotomous positions they hold mark the alternative visions of work that organize Felix Holt. These alternatives, like those represented by the shift from production to pleasure when dealing with the workers, are mapped appetitively by the opposite pleasures each affords. If Felix Holt turns to the pub to explore workers' pleasures, when looking for bourgeois pleasures its haunt is (figuratively) the bedroom, the realm of sexual desire. Through the central female figure of Esther Lyon we are given a litmus test for evaluating the different pleasures identified with Harold and Felix and the alternative social visions manifest in them.

Throughout the novel Esther functions as a liminal figure. In terms of her class identification, she can be read as the representative petit bourgeois. The product of an aristocrat and a sailor, she operates from within an indeterminate class position, liable to be as swayed by the class interests of the aristocracy (in the figure of Harold Transome) as by those of the working class (identified falsely, as we have seen, with Felix Holt). Esther's sexual desires and her eventual capitulation to Felix serve as cautionary political allegory. Torn between Felix and Harold Transome, Esther's ultimate acceptance of Felix mirrors the transformation desired by the text for the working class. They, like Esther, the message seems to say, should accept their proper function within the body politic, that of accommodation to current social conditions in the interests of the health of the nation as a whole.

The mechanics whereby the gendered body of Esther is made part of this "organic" national body reveals the violence and domination underlying the seemingly benign picture of accommodation. Specifically, the romantic plot of Felix Holt makes explicit the link between culture and power, a link obfuscated in the realm of work and production. By looking at how power circulates through the figure of Esther we can recover the missing link, the (repressed) body, upon which English culture and imperial power is written.

Esther spends the greater part of the novel in a condition of conflicted indecisiveness, at a juncture where she must choose between the initially illusive pleasures and privileges of the aristocratic "queenly" life and the hardworking, duty-bound self-sacrificing ethic of Felix's artisanal "vocation." Thanks to the convoluted legal subplot of entail which cedes to Esther legitimate rights to the Transome estate and with it any potential cross-class sexual conflict, Esther can make what looks like a voluntary choice between her two lovers. It is crucial that this is a voluntary choice; what is at stake is the principle of self-regulation.

On one level, Esther's education, her private journey through successive stages of personal development, can be read as a microcosm of the modern narrative of "inevitable progress" as she learns to discard the Romantic texts she initially identifies with in favour of the "realism" Felix Holt embodies a process built upon a necessary disillusionment, and moving toward the "disinterested objectivity" of scientific rationality:

The favourite Byronic heroes were beginning to look something like last night's decorations seen in the sobre dawn... if Felix Holt were to love her, her life would be exalted into something quite new-into a sort of difficult blessedness, such as one may imagine in beings who are conscious of painfully growing into the possession of higher powers. Romanticism is clearly not the suitable genre for this awakening.

The final death knell to any sort of Romantic utopia comes when Esther's vision of Oriental love is shattered by Harold's informing her that his Greek wife had been a slave: "Hitherto Esther's acquaintance with Oriental love was derived chiefly from Byronic poems, and this had not sufficed to adjust her mind to a new story, where the Giaour concerned was giving her his arm.

She was unable to speak". The identification of Harold as Giaour is an odd one. At once it both situates him within an Oriental narrative as Christian, no doubt, but labeled as such from within a non-Christian, Muslim perspective, and it radically severs Esther's identification with that narrative. The moment the Orient, even if only metaphorically, takes on flesh and blood, the pleasures it seemed to afford Esther lose their allure. So much so that when Harold names Esther "the empress of [her] own fortunes-and more besides," a rather befuddled Esther replies: "Dear me... I don't think I know very well what to do with my empire".

While Esther will ultimately reject this role of empress, Harold's relationship to her maps the novel's vision of East/West relations. As the revelation that Harold's wife was a slave makes clear, the validation of the English woman comes through the dehumanization of the non-European woman. The contrast is meant to show Esther that "her own place was peculiar and supreme". At the same time, however, the situating of Harold's Eastern experience in Greece, as opposed to India or Africa, falsely separates Harold's venture from the British imperial enterprise. Harold is figured more as an adventurer than a colonist or imperial administrator, thereby separating the work of empire from its socioeconomic moorings. What these two figurations suggest is a subtle distinction between different operations of cultural and economic power.

When such force is meted out genteelly in the interests of its larger (legitimatizing) cultural project then it appears to lose its nasty repressive edge and regain its status as lofty "cultured" ideal. As Esther remarks about Harold Transome's mode of governance on his own estate, what is so impressive is the naturalness-due to his gender-of his domination, "the masculine ease with which he governed everybody and administered everything about him, without the least harshness, and with a facile good-nature which yet was not weak".

Any show of brute force or direct repression, however, must remain invisible. In other words, Harold's attempt simultaneously to devalue the worth of his Eastern wife and increase Esther's value backfires precisely because of the directness of exchange it exposes. The entrance of money and, with it, an openly exploitative exercise of power demystifies the more finely veiled traffic in women in the patriarchal kinship system. Against the individual and opportunistic pleasures driving Harold's sexual pursuits, the text invites us to see Esther's final union with Felix as the opting for an "authentic" culture, unsullied by the crude and instrumental market forces of buying and selling. Yet the mechanics of their union, rather than providing any real alternative to such forces, simply dresses up the workings of cultural domination in a finer, more veiled frippery.

For what Esther chooses in Felix is nothing short of the Law:

He was like no one else to her: he had seemed to bring at once a law, and the love that gave strength to obey the law.... The first religious experience of her life-the first self-questioning, the first voluntary subjection, the first longing to acquire the strength of greater motives and obey the more strenuous rule-had come to her through Felix Holt. No wonder that she felt as if the loss of him were inevitable backsliding.

Esther is successively "stung," "shaken in her self-contentment," filled with mortification and anger, and the "sense of a terrible power over her that Felix seemed to have as his angry words vibrated through her"-feelings that become "almost too much for her self-control". And, on the next page: "she revolted against his assumption of superiority, yet she felt herself in a new kind of subjection to him. He was ill-bred, he was rude, he had taken an unwarrantable liberty; yet his indignant words were a tribute to her: he thought she was worth more pains that the women of whom he took no notice".

In short, Felix, as pedagogue and master, wields the phallus and penetrates Esther's being, causing her to accept her own lawless lack in her voluntary subjection to his superiority. Crucial to our reading of Esther's education and its relation to the culture of imperialism is the way in which this process of personal subjection is internal, regulated by the self, and involving a recognition on Esther's part that she is indeed inferior to Felix and thus subject to his superior powers.

Such internal regulation conveniently alleviates the necessity of external repression altogether as the "colonizer"-in this case, Felix-is thoroughly absorbed into the consciousness of the "colonized." As Gilles Deleuze and Felix Guattari argue, Oedipus is the figurehead of a psychology that corresponds well to such an imperialism. It is "colonization pursued by other means, it is the interior colony, and we shall see that even here at home... it is our intimate colonial education". In a word, Oedipus is what teaches us to desire our own repression. The culmination of this colonial mentality is achieved when Esther finally relates to Felix's words as if they were her own, realizing that they "at last seemed strangely to fit her own experience".

The powerlessness inherent in such a recognition is clearly marked in the novel as a condition specific to women. In this respect, Eliot is often heralded by critics for her proto-feminist representations of the plight of women in patriarchal society. But her understanding of the desires denied women is itself equally problematic. That is, for Eliot, there is a fundamental connection between power and culture that remains unquestioned: the desire to rule or to dominate is never in and of itself critiqued; instead it is always a question of how that rule is exercised.

And when that rule is suitably cloaked in a domesticated, naturalized hierarchy of duties or functions, it masks any relation to the naked power relations underlying its operation. Indeed, at the end of the novel, Eliot recreates Esther's and Felix's past for us, to the extent that all of Esther's feelings of subjection and humiliation become but pleasant lover's pleasures: "They smiled at each other, with the old sense of amusement they had so often had together".

It is just such pleasure, entailed in Eliot's version of "authentic" culture, that greases the machinery of domination, both on England's shores and beyond. This vision of domestic pleasure, so clearly meant to offset that other image of pleasure which Felix Holt gives us, that of the miners and their pubs, more potently underscores the way in which pleasure itself, and with it labour-whether in the direct form of economic domination or the more mediated domain of culture-is severed from reality, excluded from the public sphere, by the mechanisms of power fueling England's cultural project of nationhood.

In his study of the Bildungsroman, Franco Moretti reads Felix Holt as symptomatic of the end of this symbolic form which "had always held fast to the notion that the biography of a young individual was the most meaningful viewpoint for the understanding and the evaluation of history". This form, now insufficient to the new project at hand-the representation of the masses or the "collective"-is superseded by one in which the individual figures merely as a part of the whole. Within such a framework, Felix's vocation is seen as originating from an "ethnic or social partiality." Once the biography of the individual can no longer capture history, the narrative opts for the building of enclaves or sub-cultures which preserve "communal" values at odds with the larger dynamics of the "great world."

This transition occurs as an effect of larger historical processes, namely the sacrifice of individuality which typifies the "age of the masses." For Moretti, then, the failure of Felix Holt as a novel rests in the conflict between these two structures: Eliot, by attempting to tell her tale of the masses, yet with only the worn-out, historically outdated narrative form of the Bildungsroman at her disposal, is unable ultimately to represent her collective subject. Her novel, flawed not from lack of writerly skill, but because it lies on the cusp of a historical transition, marks this transition that has not yet found a form adequate to its representation.

But what this analysis fails to take into account is the way in which Eliot sets the partiality of Felix's view and the domain of his actions within the larger social dynamic of change and progress. As the "Address to Working Men" impresses upon us it is precisely in the interests of society, of

Gesellschaft as Gemeinschaft that "revolutionary" views such as those identified with an organized working class must be domesticated within the confines of a national English culture.

In order to ensure the survival of the social organism, to use Eliot's own metaphors of organicism, each part must recognize and perform its function in relation to the body as a whole. Within such an organic view of the nation, there can be no cultivation of sub-cultures, for each part of necessity is always integral to and inseparable from the whole. Rather in the interests of this national body, of nationalism, the validation of what Moretti reads as the sub-culture of Felix's position must remain sub.

One final indication of the shift from a regional communal identification to a broadly British nationalist one is evident in the inscription which opens Felix Holt:

"Upon the Midlands now the industrious muse doth fall, The shires which we the heart of England well may call.

My native country those, which so brave spirits hast bred,

If there be virtues yet remaining in thy Earth, Or any good of thine thou bred'st into my birth, Accept it as thine own, whilst now I sing of thee, Of all thy later brood the unworthiest though I be."

This poem, a slightly altered version of a passage from The Thirteenth Song of Drayton's Poly-Olbion, contains a significant revision. Whereas Drayton speaks of only one "shire"-Warwickshire-Eliot harkens to a plurality of shires; these shires together comprise her "native country" of England. In essence, Eliot remakes this poem about regional pride into something akin to a national anthem. Much like the narrative of Felix Holt as a whole, the present is here rewritten in the past with all traces of difference or conflict essentially erased.

In a sense, then, nationalism, or the identification of oneself as part of a nation, is the linchpin between (the dissolution of) community and the modern state. In place of the ruptures and discontinuities of self and community, national identification reinscribes a notion of wholeness and continuity. As such, nationalism is that which mediates between the seemingly knowable past and an unknowable present and future. It is that which bridges the representational gap in Felix Holt, the tension between the prophetic and the narrative.

In the novel, as we have seen, this mediation takes two forms: the one, represented by the figure of Felix Holt himself, functions by dint of his placement in a realm removed from daily life. The other, represented by Esther, and by extension the working class, gives us a brief glimpse of another possibility, of the existence of chaotic desires, of a discontinuous sense of self, of the nonidentity of reason and reality, subjects and objects, of the internal splits and ruptures that make Esther feel as if her thoughts and her life were a "heap of fragments." It is this possibility that the prophetic register of Felix Holt shuts down; the force of Eliot's text works to bind these fragments together into a unified form.

Hence the crucial role of education in the novel: Esther and the working class require education precisely in order to bring them within the national fold. In the face of an unnarratable, unrepresentable present, Eliot slips into the prophetic mode; she must prophesy the unity of a nation to be created. Thus, whereas the prophetic mode in which Felix Holt functions writes an uninterrupted history of progress in the guise of culture, the narrative process of integration-of both the workers as a class and Esther as a woman-into that history reveals a residue of labors and pleasures yet to be redeemed.

While at some level, Eliot's Felix Holt registers this uncomfortable fit-between labour and pleasure, between the narrative and the prophetic-it ultimately resolves such discomfort by rendering invisible that which does not "fit." In this sense, Felix Holt truly is a modern Odyssey: like Adorno and Horkheimer's analysis of the dialectic of Enlightenment, Felix Holt enacts a narrative of instrumental rationality which defines labour narrowly in the realm of a capitalist work ethic that by its very nature denies pleasure and desire.

1 Jameson, in the context of discussing Lukics's conception of totality, refers to the notion of ideology It posits in terms of strategies of containment. As Jameson argues 'Lukics's achievement was to have understood that such strategies of containment-which Marx himself described principally in his critiques of classical political economy and the ingenious frames the tatter constructed in order to avoid the ultimate consequences of such insights as the relationship between labour and value-can be unmasked only by confrontation with the ideal of totality which they at once imply and repress"

Recent feminist post-structuralist critics have attempted to address this problem specifically in relation to the construction of the nineteenth-century novel. Amstrong, for example, tries to bring the public and private spheres politics and sexuality, back into relation by historicizing the split between them She argues that it was precisely during the nineteenth century that the project of gendering subjectivity outside of and separate from "pol acquired its political significance.

She goes on then to claim primacy for the domestic front as the privileged site of ideological battle (and eventual victory) for middle-class dominance.

Given this exclusion, Negt and Kluge characterize the bourgeois public sphere as an illusory synthesis of the totality of society. They posit that this synthesis is premised significantly on the denial of large realme of social experience outside of or counter to the bourgeois public sphere, namely the self-experience of the maese, whose experience constitutes an alternative or proletarian public sphere.

As Negt and Kluge describe this process of disquallfication, 'the proletarian context of living does not as such boe lose Its experiential value; however the experience bound up in it is rendered 'incompehensible' in terms of social communication: ultimately, it becomes a private experience nil.

For a discussion tracing our critical lineage back to Arnold and the autonomy he assigns culture.

There are any number of examples later in the century of

the thematic of the colonial invading England's island, ranging from Sherlock Holmes detective stories (see especially Doyle, Tlr Sign of Four to narratives of the Englander "gone native. Like representations of the working class In the industrial novel, they reflect a palpable sense of cultural anxiety over the breaking down of clearly dem rc ted internal/ external social and spatial boundaries.

This series of displacements from the sphere of production to the domestic and national spheres typifies the structure of the industrial novel generally. Industrial novels exemplifying such a dynamic include Elizabeth Gaskell's Mary Ilarion, Charlotte Bronte's Shiley, Benjamin Disraeli's Sybil, and Charles Dickens's Hard Times.

In 1841 rapid coach from London to Exeter took eighteen hours In 1815 the same journey by rail express took six and a half hours.

This distinction between the process and experience of change is crucial to how Eliot will attempt to represent history in the novel, something I develop later In the essay. In its simplest form this distinction involves the difference between reading the processor or history of change as a diachronic, continuous narrative of development and progress and seeing history as a series of fragments and ruptures, as a narrattive of discontinuity in which the past is not simply dvely read to confirm the present.

I am here drawing on the work of Benjamin who distinguishes these two reading of the relationship between pat and present as the difference between historicism and historical materialism. Whereas historicism for Benjamin, "gives the 'eternar image of the past historical materialism "supplies a unique experience with the past". In the face of the general absence of literary representations of industrial work and industrial workers, Robbins suggests that we need to look elsewhere for representations of "the people," namely to the depiction of servants. But as I will argue It is this very absence which shapes how the realist novel represents "the people."

The epigraph to this chapter opens with the following

poem about truth: "Truth is the precious harvest of the earth./ But once, when harvest waved upon a land,/The noisome cankerworm and caterpillar,/Locusts, and all the swarmlng foul-born broods,/Fastened upon it with swift, greedy jaws,/ And turned the harvest into pestilence,/Until men said, What profits it to sow?" When John Blackwood sent Eliot her proofs of "Address to Working Men" he added a note clarifying that the charge that the new franchise makes the working man the master was made as a sarcasm in the House. Eliot responded in a letter on December 7, 1867: "I agree with you about the phrase, 'masters of the country.' I wrote that part twice, and originally I distinctly said that the epithet was false. Afterwards I left that out, preferring to make a stronger argumentum ad hominem in case any workman believed himself a future master"

It was at the behest of her publisher that Eliot wrote the "Address to Working Men" in November, 1867. Blackwood got the idea after hearing Disraeli's Edinburgh "address to the working men" in defence of the Second Reform Bill. In terms of the larger argument I am making as to the ambivalent narration of past and present in Felix Holt, the significance of the address lies in its historical continuity with the novel. Whereas the novel purportedly portrays the changes of 1832 its formal concerns are those of the 1860s.

Although there is a slight discrepancy in the time frames of Williams and Brantlinger the distinction they draw is essentially the same: the first period of reform is identified with middle-class rights and the ensuing crisis of Chartism in the 1840s, and the second with the crisis of suffrage surrounding the second Reform Bill. In the following discussion of the rising importance of culture in debates about reform I am paraphrasing Brantlinger's argument. Hobabawm also notes the shift in class alliances but in the broader context of Europe as a whole.

In terms of continental politics he marks 1848 as a turning point for the bourgeoisie. As he argues, 1848 failed because ultimately the struggle was not between the old regimes and the "forces of progress," but rather between "order" and social revolution. Moderate liberals made the discovery that revolution was dangerous, and that their economic demands could be met without it, ie. through reform: the bourgeoisie had ceased to be revolutionary class. On the signifigance of 1848.

Moretti interestingly traces this emphasis on cultural continuity back to the singular nature of the English Revolution, suggesting that 1642 and 1688 figured as "revolutionary" in the etymological sense of the word: rather than a revolutionary break between an aristocratic past and a newly-emerging bourgeois present (as in France 1789), the English Revolution reestablished or restored rights deemed temporarily lost, circling back toward English origins not forward to a revolutionary new future.

In the context of the development and analysis of the Bildungsromers, Moretti argues that this had profound effects on the British form of this genre.

Chapter 11

The "Aye" of George Eliot's Adam Bede: Christian Ethics

The greatest recent event — that "God is dead," that the belief in the Christian God has ceased to be believable — is... cast[ing] its shadows over Europe. For the few, at lease, whose eyes....are strong and sensitive enough for this spectacle... What must collapse now that this belief has been undermined... [is] our whole European morality.

Dr. Richard Niebuhr writes, in his introduction to Eliot's translation of Feuerbach's The Essence of Christianity, that Eliot "sought to retain the ethos of Christianity without its faith, its humanism without its theism." In her first full novel, Adam Bede, Eliot succeeds at doing this. By replacing God's all-seeing eye with a plethora of human eyes, Eliot depicts characters in the close-knit community of Hayslope who don't need God to be good Christians, who can hold their standards without their faith.

Eliot begins with the simplistically Christian notion that God can see everything. Adam, our title hero, sings a tune in chapter one that refers to "God's all-seeing eye,". Meanwhile, Bessy, a local Hayslope country girl, feels that "Jesus [is] close by looking at her, though she cannot see him". According to this model, a person must act morally otherwise God will know through sight and he will punish her. But, Eliot abandons these sorts of references to an all-seeing God by chapter four in favour of a structure that does not require God's eye. On the most basic level, Eliot is continually describing the physical eyes of her characters, and reminding us of their presence, although she gives up talking about God's eye.

Adam's eyes, for instance, are "keen and dark," we are told over and over. Likewise, Hetty's eyes are "dark," Lisbeth's eyes are "dim," Mrs. Poyser's are an "arctic blue-gray," Arthur Donnithorne's are notably adjective-less, Seth's are "confiding and pale," and Dinah's are always "gray," and usually "mild." Hetty is blatantly contrasted with Dinah through the look of their eyes) just as Adam is with his brother, Seth. Hardly a page passes in the entire novel where an eye is not mentioned. We are constantly reminded of the characters' perpetual watchfulness.

Furthermore, Eliot undermines the necessity of God's authority by directly replacing it with earthly authorities. "The eye of Mrs. Poyser" is one of these physical enforcers of Christian ethics. Mrs. Poyser notes that her servants "want somebody's eye on 'em constant if they're to be kept to their work". The human eye is what keeps them set on the work that their alleged God wants them to do. Bartle Massey is another authority as a teacher "whose eyes had been glaring at [his students] ominously through his spectacles for a few minutes"). One supposes he has the same influence on them as Poyser on her underlings.

The society as a whole is yet a third of these earthly authorities steadfastly passing judgment and keeping control with its "all eyes." The society show its capacity to do this at every public event, including Arthur's birthday celebration, church, the trial, the execution, and the wedding. Eliot's characters are, as it were, within the confines of Foucault's "panopticon." Everyone has the responsibility to watch everyone else in order to keep the society morally (or at least ethically) intact.

Dinah, the novel's central heroine, a female Methodist preacher, has a presence which is exactly human, although she, and others, associate her with "God." Trying to convince Dinah not to leave Hayslope, her aunt, Mrs. Poyser, tells her that Bessy, a girl Dinah turned against vanity, will "no more go on in her new ways without you than a dog 'ull stand on its hind-legs when there's nobody looking". Although it is Dinah's stated goal to help her fellows to accept God's ever-present gaze, all she succeeds at doing is getting them to cower to her authority or the community's approval. Even when Dinah convinces Hetty to confess to her crime of baby killing to "Jesus," Hetty is actually responding to Dinah alone. "Hetty kept her eyes on Dinah's face" and "Dinah felt a deep joy in the first sign that her love was welcomed by the wretched lost one". God's eye is not present, but Dinah's human eyes are, and they alone are the catalysts for human repentance and change.

Intense eyes follow the transgressive love affair between Arthur and Hetty as well. Hetty feels that Arthur's "eyes... seemed to touch her" When trying to avoid falling in love with Hetty, Arthur reasons to himself that "he must not see her alone again", and then, recanting, says that he "must see her again". Here the eyes reveal themselves as active participants, not just passive on-lookers. They have the capacity in and of themselves to transgress physical boundaries and set love in motion. Similarly, they can control behaviour and dictate ethical propriety.

Eliot also takes advantage of her audience's attentive eyes in relation to her fictional world. She pulls her reader into the active role of the watcher by prefacing her work with Wordsworth's verse, "So that ye may have/Clear images before your gladdened eyes". On the same note, she begins the novel itself, saying that she will "show" her readers "visions." Immediately, she forces her reader into the omniscient position of God, the one who will know all the text from there until the happy ending. Seemingly as a reminder of this important purpose, the reader is told that while Hetty is peering narcissitically into her mirror, she feels she is being watched by an "invisible spectator". Most superficially, this invisible figure is Hetty's ill-suited suitor, Arthur. However, on a more concrete level, she is actually being watched by the reader, who is in the bedroom with her on some level.

Most powerfully, Eliot directly addresses her reader with the responsibilities she has in a sort of manifesto on literature, which she lays out in chapter 17, "In Which the Story Pauses a Little." "You," she writes, addressing her reader dead on, "would be likely to turn a harder, colder eye... on the real breathing men and women, who can be chilled by your indifference... who can be cheered and helped onward by your... brave justice".

Her characters, she claims, are reliant on the reader much like a Christian is reliant on Jesus' mercy and fairness. Again, the religious is replaced by the secular. Eliot brings her audience into the watching-game, and thereby she morally affects us. If these characters are always watching each other, and we are always watching them, we feel, then, that there is perhaps someone always watching us and that we should behave properly. She imbues her reader with a paranoia that, if the story's moral sticks, will remain.

Scenes wherein that which is not supposed to be seen is seen bolsters this feeling that we cannot hide from acting morally (as opposed to being moral) despite the possible absence of the divine. The most forthright example of this is when Adam inadvertently witnesses Arthur kissing Hetty in the woods. Adam watches Arthur approach him from the kiss "with eyes in which amazement was fast turning to fierceness". Although Arthur is successfully avoiding God, he cannot hide from humanity. Adam's eyes absorb and judge the event, and then punish him for it with a beating. Little Totty partakes in such an activity alongside Adam a little earlier in the text when she "opened her eyes... and with her right [arm] caught at the string of brown beads round Hetty's neck". With the act of opening her eyes, Hetty begins the process of revealing to Adam Hetty's dishonorable state. Totty's eyes essentially penetrate Hetty's dress in spite of Hetty's attempt to hide her locket within it. Eliot depicts human eyes seeing within the human breast; a place it seems that only the privileged God should be able to access.

The reader, too, is made a spy at the Hall Farm, seeing that which the players don't know she can see. "By putting our eyes to the rusty bars of the gate," Eliot secretly tells her reader, "we can see the house well enough, and all but the very corners of the grassy enclosure". The eyes invade space they have not been invited onto, without being seen themselves. They "trespass," as Eliot says. This furthers in us the feeling that everything is being watched by judgmental human eyes, whether we know it or not. We "integrate" ourselves into the story we are reading, says John Goode in his essay on Adam Bede, "through the provision of a moral absolute" (Goode 35). That is to say, we provide for each other and ourselves the foundation on which socially acceptable behaviour, otherwise known as "moral" behaviour, rests.

Eliot goes so far as to make quite definite connections between the eyes' gaze and doing right. Arthur's eyes are not described with adjectives because he is wishy-washy, and doesn't particularly enforce any moral code on himself when it is necessary. In fact, Eliot describes him "resolutely turn[ing] his eyes away from any bad consequence". Likewise, in the church setting, Eliot points us to the "black-eyed youngsters". They are "black-eyed" because they haven't yet absorbed the Christian morality into their vision and therefore don't yet perpetuate the moral system within which they live.

Eliot's two primary heroes, Adam and Dinah, the ones who receive the novel's awkwardly happy ending, come together ultimately on a hilltop. Adam "chose this spot... because it was away from all eyes" and yet the other reason, which he does not give, must be that his eyes and hers are the only ones that can see from there, and they can probably see a good deal of the space below. Eliot places them at a superior vantage point thereby representing their superior moral positions. These righteous humans are sitting 'on high' instead of God. But, it is no Tower of Babble, it is right, for humans must take on the omniscient eye in order to support Eliot's notion that, as Niebuhr puts it, she can maintain "the ethos of Christianity without its faith."

Hetty internalizes the moral import of the eyes by experiencing the curse of seeing "Nothing but the place in the wood where I'd buried the baby...," she cries to Dinah, "I see it now!". The whole community then turns their damning eyes onto Hetty both in the courthouse as she stands "like a statue of dull despair", and as she is being carted out for hanging, they "gaze" (. It is her own vision, and that of her community, that condemns her. There is no need for God's classically omniscient eye to intervene.

Eliot tells us even more bluntly at one point that she is a proponent of human-divine interchangability. When hearing a "human sob," this narrator claims it is "no wonder man's religion has so much sorrow in it: no wonder he needs a suffering God". Here human emotions are equated with the invention of religion. Humans created a suffering God so they would feel better.

Eliot simply reverses the process in Adam Bede by giving humans' their moral eye back. The way Eppie replaces the gold in Silas Marner, so too humans replace God in Bede. The system remains generally the same, only the object/subject shifts. Along the same line, Eliot (let's assume she is the narrator) comically steps away from her tale for a moment and says, "One begins to suspect at length that there is no direct correlation between eyelashes and morals" The fact that this statement is in precise opposition to what I am arguing, and the fact that Eliot says it at all, suggests that it is an admission in negative terms. In Eliot's fiction, she is basically admitting, the two can be equated.

All these eyes, seeing through the traditional, unquestioned prism of Christianity's morals, reinforce that same morality without the need for an actual belief in the all-powerful omniscient eye of God. Essentially, Eliot pulls the cloth (of God) from under the outgrowth of Christian ethical codes with such dexterity that she does not disrupt the system itself. As the author Eliot moves her fictional community seamlessly from theism to agnosticism, so too does she value such a replacement in her own life as Marian. In 1856, just three years before publishing Adam Bede, she speaks of Goethe as "eminently the man who helps us to rise to a lofty point of observation, so that we may see things in their relative proportions."

Here, we see her maintaining moral absolutism by referring to objectively defined "proportions." Eliot replaces the god figure, classically sitting at the "lofty point of observation," with people. She doesn't explicitly place Goethe there at all, she says instead that he helps us (humans, that is) to arrive there together. It seems that in Adam Bede she is trying to accomplish the same feat. This is not an essay about perspective, it is an essay about objectivism and absolutism as defined by the collective human eye as opposed to the single omniscient and divine eye.

Of course, this analysis leaves me with a glaring question. Why does Eliot hold onto the morality defined by Christianity after surrendering its God? Why doesn't she re-evaluate that structure as well, rather than holding onto it by transferring authority? Why bother dismissing God if the visible fabric remains static? Perhaps she's being pragmatic — perhaps she fears anarchy in the wake of a passing God.

Chapter 12

George Eliot and the Fetish of Realism

On 29 May 1856, while at Ilfracombe with George Lewes, Marian Evans watched the local celebration of the end of the Crimean War. In her account of the incident, she describes a parade, an outdoor tea, and other examples of local eccentricities, and then refers to the event as a "bit of primitive provincial life". This association of primitivity with provincialism is deliberate. She and George H. Lewes were in the middle of a naturalist expedition to collect specimens of mollusks and anemones, a biological form of "primitive" life, and her observations of the Ilfracombe natives conflate zoological and social life: she describes the village houses as "barnacles clustered on the side of a great rock" and comments on "the strong family likeness between ourselves and all other building, burrowing house-appropriating and shell-secreting animals".

But the primitivity of provincial life was much on Evans's mind at that particular moment for non-zoological reasons as well. She encountered the village celebration as she was writing her article on W.H. Riehl's ethnographic study of provincial life.

She had started reading Die burgerliche Gesellschaft and Land and Leute only four weeks earlier. On 13 May 1856 her journal notes gloomily: "Began my article on Riehl this morning with rather despairing prospects" (Harris and Johnston 60). She finished it on 5 June 1856, less than a week after the village celebration. So her comment on provincial primitivity reflects an immersion in the ethnographic subject matter she describes in her article, "The Natural History of German Life," of which she had a living example before her in Ilfracombe life.

But what does "primitive" mean? In his New Science (1744), Giambattista Vico described the times of the earliest cultures as a period when people imbued the inanimate world around them with life, and thus lived in a universe of "animate substance. Other writers followed this lead, but it was Auguste Comte who cemented this association between primitives and perspective.

Comte established this association in Cours de philosophie positive, published 1830-1842, in which he defines his narrative of universal social development. He calls the earliest stage "Primitive Fetishism" because of its superstitious tendency to invest objects with spirits. As he tells the story, the first chapter "could begin no otherwise than by a complete and usually very durable state of pure Fetichism, which allowed free exercise to that tendency of our nature by which Man conceives of all external bodies as animated by a life analogous to his own". In the nineteenth century, primitivism was virtually synonymous with fetishism.

As Evans's comment on Ilfracombe shows, the sign of primitivism was also capable of being imported back into civilized life, in a form of reverse colonization. Children, the uneducated-any group seen as early in the developmental narrative-could be tagged "primitive" through their representation as fetishistic. This transposition of ethnological themes onto contemporary life is a form of domestic primitivism: the use of ethnographic narratives of social origins to explain elements of modern life. Because of the structure of fetishism-it was thought of as a failure of objective or rational perception-it was useful in the domestic context as a mode of social critique.

In her novels, George Eliot uses domestic primitivism to represent Victorian life as a reversion to an earlier stage of social development, most familiarly in her portrayal of the Dodsons in The Mill on the Floss.' The practice continued throughout her writing career. More than a decade after the Ilfracombe expedition, George Eliot wrote on 22 March 1868 to Sara Hennell, "I am reading about savages and semi-savages". Her notes at the time demonstrate an immersion in the study of primitive culture: she transcribed quotes from John Lubbock's Pre-Historic Times (1865), which she read in 1868, and from Edward B. Tylor's Researches into the Early History of Mankind and the Development of Civilization (1865).

In her "Notes for Felix Holt and Other," she annotates a reference to Tylor's Researches with the blunt comment, "for savage customs and ideas". Evidently, she was studying up on the essentialized attributes of primitives, intending to bring them to bear in her representation of working-class life in Felix Holt. George Eliot's realism was thus, in part, a domestic version of Victorian ethnography Knoepflmacher long ago observed, "Instead of faithfully copying the circumstances of external life, George Eliot arranged reality to make it substantiate her moral values". Similarly, her research for Felix Holt led her to substantiate assumptions about the moral values of primitive society in her representation of English working-class life, and we see an early variant of the same process at work in the Ilfracombe passage.

George Eliot was only one of many prominent Victorian writers to adapt the ethnological concept of primitivism to domestic national life: both Carlyle and Arnold used it similarly. However, her representation of it is uniquely complicated by her position as a novelist and particularly by her theory of novelistic realism. She develops that theory in her early essays and reviews, and in them it becomes clear that the effect of her realism relies on the same fetishism that it critiques. In other words, while fetishism in George Eliot's writing serves as a signifier for primitivism, it also plays a significant role in her own ideas about the project of realism. As I will argue here, the representation of fetishism in her writing exists in a paradoxical relationship with the fetishism of her theory of representation.

Long before Vico's general claim, specific primitive cultures were identified with fetishism. As Pietz has pointed out, fetishism historically "originated in the cross-cultural spaces of West Africa during the sixteenth and seventeenth centuries". The term "fetish" originally was used by Renaissance traders to describe objects used in religious practices by tribes on the Guinea Coast of Africa. The objects, traders imagined, were being worshiped as gods. This continued into the eighteenth century, when European writers were separately disputing the significance of recently discovered objects from Egyptian antiquity that appeared to show people worshipping man-made artifacts.

These two historical strands came together in a controversial book by Charles de Brosses, Du culte des dieux fetiches (1760). De Brosses-a minor French aristocrat who never set foot in Africa-held that West African fetishism was an example of the earliest stage in the universal progression of social development. He used the traders' accounts of contemporary "primitivism" to interpret the objects from Egyptian antiquity and, through historical analogy, established the concept of a universal primitive fetishism. In the process, he outlined the epistemology of the fetish that most subsequent writers followed. Writers who interpreted the objects as symbols for African gods were wrong, he argued. Instead, he interprets the objects as "fetishes, whose sacred character coincides with their physical constitution and appearance". The objects thus do not represent gods but are gods.

De Brosses's work had repercussions well beyond ethnology. A young Karl Marx read a German translation of Du culte des dieux fetiches in 1842-1843 and later incorporated it into his economic theory. And the French psychologist Alfred Binet adapted de Brosses's religious fetishism to sexual pathology in 1887, after which it was taken up by Krafft-Ebing and then Freud. But, within ethnology, de Brosses's theory of primitive fetishism dominated nineteenth-century thinking about the earliest stages of human development, largely due to its adoption by Comte, and it is through Comte that George Eliot's usage derives As the historian Hodgen has noted, de Brosses's "doctrine was not only widely disseminated but became, in the thirties of the nineteenth century the slender 'factual' foundation of Auguste Comte's primary, fetishistic, or theological stage in the development of society".

Comte divides social development into three progressive stages: the "theological," the "metaphysical" (which included the Europe of his own day), and ultimately the "positive," or utopian, stage yet to come. Fetishism marks the earliest point in this sequence. He explains that humans, in their encounters with inexplicable events, "conceive of the production of unknown effects according to the passions and affections of the corresponding being regarded as alive; and this is the philosophical principle of fetichism". In the state of "gross fetichism," humans imagine all objects, whether living or not, "to be animated by passion and will"Through this unaware act of projection, the early human is enabled "passively to yield to his propensity to transfer to outward objects the sense of existence which served him for an explanation of his own phenomena, and therefore for an absolute explanation of all out of himself".

The external world thus was composed entirely of fetishes, and this explanatory principle allowed early humans to make sense of their chaotic experiences. This fetish-worship differs fundamentally from "the adoration of images". As in de Brosses, the fetish is a non-symbolic object because its supernatural quality is "inseparable from the object in which it resides". So fetishes are distinct from the polytheistic gods, which appear in the second phase of the theological stage. These gods are abstractions that do not reside in concrete objects, and thus are represented by idols that are not themselves gods. As society develops, Comte argues, this primary fetishism never entirely disappears.

Like Charles Darwin's concept of "rudiments" or Edward Tylor's "survivals," Comte's primitive fetishism operates in later stages as a residual; all ages have "very marked traces... of the original fetichism, however it may be involved in metaphysical forms in subtle understandings". It remains in evidence even in nineteenth-century life: when someone looks at a malfunctioning watch, he or she imagines it to be a capricious being, while knowing rationally that it has no life of its own.

Because fetishism is the product of a relationship between Europeans and Africans within the contact zone, the fetish cannot be understood adequately as a positive thing in itself. Instead, it needs to be conceptualized as an expression of the relationship in which it comes into being. In schematic form, that relationship exists between three points. From the earliest travel narratives, the representation of fetishism has involved a triangular relationship between: a) a material object of some kind, b) a local who attributes supernatural qualities to the object, and c) an outsider who contradicts the local to reassert the simple materiality of the object.

In schematic terms, the three positions can be labeled as follows: the fetish, which can be either a thing or an idea; the fetishist who "worships" the fetish; and the subject. This last position is occupied by a critical spectator who interprets the fetishist's relationship to the fetish as a form of false evaluation. Fetishism entails a commentary on an attribution of false or erroneous cultural value. However, there is a dialectical complication that follows from this apparently simple triangular scheme. In asserting the falsity of the fetishist's values, the subject simultaneously asserts the truth or accuracy of his or her own values.

In this relationship, the claim that an object is a fetish, and thus overvalued as possessing qualities it lacks, also implies that non-subjective value does exist elsewhere, in other objects. By establishing the grounds of truth within his or her own cultural values, the subject thus becomes vulnerable to the claim of fetishism by another outsider. And so the critic of the first level comes to occupy the position of the fetishist in an alternate fetishistic triangle. Dialectically, the subject becomes the fetishist in the act of evaluating the fetish as such.

And, in this manner, the critique of fetishism produces the secondary fetishization of the critic's values. Representations of fetishism, as Slavoj Zizek has argued, always occur within a dialogue that entails competing claims of fetishism, in which the critic and fetishist become structurally interchangeable. Thus, the discourse of fetishism is never about the fetish as such, but rather is about the sequence of relationships that produce the notion of fetishism. While this kind of discourse tells us little about the cultural values of the local fetishist, it can indicate a great deal about the subject's cultural values.

George Eliot, like many English intellectuals in the 1840s and 1850s, was enthusiastic about the new ideas in Comte's Cours de philosophie positive." The diffusion of those ideas in England began in earnest in 1843, when John Stuart Mill published his A System of Logic, which uses many of Comte's ideas. After this date "intellectual Englishmen no longer had any excuse for not knowing the philosophy of Auguste Comte, for Mill makes absolutely clear his debt to the French thinker" A young friend of Mill's, Lewes first made his mark as a popularizer of Comte's ideas in his Biographical History of Philosophy (1845-1846).

Written as an accessible primer to philosophy in "Knights's Weekly Volume Series," its one-shilling installments reached an audience well beyond the intellectual circle that knew Mill's Logic. Lewes continued his work on Positivism, and, in 1853, just months after he and Evans became lovers, he finished his explanation of Cours, published later that year as Comte's Philosophy of the Sciences.

That George Eliot was well versed in Positivism by this date is certain, but it is also clear that her familiarity with Comte's philosophy predates the relationship with Lewes by several years. In an 1849 letter, she mentions lending out a copy of Mill's Logic. In 1851, she refers to it as her "reference book". She moved to London from Coventry in January 1851 (when she changed her name to Marian Evans), and, during that first year, she was already actively promoting Comte's writing; we know, for example, that she urged Herbert Spencer to read Comte.

Her first printed reference to Comte appears in a review of Robert William Mackay's The Progress of the Intellect, which appeared in the January 1851 Westminster Review, that she wrote before the move to London. She takes issue with Mackay's narrative of religious development. He positions "the primitive period of myth" as a degeneration from an original "monotheistic or pantheistic impression," rather than being "a step in advance of fetishism". The Christian orthodox position, based on Genesis, held that monotheism was the original form of worship, and this is the narrative that Mackay endorses. Both de Brosses and Comte countered this view with their theory of an original fetishism. And so, in this passage, George Eliot defends the positivist narrative of development. This apparently minor point helps to establish the context for her criticism of Positivists, for their inattention to the importance of the past.

Comte's followers "are prone to under-rate critical research into ancient modes of life and forms of thought.... But it would be a very serious mistake to suppose that the study of the past and the labours of criticism have no important practical bearing on the present". Rather than a substantive disagreement with the Positivist theory of development, the complaint insists on its broad applicability to analyses of the present. Contemporary life is littered with survivals from antiquity, "lifeless barbarisms" or "petrifications from distant ages". Study of the past is essential to recognize them, and thus to understand the present. She explains: "We are in bondage to terms and conceptions which, having had their root in conditions of thought no longer existing, have ceased to possess any vitality, and are for us as spells which have lost their virtue".

These lifeless concepts are idola theatri, a term that harks back to Comte's fetishism as the attribution of life to lifeless artifacts. We can identify the primitivism of Ilfracombe's celebration in its own idola theatri: the "melancholy foot-races" and "feeble fire-works". In contrast to these listless residues, she notes how "fine" it was to see the bonfires, which "made one think of the times when such fires were lighted as signals to arm-the symbol of a common cause and a common feeling". Their vitality lies in the past, however, and they survive as fetishized petrifactions that keep Ilfracombe natives in bondage to the primitive.

Her engagement with Positivism was subsequently modified, as others have noted, by her translation of Ludwig Feuerbach's Das Wesen des Christenthums. She took on this project at the end of 1853, when she gave up her editorship of the Westminster Review. It was published less than a year later, in July 1854, marking the first time the name "Marian Evans" appeared in print. Her affinity for Feuerbach's philosophy is well known, but, by looking briefly at Feuerbach's ideas, we can see that his anti-theological humanism is premised on a radical critique of fetishism in modern life.

Compared to Comte, Feuerbach dramatically widens the reach of fetishism. Instead of a survival from the most distant stage of social development, fetishism becomes the essence of modern Christianity, and so is reinstated at the centre of cultural life in developed society. In this respect, Feuerbach's attitude toward fetishism resembles Comte's less than that of Marx, whose commodity fetishism is an essential part of industrial capitalism. With Marx, Feuerbach shares a base in German materialist philosophy: "I do not generate the object from the thought, but the thought from the object.... I attach myself... only to realism, to materialism," he writes. And this engagement with realism accounts for part of Feuerbach's interest to the translating Marian Evans, then in the process of defining her own realist values.

The two authorial voices-her translation, his original-intermingle in this text, as Beer notes: "These are George Eliot's words as well as Feuerbach's". And this intertextuality is underscored by George Eliot's well-known comment in a letter written while finishing the translation: "With the ideas of Feuerbach I everywhere agree...". The Essence of Christianity begins from the position that "Religion is the dream of the human mind". Religion's illusory quality is no reason to ignore it. On the contrary, "in dreams we do not find ourselves in emptiness or in heaven, but on earth, in the realm of reality". The content of the dream is meaningful as a guide to the beings that imagine it, and Feuerbach goes on to argue that religious belief is a projection of human ideals onto an imagined, external entity. Were a bird to imagine God, then God "would be a winged being". As societies develop, the anthropomorphic image develops.

"So long as man is in a mere state of nature, so long is his god a mere nature-god-a personification of some natural force. Where man inhabits houses, he also encloses his gods in temples". Thus the image of God depends on the developmental stage of the society that produces it. However, in a complication of this pattern, humans reverse this projection and imagine themselves as subordinated creations of the God they have themselves invented. As Evans translates: "Man— this is the mystery of religion-projects his being into objectivity, and then again makes himself an object to this projected image of himself thus converted into a subject". Thus "he thinks of himself... as the object of an object, of another being than himself'.

In both Feuerbach's philosophy and George Eliot's fiction, realism hinges on the unmasking of this illusory sequence and the restoration of the human to her rightful place. Those attributes that most define God as the ideal moral being-sympathy, compassion, love-are eminently human qualities: "God is love," Feuerbach (and Evans) writes, and from this concludes that God is an externalized embodiment object of humanity's own essence. Realism demands that those essential attributes be represented as located within humanity, rather than falsely attributed to a deity. And it is out of this imperative that both Feuerbach's and George Eliot's humanism spring.

The idea of God in The Essence of Christianity thus comes about in three stages: 1) humans project their own qualities onto an external object, forget that it was a projection, perceive the object as actually possessing those qualities. This is, of course, the process of fetishism in action, exactly as described by Comte, and so Feuerbach's materialist critique of religion defines realism as the antidote to fetishism. This juxtaposition is a characteristic feature of George Eliot's essays and reviews.

In some, she unmasks the fetishist, and in others she praises writers who themselves unmask fetishistic beliefs. The former can be seen in her last extended article, "Worldliness and Other-Worldliness: The Poet Young," which appeared in January 1857.

In it, she demolishes the reverence with which Edward Young's Night Thoughts was held, and represents the poet as a self-centered sycophant. "Young has no conception of religion as anything else than egoism turned heavenward". The fetishistic act of projection and the egoistic inability to differentiate inner perception from external fact merge in her analysis of Young. Thus, even as she is just beginning to write fiction-the article is written simultaneously with her first story, "The Sad Fortunes of the Reverend Amos Barton"-she is already using the concept of primitive fetishism to represent individual immaturity in her non-fiction articles.

Eliot heaps praise on writers who unmask modern fetishistic assumptions. Her 1851 review of William Rathbone Greg's The Creed of Christendom lauds it for countering religious fetishism with a healthy dose of realism. Calling it "an introductory manual of biblical criticism," she argues that his book clears "away the dazzling haze with which the inspiration dogma invests the biblical writings" by treating the canonical writings as historical documents, rather than as revelations "dictated or suggested by God". This historicist move defetishizes scripture. It also pointedly de-fetishizes the living god: the biblical Jesus becomes redefined as "humanity in its divinest phase," but is no longer considered himself a god.

Two feminist writers come in for similar praise in the 1855 review, "Margaret Fuller and Mary Wollstonecraft." George Eliot contrasts the "doll-Madonna in her shrine" with the reality of women's ignorance in an age that discounted female education. While Feuerbach described humans as diminishing themselves in the process of projecting their best qualities onto God, George Eliot describes Victorians as deifying women in order to avoid "looking up to our wives".

Deification in domestic relations becomes a form of

disempowerment: Sit divus, dummodo non sit vivus (let him be a god, provided he be not living), said the Roman magnates of Romulus; and so men say of women, let them be idols, useless absorbents of precious things, provided we are not obliged to admit them to be strictly fellow— beings, to be treated, one and all, with justice and sobre reverence. George Eliot contrasts this doll-fetish ideology with the realistic treatment women receive in Fuller's and Wollstonecraft's two works; for both authors, the "ardent hopes of what women may become do not prevent them from seeing and painting women as they are".

The critique of fetishism in George Eliot's early novels is less censorious than in her non-fiction. Typical is the compassionate description of Mrs. Tulliver weeping over her "Teraphim, or Household Gods". She sits alone in the storeroom, where "her linen and all her precious 'best things'" are spread out before her. "'But I shouldn't ha' minded so much if we could ha' kept the things wi' my name on 'em,'" she explains, referring to the tablecloths she had marked with "a particular stitch". In Feuerbachian fashion, Mrs. Tulliver's grief is not simply over the loss of her material god but of a god that bears the marks of her own invention. Within this scene Maggie plays the role of anti-fetishist. She upbraids her mother and brother for caring more about "table-cloths and china" than "her father, who was lying there in a sort of living death". The first, then, are re-evaluated as material objects, while the second-her paralyzed father himself transformed into an object-has his aliveness reasserted.

George Eliot's most familiar, explicit reference to fetishism occurs earlier in the same novel. Instead of the seclusion of Mrs. Tulliver's storeroom, Maggie is sobbing in her attic sanctuary, engaging in her own ritual: "here she kept a Fetish which she punished for all her misfortunes". This doll, "now entirely defaced by a long career of vicarious suffering," contains the spirit of Aunt Glegg, and Maggie's revenge has to be moderated. Used to driving nails into its head, she "reflected that if she drove many nails in, she would not be so well able to fancy that the head was hurt when she knocked it against the wall". Rather than a living fetish, the doll is at the threshold of being reduced to its sheer materiality as splinters of wood.

So the child moderates her revenge and "soothe[s] herself by alternately grinding and beating the wooden head". The narrating voice adopts the anti-fetishist stance here-a stance that is strongly compassionate, while also detached. The narrator's language suggests an indulgent humour in the representation of Maggie: to be "soothed" by the violent actions of "grinding and beating" is a primitive image of catharsis, one well suited to representing the irrational passions of an undeveloped fetishist. This passage, along with the previous one, contrasts the highly developed narrator's voice with the primitive fetishism of the Tullivers, but it is a compassion that, in this light, parallels the benevolence of the colonizer for the colonized, the advanced society for the undeveloped, or the Ilfracombe tourist for the primitive provincials.

Maggie's fetish doll is not George Eliot's first reference to fetishism, though it resembles it in its structure. Much earlier, in her Coventry days, Mary Ann Evans used the term to describe herself. In November 1843, she attended the marriage of Charles Hennell, brother of her Coventry neighbour Cara Bray and author of the book that led to her break with evangelicalism, Inquiry Concerning the Origin of Christianity. Hennell was marrying Rufa Brabant, then in the process of translating D. F. Strauss's Das Leben Jesu into English, a project she soon turned over to Mary Ann." Following the wedding in London, the 24-year-old Mary Ann went for a six-week stay in Devizes with Rufa's family, beginning 7 November.

While there, she was flattered and flirted with by Dr. Robert Brabant, then in his 60s. The blind Mrs. Brabant became jealous, and, by the time Rufa returned from her honeymoon, matters were uncomfortable enough that Mary Ann left two weeks early for home, on 4 December.

The exact nature of her feelings is unknown, but the incident caused concern at the time to Cara Bray and her sister,

Sara Hennell, and it is in a subsequent letter to Sara that Mary Ann reflects on her behaviour:

> I begin to be of your and Cara's opinion anent Dr. B[rabant].... If I ever offered incense to him it was because there was no other deity at hand and because I wanted some kind of worship pour passer le temps. I always knew that I could belabour my fetisch if I chose, and laughed at him in my sleeve. Even that degree of inclination toward mock reverence has long since passed away....

Like the narrator of Mill on the Floss, the narrating subject of the letter positions the younger fetishist at a distance and frames her worship of the fetish object as a product of her immaturity. But the example is, of course, much closer to home. Here, interpreting subject and fetishist are one and the same, and the letter recognizes this in its hint of defensiveness, as if to deny that this was true infatuation, but was rather a consciously created artifice for her own entertainment.

The representation of fetishism in George Eliot's writing is complicated by the anti-representational nature of the fetish. Comte gestures toward this problem when he speculates: "If Man had been no more capable than monkeys and carnivorous animals of comparing, abstracting, and generalizing, he would have remained forever in the rude fetichism which their imperfect organization forbids their surmounting". To abstract and compare are forms of representation, and as such they signify the end of fetishism to Comte, because representation makes possible the more advanced symbolic meanings found in idol worship, in which the signifying object is distinct from its signified spirit. No such distinction exists in fetishism, where object and spirit are one and the same, fused in an unmediated anti-symbolic relationship.

As Carabelli has argued, fetishes are "perfectly aniconic... in the sense that they do not represent divinities, but are divinities". Thus, rather than being a representation of meaning, the fetish is meaning itself. Theoretically, this communion of signifier with signified, of object with spirit, cannot be directly represented, because representation itself undoes the anti-representational essence of the fetish. To represent a fetish is to turn it into an icon or symbol-precisely what it is defined against. While we have a variety of words for fetishes, these words assert, in the act of signifying, that the fetish can be represented-the sign fetish, after all.

As if to acknowledge this problem, the most frequent metaphorical vehicle used in representing fetishism is the image of the object that comes to life. Karl Marx explains, for example, that fetishism occurs when "the products of the human brain appear as autonomous figures endowed with a life of their own". In commodity fetishism, products appear transformed by their entry into exchange relations. A wooden table is just a table:

But as soon as it emerges as a commodity, it changes into a thing which transcends sensuousness. It not only stands with its feet on the ground, but, in relation to all other commodities, it stands on its head, and evolves out of its wooden brain grotesque ideas, far more wonderful than if it were to begin dancing of its own free will.

Using the same metaphor, Comte represents fetishism as if the material world were alive in every tree and rock. Similarly, Tylor illustrates fetishism with a story (originally from Charles Darwin) of "two Malay women in Keeling Island who held a wooden spoon dressed in clothes like a doll; this spoon had been carried to the grave of a dead man, and becoming inspired at full moon, in fact lunatic, it danced about convulsively like a table or a hat at a modern spirit-seance". All of these are examples of what Zizek, in "Fetishism and Its Vicissitudes," calls the "paradox of moving statues, of dead objects coming alive and/or of petrified living objects" that comes into play when "the barrier which separates the living from the dead is transgressed". And both sides of that paradox are evident in Mill on the Floss in its juxtaposition of the immobile Mr. Tulliver with Mrs. Tulliver's vibrant household objects.

While fetishism and representation are essentially inimical to one another, this opposition can magically evaporate when representation ceases to be pure representation-a disembodied set of abstractions-and begins to take on the quality and status of an object in its own right. An ornate book, finely bound in kid leather and gold-stamped, contains its representation within an object of insistent materiality. And, to a lesser degree, all books in circulation are similar objects. Were such a representation-as-object imagined to be alive, the triumph of fetishism in its rivalry with representation would be complete. Such is the case in the realist novel. The rise of realism in philosophy is a familiar story in which classical generality yields to realist particularity.

In the epistemology of realism, particulars are significant in their relation to an assumed overarching general design, and so particulars become meaningful as a way to access that larger general truth. Ian Watt's definition of formal realism, for example, holds that the novel "works by exhaustive presentation" in order to "make the words bring [the] object home to us in all its concrete particularity". Through this generous heaping of particulars, fiction produces the illusion that "the novel is a full and authentic report of human experience" The realist use of particularity thus encourages the reader to attribute a kind of life to the narrative, to imagine that behind or within this inert body of words resides a living spirit.

Major critics of realism in Watt's generation insisted that the critical assessment of realism hinged on the extent to which a novel succeeds at becoming "an imitation of life". Novels "must give us a sense that what is being conveyed across to us by the words on the page is life..." Such phrases refer to the mimetic capabilities of representation, but the same words describe an object that succeeds only by coming to life. Thus, Harvey, whose criticism centers on "the question of mimetic adequacy," writes that "Dreiser... still has the power of deeply moving the reader because the life he has imagined is indeed alive". As an aesthetic criterion of evaluation, this requirement ties the success or failure of the object to a form of hypostasis.

Critics avoid the problem of fetishism by retaining the distinction between representation and represented object. But it is the business of realism in the novel to obscure that distinction, through its heaping of particulars, so that a "report of human experience" can become "full and authentic," even when there is no historical experience to report. Realism in the novel thus works by creating an illusion of life, and in this function we can say that the realist object always strives to attain the status of the fetish. While the language of fetishism is implicit in twentieth-century appraisals of realist novels, it is more emphatic in the theory of Victorian realism to which George Eliot and her contemporaries subscribed.

In Modern Painters, John Ruskin insists on the importance of particularity. "Nearly every other rule applicable to art has some exception but this. This has absolutely none" Neither fuzzy nor hazy, art is to have a crystal clarity in its treatment of details, and thus "all great drawing is distinct drawing" Students of erotic fetishism, from Alfred Binet forward, have defined the obsession with detail as a form of fetishism.However, in Ruskin's own writing, the detail is not valued as an isolated particular.

His theory describes an aggregate effect of accumulated details rather than isolated ones. He argues, for example, that an artist's selection among available details is made by choosing "the most necessary first, and afterwards the most consistent with these, so as to obtain the greatest possible and most harmonious sum". As his argument develops he consistently emphasizes the accumulation of details; from this aggregate perspective, detail takes on a new importance. Rather than being individual representations details become presentation in the "sum" that they make.

Ruskin talks about details as if they were units of embodied Truth (now with a capital T), Truths so concrete that one could actually count them: "great art... includes the largest possible quantity of Truth.... Thus, he continues, "the difference between the great and inferior artists... may be determined at once by the question, which of them conveys the largest sum of truth?" That sum is not only quantitatively greater but qualitatively greater than its parts, and the key element in that qualitative distinction is the hypostatization of art: through their aggregation, realist particulars take on an illusion of concreteness that transforms them from representation to an embodiment of truth. That sum of truth is directly associated with the spirit world.

Ruskin defines truth as fidelity to nature, so that details can be true or false, "while the picture is considered as a statement of facts". But Ruskin's nature is a providential one rather than a sheer materiality. Objects in the natural world have meaning as signs-however unclear-of the hidden providential design. The value, then, of incorporating the greatest amount of detail in art is that the artist represents a providential text, and the more of that text that can be included, the greater the possibility of getting it right. In this sense, Ruskin's call for the "largest possible quantity of Truth" is a prescription for the greatest potency of the spirit in the realist object.

What happens, then, when the viewer or reader comes into contact with this object? In defining the technical qualities of greatness in art, Ruskin explains "why the word 'Great' is used of this art. It is literally great. It compasses and calls forth the entire human spirit, whereas any other kind of art, being more or less small or narrow, compasses and calls forth only part of the human spirit". This doctrine centers on a universal spirit, unlike the ancestral spirits of West-African religious beliefs, and yet the relationship he asserts between spirit and object is similar. The fetishistic quality of the object is evident first in the claim that the object "compasses" the spirit so that it becomes a residence for a spirit that is now "in" the object.

But that fetishism is also implicit in the active power Ruskin attributes to the object: as able to "call forth" a spirit within the viewer. In the interaction between viewer and object, the providential spirit of nature acts directly on the viewer, whose inner spirit reacts in a kind of ethereal vibration to the greater spirit contained, in varying potency, within the object. This language suggests an object that actually radiates a supernatural force, as if through a halo-effect that influences all who come in contact with its great spirit. To an African out of Comte's book, one might imagine, Ruskin's "great art" is a powerful fetish, indeed.

This hypostatization is widespread in George Eliot's writing on realism, and it becomes most pronounced when she comments on the effect of art on its audience. In these remarks, the value of realism is routinely premised on its ability to transform the artifact into an object of quasi— supernatural powers. Her 1849 review of J. A. Froude's novel, The Nemesis of Faith, describes this function dramatically:

On certain red-letter days of our existence, it happens to us to discover among the spawn of the press, a book which, as we read, seems to undergo a sort of transfiguration before us. We no longer hold heavily in our hands an octavo of some hundred pages...: but we seem to be in companionship with a spirit, who is transfusing himself into our souls, and is vitalizing them by his superior energy....

Chapter 13

George Eliot and the Production of Consumers

In 1866, George Henry Lewes wrote that "it is a pity that [Felix Holt] isn't quite ready for publication just in the thick of the great reform discussion so many good quotable 'bits' would be furnished to M.P.s" (Eliot, Letters 8: 374). The absence of George Eliot quotations from that debate has been more than compensated for by their ubiquity in other venues. Before her death, excerpts from Eliot appear in an anthology, on a calendar, in four schoolbooks, on an army officers' examination, in a sermon, in one reader's copy of the New Testament, and as epigraphs to a socialist treatise and an abridgment of Boswell's Life of Johnson. In the years immediately following, her works are excerpted in a Zionist tract, provide chapter mottoes for at least one novel, and appear in anthologies ranging from booklets for the pocket to albums for the sofa-table (see Zionism).

Readers' fondness for quoting Eliot can ultimately be traced to the structure of her own narratives, punctuated with epigraphs and self-contained digressions. But it originates more directly in the publishing venture of one of her fans. In the year in which Middlemarch appears, the publisher Blackwood also brings out a daintier volume-the Wise, Witty, and Tender Sayings in Prose and Verse Selected from the Works of George Eliot-edited by a sycophantic young Scotsman named Alexander Main. Three more editions follow over the next eight years, updated each time a new book by Eliot herself appears.

Meanwhile, at the end of 1878, in time for Christmas presents, Main assembles a new series of quotations for the George Eliot Birthday Book, a diary decorated with a "thought" from George Eliot for every day of the year.' The fact that every new book by Eliot prompts a new edition by Main means that Daniel Deronda and the Impressions of Theophrastus Such are both written in the expectation of being excerpted. And because buyers of the Sayings and Birthday Book constitute only a fraction of the readers who know of their existence, Main's anthologies shape the way Eliot's work is perceived even by those who refuse to read her at less than full length.

This article examines the effect of that awareness on George Eliot-and on her readers, reviewers, and critics. Anthologies redefine the genre of Eliot's oeuvre and the gender of its author in contradictory ways: they sanctify the novel by classifying Eliot as a poet, and bracket her with male predecessors while marketing her to women. In training their readers to sift Eliot's reusable wisdom from her ephemeral plots, anthologies replace the novel's difference from other genres by a gendered difference within its own public. Nineteenth-century reviews and twentieth-century criticism characterize Eliot's work more explicitly as peculiarly quotable, even as-like Eliot herself-they question the ethics of appropriating others' words.

Their ambivalence about Eliot's lapidary generalizations marks a shift away from traditional assumptions about the relation between plot and pleasure which replaces the figure of the self-indulgent female reader about whom eighteenth-century critics had worried with a new figure of the self important female sage. Reviewers' anxiety about the dependence on representative quotation that they share with anthologists raises questions about the rules of textual evidence that twentieth-century criticism has yet to resolve.

Few novels are quarried for anthology-pieces before George Eliot's. Victorian anthologies are dominated by more serious genres: lyric, the essay, and drama (or rather, Shakespeare). In that context, the very act of excerpting Eliot implies that the novels, or the best parts of the novels, are not narrative at all. Alexander Main's assertion that Middlemarch "is really a prose-poem much more than a novel in the ordinary sense of the word" tells us less about the form of that text than about the anthology-piece as a form. The preface to the Sayings defines Eliot's achievement in terms of genre: What Shakespeare did for the Drama, George Eliot has been, and still is, doing for the Novel.

By those who know her works really well, this branch of literature can never again be regarded as mere story-telling and the reading of it as only a pastime. George Eliot has magnified her office and made it honourable; she has for ever sanctified the Novel by making it the vehicle of the grandest and most uncompromising moral truth. (Sayings ix; emphasis added) By defining "story-telling" as "only a pastime," Main reduces narrative to the dispensable "vehicle" by which "truth" is conveyed.

And he does dispense with it. Main's comparison of Eliot with Shakespeare invokes a dramatic model that the second edition of the Sayings borrows more obliquely, adding several dialogues from Middlemarch and eliminating the narrator's voice by the double expedient of deleting speech tags and transposing the narrative into stage directions. Thus, "Mr. Bulstrode, alone with his brother-inlaw, poured himself out a glass of water, and opened a sandwich-box" (Middlemarch 155) becomes: Mr. Bulstrode (pouring himself out a glass of water, and opening a sandwich box). -I cannot persuade you to adopt my regimen, Vincy?

Mr. Vincy. -No, no; I've no opinion of that system. Life wants padding. When the narrative voice does appear outside of these parentheses, it is presented not as the narrator's but as the author's: each chapter begins with a section entitled "George Eliot (in propria persona)"-truncated, in the 1878 Birthday Book, to "George Eliot." Main's refusal to recognize free indirect discourse allows him to pad these sections out by misattributing to the "propria persona" statements that the novels themselves locate in the perspective of a character.

Thus, Main's saying that "People are so ridiculous with

their illusions, carrying their fool's caps unawares, thinking their own lies opaque while everybody else's are transparent" misquotes a passage that originally read:

[Mary] sat tonight revolving, as she was wont, the scenes of the day, her lips often curling with amusement at the oddities to which her fancy added fresh drollery: people were so ridiculous with their illusions, carrying their fool's caps unawares, thinking their own lies opaque while everybody else's were transparent. By transposing the past tense to the present, Main turns what the novel presents as Mary's thought into a general truth with no verbs marking when or to whom it occurs. Eliot's complaint about a different anthologizer could also be applied to Main: "You observe that he is so unreflecting as to take the words put dramatically into the mouths of my characters as the expression of my own sentiments."

But drama and the essay are not the only genres that displace the novel. Main crowds it out more literally by over-representing both Eliot's poems (one-seventh of the 1873 edition) and verse epigraphs taken from the novels (of which he includes exactly half). Even within the chapter devoted to verse, Main includes a disproportionate number of the "songs" that punctuate the narrative of The Spanish Gypsy (which will later be excerpted, with musical settings, in yet another volume). Eliot herself encourages this bias.

The only two quotations that she requests Main to include in the Birthday Book are both epigraphs; and she asks him quite explicitly to slant the collection away from prose narrative and toward verse epigraphs, insisting that "there should be a good sprinkling of the best quotations from my Poems and poetical mottoes." When a century later William Bennett includes two quotations from Eliot poems in his Book of Virtues but none from her novels-implying that prose fictions have no place in an anthology even when they render an author too famous to exclude-he simply repeats the 1872 anthology's redefinition of Eliot as a poet.

Main's preface announces his generic agenda from the beginning: "Nor is it only as a novelist that George Eliot has claims upon our closest attention and our deepest regard....

The Legend of Jubal,' 'Armgart,' and 'The Spanish Gypsy so massive in structure, so lofty in tone, so rich in thought, fairly entitle their author to a foremost place in the ranks of British poets" (Sayings x). Main plans a second anthology to grant Eliot that place. Two years after the Sayings appears, he writes to its publisher offering "to make a new selection of English lyrics, from Shakespeare and Spenser to Browning & George Eliot, under the title: 'The Spirit of British Poetry,"' which, he suggests, "might very easily, and I think, very properly, be made uniform with the first edition of the Sayings."

By making one anthology "uniform" with the other, Main erases the difference between George Eliot and her male predecessors. Eliot herself asks for her Sayings to be republished in a form modeled after Matthew Arnold's Wordsworth anthology: "I have been examining the actual volume, and it seems to be capable of sufficient compression by substituting a thinner paper-still fine and tinted, but as thin, for example, as that of Matthew Arnold's Selections from Wordsworth". Like Main, Eliot uses the anthology as a tool to inscribe herself within a poetic tradition.

In other words, although Main claims that Eliot has made the novel a serious genre, his anthology de-novelizes Eliot as strenuously as earlier abridgments like Charles and Mary Lamb's Tales (1807) had novelized Shakespeare. The Lambs use the model of the novel to reduce Shakespeare to a smaller, domestic, feminine scale; conversely, the preface to the Sayings invokes Shakespearean drama to "magnify" Eliot's "mere storytelling" into something more "grand." Where the Lambs redefine Shakespeare as a children's writer, Main helps to position Middlemarch as what Virginia Woolf would later call "one of the few English novels for grown-up people" While the Lambs modernize Shakespeare by transposing his plots into a genre that postdates them, Main attempts to grant a living novelist the status usually reserved for dead poets.

Ultimately, however, Main's anthologies do not so much substitute one genre for another as scramble generic signals to a poim where "lyric" ceases to designate anything more specific than "anthology-piece." Main's unsuccessful plan to yoke Eliot with Shakespeare under the rubric of "British Poetry" makes clear that the novel is not the only genre that anthologies rename. The proposed "selection of English lyrics, from Shakespeare and Spenser to Browning & George Eliot" which Main later revises to read simply A Selection of British Lyrics from Shakespeare to George Eliot-begins the history of "lyric" with a dramatist and ends it with a novelist.

The title makes no sense unless we remember that Shakespeare had already been redefined by earlier anthologies as a writer of lyrics. Thomas Percy's decision to excerpt only the songs from Shakespeare's plays in his Reliques of Ancient Poetry (1765) is repeated by later collections like Robert Bell's Songs from the Dramatists (1854) and A.H. Bullen's Lyrics from the Dramatists of the Elizabethan Age (1889), and by the overrepresentation of songs in Palgrave's Golden Treasury (1861).

Victorian editors deny the dramatic status of the plays more obliquely than the Lambs, by isolating Shakespearean anthology-pieces from other dramatic texts. Put differently, Shakespeare provides Main with a precedent for excerpting works in a genre that anthologies otherwise exclude. Vicessimus Knox's influential Elegant Extracts (1784) includes 112 pages of Shakespeare and only 23 from other dramatists. An excerpt from the excerpts, Knox's abridged Poetical Epitome (1792), reduces the latter more sharply than the former.. Even more than a century later, in 1910, Henry Frowde's Moments series of pocket anthologies, which includes no novelist but Eliot and Dickens, also excludes all dramatists except Shakespeare.

In this context, Main's invocation of Shakespeare sets off a chain of generic transformations in which narrative gets displaced by drama which has already been redefined as lyric. In the preface to the Sayings, Shakespeare's name stands not only for Eliot's power to transcend genre, but for the power of anthologies to transform it. The Sayings claims for a single novelist the generic extraterritoriality that earlier anthologies had conferred upon a single playwright. The generic rule proves the authorial exception: genius overrules genre. Just as the Elegant Extracts do not grant respectability to drama but simply make Shakespeare less of a dramatist, Main's anthologies do not ennoble the novel so much as de-novelize Eliot.

In Eliot's case as in Shakespeare's, authorial identity overrules the generic criteria that normally govern admittance to anthologies-and to the canon. Main's Sayings and the anthologies that follow make Eliot's relation to other novelists as tenuous as her relation to other women. Like another admirer who describes Eliot as "the female Shakespeare, so to speak," they define her as an exception. Main's defensive claim in the preface that by ranking Eliot with Shakespeare "I would not be supposed to undervalue the writings of other novelists" confirms the accusation that it attempts to avoid: as his publisher, John Blackwood, complained, "in his preface he allows too little for all the good in Novels that have gone before". Main's claims for Eliot's uniqueness depend on the same dismissal of the novel that his preface claims to challenge.

The Sayings contributes to the substitution of individual genius for generic categories that makes one review in the Telegraph a few months later pronounce it "almost profane to speak of ordinary novels in the same breath with George Eliot's" The review could be taken to mean that Eliot is incomparable. Yet "speak[ing] in the same breath" predicts with uncanny accuracy the juxtapositions that shape Eliot's image in the decade leading up to her death. Eliot's name reappears at the front of the next anthology that Main compiles, a collection of wit and wisdom of Samuel Johnson whose preface is signed by G.H. Lewes and whose epigraph is taken from Eliot's poem The Spanish Gypsy (since Main seems unable to stop excerpting Eliot even when commissioned to excerpt someone else).

Where the preface to the first edition of the Sayings had compared Eliot explicitly with Shakespeare, the publication of the second edition within weeks of Main's Conversations of Doctor Johnson-causing the two volumes to be advertised together-gives her an even more respectable analog. The company of a conservative male essayist helps erase Eliot's scandalous past and her association with a frivolous genre. The double Lewes-Eliot signature lends weight to one reviewer's earlier criticism of Main's Sayings of George Eliot as "unendurable Johnsonese."

But the Conversations of Doctor Johnson is not the only book for which George Eliot provides an epigraph. A quotation from a different Eliot poem appears as a chapter motto in George Jacob Holyoake's History of Co-operation in England. Eliot's own revival of the chapter motto in her last three novels heightens the effect of these tributes. By 1899, the younger novelist Mary Cholmondley can signal her allegiance to Eliot simply by prefacing with mottoes-several excerpted from Eliot-each chapter of a novel whose heroine writes long periodic sentences interspersed with epigrams and criticized by her brother, "who had the same opinion of George Eliot's works".

As Lewes reports to Main, quotations from Eliot also appear in the front of a fourth, more sacred book: "I may also tell you-quite in private of course-what I think will please you almost as much as it did me: Mrs. Cowper Temple told Mrs. Lewes that she had copied passages from 'Romola' into her New Testament" (. Lewes has reason to think that the anecdote will please Main, for his anthologies already render Eliot quotations sacred.

The gilt-edged pages of the Sayings and the red lettering of the Birthday Book help explain why a Swiss admirer proclaims the Sayings his "breviary" and John Blackwood's wife pronounces it "undeniable Sunday reading"." Main would have been pleased to know that an imitation of his Sayings-Moments with George Eliot-appears in 1913 in a series of miniature books between the "Sermon on the Mount" and The Imitation of Christ. Anthologies transpose Eliot's words from the most secular of nineteenth-century genres to the most sacred.

Mrs. Cowper Temple's manuscript inscription has more public counterparts. In a different letter to Main, Lewes boasts that "an orthodox West-End preacher" has quoted

Middlemarch in a sermon. He responds to Main's initial proposal of an anthology by describing another reader's project of larger-scale inscriptions: "Some years ago a lady suggested that 'texts' should be selected from [Eliot's] works to hang up in schoolrooms and railway waiting rooms in view of the banal and often preposterous bible texts, thus hung up and neglected. Your idea is a far more practical one". Yet the first fantasy has not proved entirely impractical: in the year following the American broadcasting of Middlemarch, one college has plastered the New York subway with advertisements reading (apocryphally?) "'It is never too late to be what you could have been.' George Eliot, Middlemarch."

Although the project of inscribing Eliot's words in railway stations is not realized until much later, Eliot quotations do enter the "schoolroom" (as Lewes puts it) before her death. By 1879 she has given permission for her works to be extracted in four schoolbooks, defending "well-chosen extracts" as "really useful to the works from which they are taken."In 1874, Main reports that a schoolmaster has agreed to buy multiple copies of the Sayings: "he means, of course, to use them for school prizes-not a bad way of circulating a book of the kind; for prizes are always shown off, you know."'

And in the same year, an excerpt from Middlemarch which had already been quoted in the second edition of the Sayings reappears on an examination for military officers, which gives as essay topics a choice between "compar[ing] Cromwell and Napoleon, as generals and as statesmen," or discussing Will Ladislaw's assertion that "to be a poet is to have a soul in which knowledge passes instantaneously into feeling, and feeling flashes back as a new organ of knowledge."

Eliot knows very well that authors' reputations are colored by the places in which excerpts from their work appear: she expunges a Whitman epigraph from Daniel Deronda "not because the motto itself is objectionable to me-it was one of the finer things which had clung to me from among his writings-but because, since I quote so few poets, my selection of a motto from Walt Whitman might be taken as the sign of a special admiration which I am very far from feeling". Where Eliot's own chapter mottoes invoke a literary tradition, readers' eagerness to appropriate her work-in the inscriptions in the Bible, the quotation in the sermon, the question on the officers' exam, the examples in the schoolbooks, and the epigraphs to Johnson, Red Pottage and the History of Cooperation in England-makes clear that novels can borrow weight not only from the texts that they quote but from the texts in which they are quoted.

AVOID

By the 1870s, Eliot is defined by the company she keeps. Her refusal to quote Whitman reflects an awareness that quotation consecrates, but also a fear of guilt by association. The excerpting of her own work brings both possibilities home. Eliot's participation in that project remains deeply ambivalent: she pressures her publisher to bring out Main's Sayings and suggests specific quotations for inclusion in his Birthday Book, but disclaims responsibility for the anthologies whose publication she authorizes and whose contents she supplies.

Her letter authorizing Main's Birthday Book describes birthday books parenthetically as "the vulgarest thing in the book stalls". When she writes to Main describing as "dolting and feeble" the Tennyson Birthday Book which provides him with a precedent, she adds a pointed qualifier: "This is not the Poet's fault". The corollary is presumably that the fault lies with the compiler-in this case with Tennyson's editor, but it would be difficult for Main not to apply the accusation to himself.

In absolving Tennyson from blame for his Birthday Book, Eliot also disclaims responsibility for hers. Lewes goes farther, asking Main to delete from the Sayings a reference to Eliot's involvement in the selection of excerpts: "it would not do for the public to suppose she had had any share in the book, beyond that of giving permission to its being executed". Lewes's fear is confirmed when a review of Daniel Deronda-a novel written in the wake of the first edition of Main's Sayings and immediately anthologized in the second-complains "that Mr. Main should, apparently with the author's sanction, collect together 'wise, witty, and tender sayings' from George Eliot's writings may be open to remark". That disapproving tone reappears a century later, when Rosemary Ashton glosses Eliot's consent to the Sayings as the triumph of personal vanity over aesthetic principle: "though she was aware that such extracting would be damaging to the artistic structure of her works... her self-distrust and love of approbation... induced her to permit it". But Eliot's self-distrust could just as easily be used to explain her resistance as her consent, for Main's anthologies heightens her anxiety about the place of maxims within her own fiction.

Her protest against Main's proposed preface to the second edition of the Sayings quickly turns against her:

If [the preface] were true, I should be quite stultified as an artist. Unless my readers are more moved towards the ends I seek by my works as wholes than by an assemblage of extracts, my writings are a mistake. I have always exercised a severe watch against anything that could be called preaching, and if I have ever allowed myself in dissertation or in dialogue [anything] which is not part of the structure of my books, I have there sinned against my own laws....

Unless I am condemned by my own principles, my books are not property separable into 'direct' and 'indirect' teaching. My chief doubt as to the desirability of the 'Sayings' has always turned on the possibility that the volume might encourage such a view of my writings. Eliot's letter begins by accusing Main of misrepresentation, but ends by accusing herself of failure. In stating that her novels should be organic wholes rather than accumulations of didactic parts, Eliot does not claim that they are.

On the contrary, the statement that "I have always exercised a severe watch against anything that could be called preaching" presupposes a danger that needs to be guarded against. Although the passage begins in the conditional mode-"I should be quite stultified as an artist"-the indicative soon takes over: "my writings are a mistake," "I have sinned," "I am condemned." All three statements suggest that Eliot feels her readers' reactions to be (to paraphrase her characterization of the Tennyson Birthday Book) "the Writer's fault."

The assertions that "I have sinned against my own laws" and "I am condemned by my own principles" outline a gulf between Eliot's aesthetic theory and the impression made upon readers (including Main and his audience) by the novels themselves. In the confession of not practicing what she preaches, Eliot reinscribes the very distinction between "indirect" and "direct" teaching that her letter sets out to deny. Main simply accentuates that distinction, with an almost parodic effect. One of the sentences that the Sayings excerpts from Felix Holt could be usefully applied to what the author of one feels about the editor of the other: "There is hardly any mental misery worse than that of having our own serious phrases, our own rooted beliefs, caricatured by a charlatan or a hireling"

But Eliot's embarrassment about Main's anthologies cannot be explained by their internal structure alone. An alternative explanation has to do with Main's audience-and with its gender. The Birthday Book is marketed quite deliberately to a vulgar public. When Eliot complains that its binding is too gaudy, William Blackwood answers that "I quite join in your condemnation of the binding but we had to consider a colonial class rather as likely to be its largest buyers and cater to their taste accordingly".

Blackwood's characterization of that "class" rephrases in geographical terms the contempt that Lewes had stated more bluntly: "The cover for the Birthday Book is startling and ornate, but we suppose adapted to the bookseller mind, and the mind of the idiots who buy birthday books!" Responsibility for the Birthday Book is banished to the colonies, far from the more civilized nation that Eliot invokes when she remarks that "entre nous, I am a little shocked at the tone" and, in another letter, "entre nous, I wish that the Preface [to Main's Sayings] had been touched with a more fastidious finger, a more scrupulous regard to mesure."

Where Eliot wants a public, Main gives her a market.

The gilt-edged pages of the Sayings literalize Main's promise of the text's "rich worth": they advertise its status as a material object and a consumer good. Eliot's criticism of the vulgar audience and gaudy binding of the Birthday Book repeats her satire in Middlemarch of readers who judge books by their covers. Mr. Trumbull, who boasts that he owns "no less than two hundred volumes in calf" belongs to the same "class" whom Blackwood blames for the "ornate cover" of the Birthday Book.

As a consumer, Trumbull values books for their bindings; as an auctioneer, he prices a painting by its frame and a book by its lettering, "no less than five hundred [riddles] printed in a beautiful red". While the form of the riddle-book anticipates the red-and-black lettering of the Birthday Book, its self-contained fragments of wit prefigure the contents of the Sayings-in which, ironically, the passage ridiculing the riddle-book is duly reproduced.

Mr. Trumbull's description of the riddle-book as "an ornament for the table" and of his books as "calf" reminds us that what we ourselves are reading— Middlemarch—is also an object for sale. Yet his vulgarity immediately warns us to forget it. Expensive bindings denote empty heads: the traditional humiliation of finding one's books recycled for trunk-linings or curl-papers gives way to the fear of finding oneself displayed on a coffee-table. In a culture where book is to text as body to mind, books must represent their own circulation as suspect. In G. H. Lewes's novel Ranthorpe (1847), the hero is introduced reading the wares of a bookstall without buying any of them: "He cared not for rare editions, large paper copies, or sumptuous bindings.

His hunger was for knowledge; he had a passion for books-no matter what edition, what bindings; he cared not even whether they had covers at all". The willful blindness to the cover which positions Ranthorpe opposite to Mr. Trumbull or to Eliot's "colonial" readers reinforces his failure to buy; yet the placement of this scene in the first chapter means that its readers may well have just purchased Ranthorpe itself. In Middlemarch, too, the auctioneer's substitution of "volumes" for "books," and his specification of the binding and coloring, make clear Eliot's worry about the decorative and commercial uses to which books can be put-including her own.

Rosamond Vincy provides a feminine counterpart to Trumbull's taste. The only book that she is shown reading is characterized, like his, by its binding: "the last Keepsake, the gorgeous watered-silk publication which marked modern progress at that time". As the specification of watered silk makes clear, the Keepsake shares the "ornate cover" that attracts vulgar buyers to the Birthday Book-as well as its gilt-edged pages and engraved inscription plate.

Like the Birthday Book and like Trumbull's calf-bound library, the annuals subordinate contents to cover, text to book: in Thackeray's words, "the first and most important fact of the Keepsake is its binding" Eliot's protests against the luxurious material form of the Birthday Book echo the ambivalence of men who write for the annuals, like Wordsworth, who claims that "it would disgrace any name to appear in an annual" but publishes his own work in Winter's Wreath; Tennyson, who claims to have "foresworn all annuals provincial or metropolitan" but continues to contribute to them and Southey, who calls annuals "picture-books for grown children" but publishes in several including the Keepsake itself.

Rosamond's embarrassment about reading the Keepsake resembles Southey's about writing for it: "Rosamond herself was not without relish for these writers, but she did not readily commit herself by admiration, and was alive to the slightest hint that anything was not, according to Lydgate, in the very highest taste". At the same time, her reluctance to declare herself a Keepsake reader prefigures Eliot's reluctance to acknowledge her share in compiling the Birthday Book.

Eliot's reference to the annual "which marked modern progress at that time" emphasizes the ephemerality of gift books-and the datedness of the Keepsake, begun in the year before Middlemarch is set and discontinued in the year when Eliot begins to publish fiction. The phrase clinches Eliot's summary of Rosamond, earlier in the same chapter, as "that combination of correct sentiments, music, dancing, drawing, elegant note-writing, private album for extracted verse, and perfect blond loveliness, which made the irresistible woman for the doomed man of that date." The references to "that date" and "that time" reinforce Rosamond's association with literary as well as sartorial fashion. Yet while the annual is dead by the 1870s, the young lady's "album for extracted verse" is not. It survives in the blank pages of the Birthday Book, used to collect autographs of celebrities or inscriptions from friends. Rosamond's specifically feminine vulgarity suggests an explanation for the fact that Eliot resists the Birthday Book more strenuously than the Sayings: the second anthology makes clear which sex it addresses.

The Birthday Book reinforces Eliot's femininity-at the same time, however, as her androgyny. By taking a Tennyson Birthday Book as his model, Main brackets Eliot with a male poet often criticized as "feminine" or "effeminate." While Tennyson writes like the opposite sex, Main reads like them: he sets an example for a feminine audience by reading in ways that Eliot herself ascribes to women.

Even before the appearance of the Birthday Book, the Sayings places Eliot's work in the category that she had begun her career by distancing herself from: "Silly Novels by Lady Novelists." The essay of that title, published in 1856, does not ridicule lady novelists alone. It also satirizes female readers who underline moral comments, such, for instance, as that "It is a fact, no less true than melancholy, that all people, more or less, richer or poorer, are swayed by bad example;" that "Books, however trivial, contain some subjects from which useful information may be drawn;" that "Vice can too often borrow the language of virtue;" that "Merit and nobility of nature must exist, to be accepted, for clamour and pretension cannot impose upon those too well read in human nature to be easily deceived;" and that, "In order to forgive, we must have been injured."

There is, doubtless, a class of readers to whom these remarks appear peculiarly pointed and pungent; for we often find them doubly and trebly scored with the pencil, and delicate hands giving in their determined adhesion to these hardy novelties by a distinct tresvrai, emphasized by many notes of exclamation. Evans's ridicule of these "delicate hands" draws on a tradition that represents women leaving the impress of their bodies on books: from Lady Slattern in The Rivals, who "cherishes her nails for the purpose of making marginal notes" in library books; to Dickens's sketch of girls' initials and underscorings in a circulating-library novel "whose pages, reduced to a condition very like curl-paper, are thickly studded with notes in pencil"; to Thackeray's reflection that it is a wonder how fond ladies are of writing in books and signing their charming initials!

Mrs. Berry's before-mentioned little gilt books are scored with little pencil marks, or occasionally at the margin with a note of interjection, or the words, "Too true, A.B." and so on. Much may be learned with regard to a lovely woman by a look at the book she reads in. Marian Evans's satire points back to this tradition, but also forward to the model of feminine reading that the Birthday Book will later invite. While "silly novels" provoke marginal inscriptions beside the most platitudinous "moral comments," the Birthday Book places sententious passages opposite blank spaces where readers can write.

Main himself composes the Sayings and the Birthday Book by marking the "moral comments" in Eliot's novels; and his preface, which describes her sayings as "the grandest and most uncompromising moral truth," simply translates into English ladies' marginal comments of "tres vrai." Main's anthologies make visible the same kind of abstraction that "Silly Novels by Lady Novelists" criticizes: "The most pitiable of all silly novels by lady novelists are what we may call the oracular species-novels intended to expound the writer's religious, philosophical, or moral theories."

The oracular image that leads John Morley to compare Eliot with "the inspired Pythia on the sublime tripod" owes as much to Main's taste for reading "moral comments" as to Eliot's for writing them. In a culture where (in the words of one journalist) women are expected to prefer "analysis" to "action," while men read for the plot and skip "irrelevant chatter," Main reads like a woman and writes for them too.

Eliot herself describes Main's response to her work in the same language that Marian Evans had used to criticize ladies' novels and lady readers. "Silly Novels" ridicules readers who "[under]score" "moral comments" and writers who rely on "the illustrative aid of italics and small caps," "the lucidity of italics and small caps," or "profuse italics". Eliot later attributes the same three habits-underlining, italicizing, and capitalizing-to Main.

She writes that "I have been looking through the 'Sayings' with that sort of delight which comes from seeing that another mind underlines the words one has most cared for in writing them"; but she asks Blackwood to "suggest to [Main] to avoid italics" in the second edition of the Sayings, and she tells Main (at least according to Lewes) that "your delight in italics and small caps is objectionable".

Eliot's image of Main "underlining" the passages he selects for reprinting makes the "underscoring" that she attributes to lady readers and the "profuse italics" that she ascribes to lady novelists metaphors for the process by which anthologies are compiled. Arnold Bennett would later turn Eliot's ridicule of feminine italics against her, calling her own use of emphasis "transparently feminine": "The average woman italicizes freely. George Eliot, of course, had trained herself too well to do that, at least formally; yet her constant, undue insistence springs from the same essential weakness, and amounts practically to the same expedient".

Bennett's assertion that Eliot's masculine "training" hides a feminine "essence" is absurdly circular, but he is not entirely wrong to suggest that Eliot tries to dissociate herself from the kinds of emphasis conventionally ascribed to women. In the same way that J.W. Cross's Life will later define Eliot as a masculine writer by assigning to her husband the memorializing role conventionally reserved for great men's widows, Eliot establishes her own good taste against the feminine vulgarity of her male editor and his female readers. The "picture-books for grown children" read by the "infantine"

Rosamond, like the Birthday Book whose "ornate binding" is embossed with an image of a baby, defines Middlemarch itself, by contrast, as "one of the few English novels for grown-up people." The birthday book takes over the girlish audience from whom Eliot's own work had disencumbered the novel. Yet the counterexample of Mr. Trumbull makes clear that misogyny does not explain Eliot's objection to being marketed to girls.

The problem is less that the Birthday Book addresses women than that it reduces women to consumers-just as the "private album for extracted verse" and "watered-silk" annual form Rosamond Vincy into a pattern of the young woman whose only object in life is to buy fashionable things. The Birthday Book uses literature to cement girls' friendships because its presentation plate labels it a gift and its blank spaces invite them to exchange signatures. But it inscribes those friendships within the marketplace, because the facing pages are filled with reminders of the dates on which birthday presents need to be bought for friends in turn.

The inscription plate at the front of the Birthday Book and the calendar pages facing the quotations implicate George Eliot in an endless cycle of gift-buying whose yearly rhythm repeats the planned obsolescence of the literary annuals that "marked modern progress at that time." Where Main's invocations of Shakespeare in the preface to the Sayings had defined Eliot as a classic for all time, the Birthday Book reshapes her for an age-and for a sex.

David Carroll has argued persuasively that Eliot "wishes to define moral problems and assert certain values, but the forms of wisdom literature are no longer available". But the problem could also be phrased in the opposite terms. The riddle-book in Middlemarch, the Sayings and the Birthday Book suggest that the forms of wisdom literature are all too easily available as commodities: that their availability to vulgar, young, and feminine readers discredits any wisdom that they contain.

In sheer bulk, however, the number of Eliot quotations that appear in Main's anthologies is dwarfed by the number that appear in reviews. Eliot is not unusual in this respect, for many contemporary reviews excerpt so heavily as to borrow the fragmentary form of anthologies as much as their evaluative function. What Hazlitt complained of the Quarterly Review could be extended to almost any nineteenth-century periodical: "the poetical department is almost a sinecure, consisting of mere summary decisions and a list of quotations". Marian Evans's own journalistic career is no exception. The recurrence of the verb "extract" in her reviews makes explicit the resemblance between composing reviews and compiling commonplace-books.

An article on Carlyle's Selected Essays, in which Carlyle's words outnumber her own, begins by announcing half jokingly that her review will duplicate his anthology: "To make extracts from a book of extracts may at first seem easy" A more hostile review of Dr. Cumming's work takes excerptability as a measure of worth: "Throughout nine volumes we have alighted on no passage which impressed us as worth extracting, and placing among the 'beauties' of evangelical writers". The hypothetical anthology ("beauties") from which Evans excludes Cumming forms a mirror-image of the review in which she quotes his most glaring absurdities: one singles out the best passages, the other the worst.

Yet as Coleridge complains earlier in the century, even negative reviews ultimately propagate the texts-and the passages-that they excerpt: "if in a volume of poetry the critic should find a poem or passage which he deems more especially worthless, he is sure to select it and reprint it in the review; by which, on his own grounds, he wastes as much more paper than the author, as the copies of a fashionable review are more numerous than those of the original book"

Regularly mined for judgments of individual works or stray generalizations about literature, the review remains to be systematically studied as a genre in its own right. Reviews figure only as "sources" in a tradition of reception studies that focuses on the content of readers' opinions to the exclusion of the forms which elicit those judgments in the first place: even the otherwise invaluable Critical Heritage anthologies juxtapose published reviews with private letters and diaries while excising both plot summary and illustrative quotation from the former.

Yet the convention of alternating synoptic summary with synecdochal excerpts shapes Victorian assumptions about how to read-and about the structure of literary texts. Reviews encourage readers and writers to think of texts as accumulations of self-contained anthology-pieces connected by longer passages of information or padding.

They train readers to identify portions of text as either sublime or dispensable, and writers to produce lapidary passages that can be understood and appreciated out of their narrative context. This is especially true for writers who begin their own careers as reviewers: Marian Evans's experience as a journalist makes George Eliot aware from the beginning that her work will be judged through quotation.

The omnipresence of quotations in Victorian reviews means that the bare fact that reviewers excerpt Eliot has no significance in itself. While anthologies quote Eliot more than any previous novelist, reviews do not. What is unusual is that both hostile and favorable reviews describe Eliot as peculiarly quotable while explicitly questioning the adequacy of excerpts to represent her work-and, by extension, the ethics of quotation itself. Positive reviews begin to describe Eliot's work as raw material for hypothetical anthologies long before Main's Sayings appears. In a review of Felix Holt, E.S. Dallas concludes an unbroken series of four chapter mottoes and two long quotations-a kind of miniature anthology that prefigures Main's overrepresentation of epigraphs-with the observation that "we might cull too from the talk of the characters to whom we are introduced a whole book of proverbs".

Richard Simpson praises Eliot for interspersing her "drama" with "a copious supply of maxims, ethical, psychological, and physiological, enough to furnish forth a 'just volume' of ana". The "whole book" and the "just volume" form mirror-images of the equally hypothetical "Beauties" from which Marian Evans excludes Cumming. Like Evans, Simpson and Dallas take the number of potential anthology-pieces as a proof of literary value.

HOUR

Other reviewers raise this possibility before ostentatiously rejecting it. The Westminster's review of The Mill on the Floss announces its determination not to become an anthology: Neither have we thought it desirable to give a collection of the quaint humorisms that abound in the first two volumes, or to make a catena of the profound and farreaching remarks which abound throughout the book; this would neither be fair to the author nor agreeable to our readers.

These beauties are for the most part so organic, that to withdraw them from their context would be to dislocate them from that vital nexus which gives them their highest charm. The refusal to make a "collection of quaint humorisms" rejects the genre of Main's Witty Sayings at the same time as it turns against the conventions of the review itself. Yet the review's attitude toward quotation is less simple than its moralistic language of "fairness" would suggest. The article terms witty passages "beauties," even though it refuses "to withdraw them from their context"; and it calls them "organic" even though it refers earlier to "the separate beauties" of The Mill on The Floss.

In terming the beauties "organic" and the novel a "vital nexus," the review anticipates the language of Eliot's own assertion that "forms of art can be called higher or lower only on the same principle as that on which we apply the words to organisms; viz., in proportion to the complexity of the parts bound up into one indissoluble whole". So does Edward Dowden's essay on Eliot in 1872. Like the reviewer of The Mill on the Floss, Dowden calls attention to the selfrestraint with which he resists the temptation to quote: "Many good things in particular passages of her writings are detachable; admirable sayings can be cleared from their surroundings, and presented by themselves.... But if we separate the moral soul of any complete work of hers from its artistic medium, if we murder to dissect, we lose far more than we gain".

Dowden's discussion of whether to quote signals a departure from the conventions of the review. But the wording of his statement that "admirable sayings can be cleared from their surroundings" can also be read more literally as a comment on the Sayings published by Main several months before. Just as Eliot's letter against Main's preface juxtaposes the assertion that "my books are not properly separable into 'direct' and 'indirect' teaching" with the acknowledgment that readers are dangerously skillful at separating the two, Dowden combines the claim that Eliot's sayings "can be" detached with the argument that they should not be. The ambivalence expressed by Dowden's weighing of "loss" against "gain" is rendered all the more acute by his recourse to a Wordsworthian tag: it takes a decontextualized quotation to defend the organic unity of the text.

Marian Evans's own reviews already question the evidentiary value of quotation. Her review of Men and Women ends an excerpt with the apology that "extracts cannot do justice to the fine dramatic touches by which Fra Lippo is made present to us, while he throws out this instinctive Art-criticism.

And extracts from 'Bishop Blougram's Apology,' an equally remarkable poem of what we may call the dramatic-psychological kind, would be still more ineffective." After praising the latter as "masterly satire," Evans adds that "the poem is too strictly consecutive for any fragment of it to be a fair specimen" Evans's denial that quotations provide a "fair" specimen or "do justice" to Browning anticipates the Westminster Review's claim that to quote from The Mill on the Floss "would [not] be fair to the author".Both define quotation as an ethical problem.

Evans's anxiety about "fragments" and "specimens" looks even further forward to an axiom at the end of Middlemarch: "The fragment of a life, however typical, is not the sample of an even web". R.H. Hutton inverts that language when he labels a quotation from Middlemarch itself "a sharp saying and a sample of many another with which every chapter of Middlemarch is plentifully strewn". Similarly, Dinah Mulock reverses Evans's claim that no excerpt constitutes a "fair specimen" of "Bishop Blougram's Apology" when her review labels a quotation from The Mill on the Floss "a mere chance specimen of [Eliot's] care over small things".

Evans's denial that fragments constitute "specimens," and Eliot's that fragments constitute "samples," calls Mulock's and Hutton's use of representative quotations into question. Henry James, who compares Daniel Deronda with "a group of little uneven ponds," faults Eliot precisely for not producing an even web: for a "disproportion between the meagre effect of the whole and the vigorous character of the different parts". A.V. Dicey, too, complains in his review of Middlemarch that "the parts are much more striking than the whole". Yet their own reviews necessarily substitute the former for the latter.

Reviewers' apologies for quoting too little or too much or for quoting at all can be explained only in part by a gradual historical shift away from quotation. The length of excerpts tends to decrease toward the end of the nineteenth century, though such trends are difficult to measure or to date. Edwin Eigner and George Worth offer no evidence for their heavily teleological assertion that "book reviews... beginning in the late 1840s were becoming self-conscious about the time-honoured practice of filling out the bulk of the articles with passages extracted from the novels under discussion. By the late 1850s most reviewers had enough respect for the integrity of a work of fiction to resist representing it through snippets".

I would date that self-consciousness much earlier, for it can be traced back to the origins of the modern periodical press itself. Less than a year after the founding of Blackwood's Edinburgh Magazine in 1817, a review in it already ends a quotation with the apology that these specimens may suffice to show the peculiarities of Mr Lamb's genius and manner; but the charm of his Poetry pervades the whole bulk of the volume, and it is as impossible fully to comprehend that charm from a few partial passages, as it would be from a few casual smiles to understand the full expression of an intellectual and moral countenance.

Three years earlier, Francis Jeffrey's review of The

Excursion makes the reviewer's practice of quoting "extracts" into the poet's fault: "while we collect the fragments, it is impossible not to lament the ruins from which we are condemned to pick them".

Conversely, another reviewer adduces the difficulty of excerpting Wordsworth as evidence of his talent: "It is almost impossible to select any passage without injury to its effect, owing to a want of that interest which the context supplies. We shall, however, venture to cite the following tender touches". Reviewers' criticism of texts for either resisting or requiring quotation reinforces their formulaic apologies for quoting themselves.

Both mark the tension between an organicist theory and a synecdochal practice. Reviewers' ambivalence about quotation and quotability, like their hostility to the anthologies that take their own use of the excerpt to its logical conclusion, points to unresolved doubts about what counts as evidence in argument and how texts can be represented in miniature. Twentieth-century criticism will inherit that dilemma along with a canon of familiar quotations from Eliot's work that bears a striking resemblance to Main's.

Reviewers' uneasiness about quotation makes their aesthetic an inverse image of Main's. They share his basic technique of dividing texts into sententious or lyrical passages that can be appreciated out of context and narrative passages that cannot. Yet while Main dismisses the latter as a "vehicle" for the former, reviewers criticize the former as intrusions upon the latter.

A.V. Dicey posits a direct proportion between the quality of sayings and the quality of narrative: "As the number of George Eliot's 'wise, witty, and tender' sayings increase, the directness with which she paints living persons diminishes". Dicey would later criticize Eliot for giving her "sanction" to the publication of the Sayings. Here he already makes Eliot responsible for Main's didacticism: by appropriating the title of the anthology, he elides the difference between Main's work and hers.

Dicey turns Eliot's organicist model of art against her.

For Dowden's reluctance to "detach" beauties and the Westminster's refusal to "withdraw them from their context," he substitutes the accusation that the beauty of the sayings deprives Middlemarch itself of unity to begin with: The parts are much more striking than the whole.... No one who admires beautiful writing or who can appreciate striking and original thoughts can fail to feel that the chorus or reflective portion of the book is full of beauty and power. To a large class of persons it forms probably the great charm of Middlemarch.... But a critic, even while he admires the reflections themselves... can hardly deny that the part taken by George Eliot as the moralizer over her own handiwork, if it gives her novel a peculiar charm, also greatly damages its whole effect....

The very brilliancy of the epigrams,... the elaborate care given to the separate parts, leaves in the mind a sense of something like strain, and makes it difficult to look at the work as a whole. That "large class of persons" is embodied by Main and his readers; but as "a critic," Dicey excludes himself from it. So does the reviewer who complains that the Scenes of Clerical Life contain too many beauties: "Almost every sentence seems finished into an epigram or an aphorism.

The pudding is often too profuse in plums-too scanty in connective dough". Where Main's preface praises Eliot's sayings as "riches," the review suggests that their richness makes the novels indigestible. The metaphor neatly reverses the traditional comparison of fiction with sweetmeats and instruction with plain food.

Earlier critics of the novel conventionally argue that-as one reviewer puts it in 1812-"books, merely entertaining, produce the same effect upon the mental faculties, which a luxurious diet does upon the corporeal frame: they render it incapable of relishing those pure instructive writings, which possess all the intrinsic qualities of wholesome, unseasoned food" (qtd. in Ferris 38-39).29 The review of the Scenes of Clerical Life suggests just the opposite: it equates fictional narrative with bland "connective dough" and moral wisdom with tempting but unhealthy "plums."

A hostile review of The Mill on the Floss takes the culinary image even further to contrast nutritious plot with dilute preaching: "We ask for meat, and she gives us pap-for a history, and she gives us sermons" (The sugar has become the pill. In 1870, an article on "The Uses of Fiction" chooses Eliot for an "example" of the problematic place of aphorisms in the novel. The essay begins by echoing Main's metaphor of the novel as a "vehicle" for "conveying" maxims, but ends by accusing the latter of "disfiguring" the former: There is no vehicle so useful as the novel for conveying odds and ends of knowledge.

If this is done with skill and grace, these chance embellishments greatly increase the pleasure one finds in reading the book. In the works of George Eliot, for example, we meet with simple phrases or sentences that are suggestive, and frequently more satisfactory than a ponderous volume.... But everything depends on the manner in which the novelist introduces these glimpses of thought, or erudition, or wit.

They must not be obtruded, or the illusion of the story is destroyed. Mrs. Poyser must find a fitting occasion for her sarcasms; or we look upon her as mere puppet, and think of the hand that is pulling the cords. If a man uses a story for the purpose of stringing together maxims or reflections, then let him say so; and we accept as a graceful sort of foil—as in the case of Sartor Resartus, or Companions of my Solitude, or Henry Holbeach—the connecting link of narrative.

The first and chief business of the novel, however, is to give us authentic descriptions of this or that section of the world; and we cannot have the face of the picture disfigured by prominent aphorisms.

This argument turns the language of the "beauty" against itself: the sayings that "embellish" at the beginning of the paragraph "disfigure the face" by the end of it. Yet even the initial praise defines maxims as ornamental, not functional. Rather than representing plot as the means to sweeten or disguise a moral, it represents narrative as the end that moralizing decorates (at best) or obstructs (at worst).

The charge that maxims interrupt the "business of the novel" restates David Masson's argument-in a more ambivalent discussion of "the interfusion of exposition with fiction" published eleven years earlier in British Novelists and their Styles-that "the proper limits within which a poet or other artist may seek to inculcate doctrine" depend on whether one accepts or rejects the consensus that "the representation of social reality is, on the whole, the proper business of the novel". But it echoes even more closely the language of a reviewer who asserts in 1865 that "a novel ceases to be a novel when it aims at philosophical teaching. It is not the vehicle for conveying knowledge. Its business is to amuse". "The Uses of Fiction" eliminates the chiasmus equating writers' "business" with readers' "amusement": its concession that sayings give "pleasure" confirms its charge that they disrupt "business."

I suggested earlier that "Silly Novels by Lady Novelists" attributes a taste for sententiousness to women readers and women novelists. Evans's gendering of the maxim appears surprising at first, for it clashes with a more traditional (but equally misogynistic) belief that women read frivolously for the plot, men seriously for ideas.

That contradiction can be explained in part by the assumption that men get their ideas from genres other than the novel. But it can also be explained, I think, by a historical shift in assumptions about the place of moralizing in fiction-and about the structure of literary works-which culminates in reviewers' distrust of eliot's self-contained maxims.

In 1751, samuel richardson prefigured main's project of extracting maxims from novels when he marketed his own collection of... Moral and instructive sentiments, cautions, aphorisms, reflections and observations contained in the history [of clarissa]. By offering his collection as a corrective to the frivolity of "young people; who are apt to read rapidly with a view only to story" richardson anticipates main's claim that "the narrative part of those letters was only meant as a vehicle for the instructive" (ix; emphasis added).

Samuel johnson echoes this logic when he observes that "if you were to read Richardson for the story, your impatience would be so much fretted, that you would hang yourself.

But you must read [Richardson] for the sentiment, and consider the story as giving occasion to the sentiment". Where Richardson attributes the desire for "story" to one marginal audience ("young people"), later critics attribute a taste for the "aphorisms, reflections, and observations" against which Richardson defines "story" to a different series of vulgar readers: in Dicey's review, the "large class of persons" who care more for individual maxims than for the continuity of the whole; in William Blackwood's letter, the "colonial class of readers" who buy anthologies of sayings rather than the novels from which they are taken; and in "Silly Novels by Lady Novelists," the "class of readers to whom [platitudinous] remarks appear peculiarly pointed and pungent."

Where Johnson had attacked the audience that "read Richardson for the story," a hundred years later the reviewer who states in the first person that "we ask for story" includes himself among it.Where eighteenth-century critics accused fiction of taking readers away from their business, and plot of distracting them from morals, Eliot's reviewers worry instead that moral discourse distracts her from the business of fiction.

And once Victorian critics have reversed the older hierarchy that subordinates the narrative to the sententious, it becomes logical to switch the gender of the two as well: to replace the figure of the self-indulgent female fiction-reader with the self-important female sage. In the process, the anthologies intended to inscribe Eliot within a masculine tradition become instead the sign of personal vanity, feminine vulgarity, and aesthetic failure.

The consequences of that reversal are still with us. A hundred years after "The Uses of Fiction" decrees that moral generalizations "must not be obtruded," W.J. Harvey is still urging readers to ignore Eliot's "authorial intrusions" and "moral comments": "These comments are a means to an end; they are one of the bridges between our world and the world of the novel. They are not ends in themselves, not the proper objects of our contemplation.

And we are meant to pass easily and quickly over these comments" Where Main calls the narrative a vehicle for the sayings, Harvey reduces the sayings to a bridge into the narrative. His claim that the moral comments are "not the proper objects of our contemplation" revives the tone of ginger distaste that critics had earlier used to describe Eliot's union with Lewes.

Twenty years later, when Dorothea Barrett celebrates Eliot's "rebelliousness and eroticism" while calling her sibylline image "unfortunate," didactic tone finally replaces sexual acts as the transgression that admirers need to explain away.

Harvey presents skipping ("passing quickly over") not only as the ideal but as an unavoidable norm. He clinches the apology that "the number and length of such [moral] comments is not as great as some critics assume" with the assertion that "the great majority of intrusive comments last for only two or three sentences and with rare exceptions are surely passed over by the impetus of any non-analytical reading".

The fact that such "intrusions" are more frequently reproduced than any other part of George Eliot's work-in anthologies, reviews, and critical studies including Harvey's own-does not in itself disprove this last argument, because quotation is always a product of analysis in the most literal sense. Yet no positive evidence can be imagined either, since the "non-analytical reading" for which Harvey speaks leaves no trace to prove what it skips and where it lingers. More fundamentally, the invitation to quicken our pace assumes that all readers can recognize those moments when the text shifts from narrative to saying.

To skip sententious passages one must first identify them, in the same way that even the silliest lady readers, according to Eliot, unerringly recognize platitudes to mark in the margin. This would suggest in turn that "non-analytical" readers identify sententious passages as systematically as do critics who adduce them as evidence, reviewers who excerpt them as specimens, and editors who collect them in anthologies. The only difference is that each group ignores what the other prizes. The nineteenth-century reversal in the relative status of narrative and sententiousness makes clear how arbitrary those markers of readerly difference are, but also how powerful. So does the association of women with each in turn. The energy with which Eliot's editors and critics distinguish those who read for the plot from those who read against it suggests that the "rise of the novel" reinforces the social and aesthetic hierarchies that it appears to challenge.

By exchanging the novel's difference from other genres for a gendered difference within its own public, Eliot's career opens the way for professional criticism of the novel in the twentieth century.

Chapter 14

Painting and Idealization of Character

Both in theory and in practice George Eliot's realism welcomed the idealization of character. "Paint us an angel, if you can," urges the narrator of Adam Bede, "paint us yet oftener a Madonna..." (17: 270). And as if to heed his own advice, he thrice associates Dinah Morris with the angel at Christ's sepulchre in Adam's new illustrated Bible ((10:162, 14:208, 51:319). By the same token, Milly Barton is "a large, fair, gentle Madonna" (2:24), and Lucy Deane in The Mill on the Floss has "a face breathing playful joy, like one of Correggio's cherubs" (VI, 9:267). As these examples suggest, George Eliot habitually idealized her characters by associating them with sacred and heroic history painting and classical sculpture. Her work well exemplifies what Jean Hagstrum calls "the unshakeable association that has existed between literary idealization and ideal form in the graphic arts" (Sister Arts, p. 8). This chapter will discuss the rationale for George Eliot's pictorial idealization of character, and relate her techniques to the revival of typological iconography in the nineteenth-century visual arts. Particular attention will be paid to Eliot's characteristic ambivalence toward such idealization as it is expressed in Middlemarch, and to her complex resolution of that ambivalence in the double plot of Daniel Deronda.

Not all Victorian novelists believed in the compatibility of the ideal and the real. Trollope, for example, assumed that the terms are antithetical. Transvaluing Reynolds's famous contrast between Italian and Dutch painting, Trollope contended in The Last Chronicle of Barset that the High Renaissance art of Italy depicts what is unreal:

We are, most of us, apt to love Raphael's madonnas better than Rembrandt's matrons. But though we do so, we know that Rembrandt's matrons existed; but we have a strong belief that no such woman as Raphael painted ever did exist. In that he painted ... for Church purposes, Raphael was justified; but had he painted so for family portraiture he would have been false." [London: Smith, Elder, (1867), II, 84:383]

This conception of realism was very different from George Eliot's. She believed that Raphael's madonnas sometimes belong in family portraiture, and she pointedly denied that the ideal is antithetical to the real. "Any real observation of life and character must be limited, and the imagination must fill in and give life to the picture," she told John Blackwood in 1861 (Letters, III, 427).

Eliot agreed with G. H. Lewes's argument, in his important essay on "Realism in Art" (1858), that the opposite of realism is not idealism but falsism. Lewes illustrates the compatibility of idealism ,with realism by citing Raphael's Sistine Madonna:

In the figures of the Pope and St. Barbara we have a real man and woman, one of them a portrait, and the other not elevated above sweet womanhood. Below, we have the two exquisite angel children, intensely childlike, yet something more, something which renders their wings congruous with our conception of them. In the never-to-be-forgotten divine babe, we have at once the intensest realism of presentation, with the highest idealism of conception: the attitude is at once grand, easy, and natural; the face is that of a child, but the child is divine ... we feel that humanity in its highest conceivable form is before us.... Here is a picture which from the first has enchained the hearts of men, which is assuredly in the highest sense ideal, and which is so because it is also in the highest sense real — a real man, a real woman, real angel-children, and a real Divine Child; the last a striking contrast to the ineffectual attempts of other painters to spiritualize and idealize the babe — attempts which represent no babe at all.

The Leweses valued highly the ideal realism of High Renaissance painting, and George Eliot strove to create a similar effect in many parts of her own fiction.

Eliot was of course no Christian, but her idealization had a rationale in the secular religion of humanity which replaced her Evangelicalism. This humanism rejected Christian theology but sought to retain the ethics, emotional culture, and social bonding of the older religion. Feuerbach, whose Essence of Christianity strongly influenced Eliot on these points, argued that since the Christian god is a projection of mankind, mankind itself should be worshipped in a religious spirit. Christian devotion should be transferred to secular subjects, and human experience should be venerated and sanctified.[7] George Eliot favored this redirection of emotion, and promoted it in her fiction by associating her characters with sacred and heroic visual] art.

Thus she attempted to hallow Romola's experience by visualizing her moral growth as a progression from "The Unseen Madonna" to "The Visible Madonna" to "the Holy Mother with the Babe, fetching water for the sick" in a plague-stricken village. Feuerbach himself suggested a didactic and affective rationale for literary pictorialism when he defined imagination as the "type-creating [bildliche], emotional, and sensuous" part of the human mind, and argued that "man, as an emotional and sensuous being, is governed and made happy only by images, by sensible representations."

George Eliot took something of a liberty when she rendered Feuerbach's term bildliche as "type-creating." But her translation points up one important element of traditional Christian thought which she sought to preserve and secularize in her religion of humanity: the concept of types. George Eliot's pictorial idealization may be viewed in the context of efforts by other nineteenth-century artists to redefine typological symbolism so that it might serve the religious and aesthetic needs of the age. Typological symbolism attracted many of the best minds of the period because it offered a way of conferring spiritual meaning upon the representation of phenomenal experience? of affirming the existence of design while yet respecting the integrity of history. Strictly speaking, a type is an Old Testament prefiguration of a New Testament truth. It is not a vehicle of allegory; a type retains its identity as a historical reality at the same time that it foreshadows the divinely ordained event which fulfills it.

The Victorians often used the term more loosely, however, to denote any exemplary moral or religious norm which finds successive incarnations in history. In the visual arts the revaluation of typological symbolism was a sign of dissatisfaction with established conceptions of sacred and heroic history painting. This dissatisfaction had grown steadily since the middle of the eighteenth century. In the later eighteenth century, history painters began boldly to combine the inherited motifs of Christian art with scenes of contemporary heroism. By the mid-nineteenth century, a creative and nontraditional typological symbolism was widely employed in English painting.

Obscure or invented incidents in the early life of Christ were made to foreshadow famous later events, and Christian types were often applied postfiguratively to secular and contemporary situations. Such symbolism is a prominent feature in Pre-Raphaelite painting, where it balances the tendency of empirical realism toward fragmentation and atomism. The iconography of the Deposition in Holman Hunt's A Converted British Family Sheltering a Christian Missionary from the Persecution of the Druids (1850), of the Pieta in Henry Wallis's The Death of Chatterton (1856), of the Madonna and Child in Ford Madox Brown's The Pretty Baa-Lambs (1852) or Take Your Son, Sir! (1857), of the emblematic pilgrimage in Millais's The Blind Girl (1856), suggests in each case a connection between a concrete historical moment and a recurrent type of spiritual activity.

George Eliot came to art, then, in an atmosphere congenial to "the notion that Types in their continuing cycles can be found in contemporary reality". Her education had introduced her to the traditional exegesis of biblical types, which was still widespread in nineteenth-century Evangelical circles. In Scenes of Clerical Life, Amos Barton finds it difficult to communicate "instruction through familiar types and symbols." Attempting to explain the Christian significance of unleavened bread, he carries the imagination of his audience "to the dough-tub, but unfortunately was not able to carry it upwards from that well-known object to the unknown truths which it was intended to shadow forth" (2:39). In "Janet's Repentance" the residents of Milby "had not yet heard that the schismatic ministers of Salem [the Dissenters' chapel] were obviously typified by Korah, Dathan, and Abiram" (2:60). George Eliot was obviously familiar enough with typological thinking to draw upon it for humorous effects.

The novelist often used the word type in connection with the representation of sublime and religious ideas in contemporary art. At Weimar she saw a portrait head of Goethe at seventy which she thought "might serve as a type of sublime old age". Also at Weimar she saw Liszt in concert, and thereafter understood why "the type of Liszt's face seems to haunt [Ary Scheffer] in so many of his compositions." She particularly recalled Scheffer's Die drei Weisen aus dem Morgenlande (1844), a picture "in which he expressly intended to introduce an idealization of Liszt" as one of the three Magi, "gazing in ecstasy at the guiding light above them." She herself thought Liszt looked like "a perfect model of a St. John" or "a prophet in the moment of inspiration" (Essays, p. 98).

This kind of idealization, which ennobles without falsifying its subject, and which associates admirable human faces with established Christian exemplars, violates neither George Eliot's atheism nor her conception of realism.

She used the word type even more revealingly when defending her presentation of Mordecai in Daniel Deronda: "The effect that one strives after is an outline as strong as that of Balfour of Burley [in Scott's Old Mortality] for a much more complex character and a higher strain of ideas. But such an effect is just the most difficult thing in art-to give new elements-i.e. elements not already used up — in forms as vivid as those of long familiar types" (Letters, VI, 223). Here is a clear statement of the rationale for the pictorial idealization of character in George Eliot's fiction: she seeks to give the new elements of her religion of humanity in forms as vivid as those of the long familiar types of traditional religious culture.

Eliot was well aware of the revaluation of typological symbolism in the nineteenth-century visual arts, especially within the German Nazarene and English Pre-Raphaelite movements.[20] She began to follow the work of the Pre-Raphaelites in 1852, when she commended Millais's A Huguenot on Saint Bartholomew's Day in May and read the famous essay on "Pre-Raphaelitism in Art and Literature" in the British Quarterly Review for November (Letters, II, 29-30, 48).

This essay helped to shape her most basic beliefs about the movement: that it represented a salutary return to nature, truth, and realism in art, but that its strengths were sapped by its weakness for medieval ecclesiasticism and archaism.

Thus Eliot had mixed reactions to the work of her favourite Pre-Raphaelite painter, William Holman Hunt. In 1856 she described him as "one of the greatest painters of the pre-eminently realistic school" (Essays, p. 268), and she remained interested in his work at least until 1864, when she sent to Sara Hennell a sympathetic critique of his Afterglow in Egypt (Letters, IV, 159). But her lack of sympathy with the theistic religious aims of Hunt's painting sometimes made her indifferent or oblivious to the workings of its figural symbolism.[21] She had no use for The Light of the World (1853) because "it is too mediaeval and pietistic to be rejoiced in as a product of the present age" (Letters, II, 156).

She praised The Hireling Shepherd (1851) for the "marvellous truthfulness" of its landscape (Essays, p. 268), but quite misread the moral iconography of the shepherd and the wench, failing to see that, like Adam Bede, the painting is profoundly critical of false and idyllic notions of pastoral; see John Duncan Macmillan, "Holman Hunt's Hireling Shepherd: Some Reflections on a Victorian Pastoral," The Art Bulletin, 54 (1972), 187-97, and chapter 8, n. 46, below. Her doctrinal antipathy probably accounts for her inability to perceive the similarity between her own mode of didactic symbolism and that of her more orthodox contemporaries. She was even less receptive to the typological history painting of the German Nazarenes, which she encountered on her trips to Berlin, Munich, and Rome in 1854-60. She was sympathetic with the early Nazarene revolt against the German neoclassical style, and once compared it (borrowing an argument from the author of "Pre-Raphaelitism in Art and Literature") with Wordsworth's rebellion against eighteenth-century poetic diction. Thus she defended "an early poem of Wordsworth's, or an early picture of Overbeck's" on the ground that "the attempt at an innovation reveals a want that has not hitherto been met" (Essays, pp. 99-100).

But Eliot strongly disliked the monumental style of history painting which Nazarene artists and their disciples began to practice in the 1820s and perfected in the 1840s; see Keith Andrews, The Nazarenes: A Brotherhood of German Painters in Rome (Oxford: Clarendon Press, 1964), pp. 29, 67. G. H. Lewes was referring to this style when he spoke of "celebrated paintings of the Modern German school ... in which a great deal is meant and very little executed, full of symbol and historical meaning, which require a long commentary before they can be rendered intelligible, and which before and after the commentary leave the emotions untouched and the eye ungratified" ("Realism in Art," p. 497). Because George Eliot's critique of Nazarene history painting is central both to the question of her pictorial idealization of character and to the meaning of Middlemarch, it is worth discussing in some detail.

It has long been recognized that Adolf Naumann, the German painter of the Rome chapters of Middlemarch, represents the Nazarene or revivalist tradition, which was the branch of German Romantic art best known in Victorian England; see William Vaughan, "The German Manner in English Art, 1815-1861," Diss. Courtauld Institute 1977, pp. 18, 25, 35. Naumann is modeled upon two identifiable Nazarenes: Johann Friedrich Overbeck (1789-1869) and Josef von Führich (1800-76). Naumann's link with Overbeck is twofold. First, Naumann portrays Mr. Casaubon in a "picture in which Saint Thomas Aquinas sat among the doctors of the Church in a disputation too abstract to be represented, but listened to with more or less attention by an audience above" (22:332).,/P.

Gordon S. Haight has noted the resemblance between this fictive painting and Overbeck's The Triumph of Christianity in the Arts (1840), a picture that George Eliot had hoped to see during her trip to Germany in 1854-55 (Haight, p. 151; fig. 7). Both of these idealized history paintings are patterned after Raphael's Disputa in the Vatican Stanze. The second link between Naumann and Overbeck is a detail of the costume worn by Overbeck on the day George Eliot visited his Roman studio in 1860 — a connection first noticed in a review of Cross's Life by Joseph Jacobs (George Eliot ... : Essays and Reviews from the 'Athenaeum ' [London: D. Nutt, 1891], p. 72). The venerable painter had on "a maroon velvet cap, and a grey scarf over his shoulders."

On display in Overbeck's studio, the Leweses saw cartoons of The Savior Withdraws from His Followers on the Hill at Nazareth (1857) and Allegory of the Arts (1860). Duly recorded in the novelist's journal (Cross, II,158), these items reappeared eleven years later as "a dove-coloured blouse and a maroon velvet cap" worn by Naumann when the Casaubons visit his studio in Middlemarch (22:327). Having seen the greatest of the Nazarenes in his own milieu, George Eliot knew how to dress a character partly modeled upon him.

Although Overbeck lived to be visited by George Eliot, he was nevertheless too old to be Naumann's sole original. The distinguished Nazarene was already forty in 1829, the year of Dorothea's honeymoon (For 1829 as the year of Dorothea's honeymoon, see Jerome Beaty, "History by Indirection: The Era of Reform in Middlemarch," Victorian Studies, 1 (1957), 173-79). Chronologically, Naumann more closely resembles Josef von Fuhrich, who was born in Bohemia in 1800 and worked under Overbeck in Rome from 1827 to 1829, helping to finish the frescoes in the Casino Massimo. One of the paintings attributed to Naumann in the novel is modeled upon a painting of Fuhrich's that George

Eliot had seen during her own honeymoon trip to Berlin in 1854-55.

Ladislaw tells us that Naumann is painting "the Saints drawing the Car of the Church" (22:326). This processional allegory recalls Führich's The Triumph of Christ. George Eliot saw the painting in Graf Raczinsky's famous collection of modern art, and described it in her journal with a charmingly Dorothean incomprehension of the iconography, which derives from Titian's Triumph of Faith:

Under this picture was one by a Viennese artist [Führich had become Professor of History Painting at Vienna] also shewing a great amount of misapplied power. Jesus sits in a chariot, drawn by a bullock and a lion (I think), Popes in their robes pushing along the wheels, and a saintly female figure — the Virgin, I suppose, sitting opposite him" ["Recollections of Berlin," Beinecke Library; for the iconography, see E. Panofsky, Problems in Titian, Mostly Iconographic, N. Y.: New York U.P., 1969, pp. 58-63].

The lion and "bullock" are, of course, two of the four evangelists drawing the chariot, and the "Popes" at the wheels are the four fathers of the church, of whom only Gregory wears the papal habit. Dorothea's ignorance of Christian iconography in Middlemarch clearly mirrors a stage in her creator's own education. Nevertheless, George Eliot was almost certainly remembering Führich's Triumphzug when she attributed "the Saints drawing the Car of the Church" to Naumann. She may also have remembered Otto van Veen's Der Triumph der katholischen Kirche in sechs Bildern allegorisch dargestellt, which she might have seen at Munich in 1858; Verzeichnis der Gemalde in der koniglichen Pinakothek zu Munchen (Munich,1858), pp. 197-200. 36 Vaughan, "The German Manner in English Art," p. 46.

The year of Dorothea's wedding journey was a year of great change in the Nazarene movement. It marked the end of the Roman phase of the movement, which had begun in 1810, when Overbeck first moved to the Eternal City to live and paint in the spirit of late medieval Christianity with his fellows in the Brotherhood of Saint Luke. After the completion of the Casino Massimo frescoes in 1829, the remaining Nazarenes disbanded to various cities in Germany, leaving Overbeck to carry on alone in Rome. By then Nazarene artists were in great demand for the decoration of public buildings and monuments, and the staffing of various academies and art institutes. Official recognition and patronage prompted a change toward a programmatic, didactic, monumental style of art suitable to the decoration of cities that had grown culturally ambitious, intensely nationalistic, and historically self-conscious. This later phase of German art, known to George Eliot chiefly through Overbeck's Triumph of Christianity and the fresco cycles in Berlin and Munich of Peter Cornelius and his pupil Wilhelm von Kaulbach, is clearly anticipated by Naumann's theory and practice of history painting in Middlemarch.

George Eliot's critique of Naumann's art involves a sophisticated version of the standard Victorian charge that modern German art contains too much mind and not enough nature. The Leweses thought of the Nazarenes and their followers essentially as Pre-Raphaelites who lacked the saving grace of naturalism. Eliot's principal objection to German monumental art was that its symbolism is insufficiently grounded in an empirically observed and represented order of nature.

This tendency to depict things "too abstract to be represented" is suggested by Ladislaw's introduction of Naumann as "one of the chief renovators of Christian Art, one of those who had not only revived but expanded that grand conception of supreme events as mysteries at which the successive ages were spectators, and in relation to which the great souls of all periods became as it were contemporaries" (22:332,326). We are meant to take this vague but grandiose neotypological theory of history painting with a large grain of salt. Idealization must not be confused with Teutonic mystification. (For a different view of Naumann's achievement, see Barbara Hardy, "Middlemarch: Public and Private Worlds," English, 25 (1976), 22.)

Naumann's pictures are open to the same objections that

George Eliot made to Wilhelm von Kaulbach's *weltgeschichtliche Bilder* when she saw them at Berlin and Munich. Kaulbach's "allegorical-historical compositions ... intended to represent the historical development of culture," she declared, "leave one entirely cold as all elaborate allegorical compositions must do."[41] Kaulbach's frescoes employ "a regular child's puzzle of symbolism," she complained to Sara Hennell; "instead of taking a single moment of reality and trusting to the infinite symbolism that belongs to all nature, he attempts to give at one view a succession of events, each represented by some group which may mean 'whichever you please, my dear'" (*Letters*, II, 454-55).

In other words, Kaulbach's symbolism does not sufficiently incarnate the ideal in the real. It ignores what Ruskin termed the naturalist ideal, and it violates Lessing's prohibition against representing events separated by time in a single picture; see *Laokoon*, sec. xviii. The engravings of "mystic groups where far-off ages made one moment" in Mrs. Meyrick's front parlor in *Daniel Deronda* (20:313) are probably reproductions of modern German history paintings such as Kaulbach's.

First articulated in the 1850s, George Eliot's reaction to Nazarene art remained relatively unchanged. Reappearing in *Middlemarch*, her critique of the indeterminacy and arbitrariness of German typological symbolism amusingly unites Mr. Brooke's fuzzy response to the "Dispute" with Will Ladislaw's parody of the "Saints." Brooke, echoing Browning's Duke of Ferrara, says to Casaubon: "And we'll go down and look at the picture. There you are to the life: a deep subtle sort of thinker with his forefinger on the page, while Saint Bonaventure or somebody else, rather fat and florid, is looking up at the Trinity. Everything is symbolical, you know — the higher style of art: I like that up to a certain point, but not too far — it's rather straining to keep up with, you know" (34:86). As interpreted by Mr. Brooke, the "symbolical" style of Naumann's "Dispute" affords more delight than instruction.

Ladislaw's parody of the "Saints" likewise stresses the

indeterminacy and arbitrariness of its symbolism, but does so more instructively:

"I have been making a sketch of Marlow's Tamburlaine Driving the Conquered Kings in his Chariot. I am not so ecclesiastical as Naumann, and I sometimes twit him with his excess of meaning. But this time I mean to outdo him in breadth of intention. I take Tamburlaine in his chariot for the tremendous course of the world's physical history lashing on the harnessed dynasties. In my opinion that is a good mythical interpretation." Will here looked at Mr. Casaubon, who received this offhand treatment of symbolism very uneasily, and bowed with a neutral air. [22:326-27]

Will's statement is not, as Richard Ellmann and others have assumed, a description of an actual project.[43] Rather, it describes a purely imaginary allegory of secular history concocted by Will to parody the symbolic pretensions of Nazarene allegories of church history. Will's fantastic "Tamburlaine" belongs to the same genre as Kaulbach's "allegorical-historical compositions ... intended to represent the historical development of culture." The point of the parody is essentially the same point that Will makes when he accuses Naumann of thinking "that all the universe is straining towards the obscure significance of your pictures" (19:290).

What weakens Naumann's history painting is precisely what vitiates Mr. Casaubon's key to all mythologies. Proceeding from dogmatic Christian preconceptions, both men approach history deductively and categorically rather than inductively and empirically. As a follower of Jacob Bryant's A New System, or an Analysis of Ancient Mythology (1774-76), Casaubon finds his key to all mythologies in the revealed truth of Holy Scripture, and seeks to interpret the pagan mythologies as corruptions of the one true myth.

Both he and Naumann read the past as a symbolic record of Christian certitudes. Their agreement on the Christian interpretation of myth and history is signified by Casaubon's decision to appear in the "Dispute" and to buy the finished painting. In Scenes of Clerical Life, George Eliot noted the bond between Nazarene art and Anglican sensibilities when she described a clergyman's study in which "a refined Anglican taste is indicated by a German print from Overbeck" (I 1: 170). One wonders whether she knew that Charles Pusey visited Overbeck in Rome in 1829 (Vaughan, "German Manner in English Art," p. 48).

To associate Naumann with Casaubon in this context is to see how Naumann's career fits the historical pattem of aspiration and failure established by the careers of the major characters in Middlemarch. Naumann's ambition to renovate Christian art is comparable to Casaubon's ambition to find the key to all mythologies. But like the mythographer, the painter is working along lines that future generations will judge to have been misguided and retrogressive.

In George Eliot's view, Naumann's achievement belongs to a reactionary eddy in the mainstream progression of nineteenth-century painting toward a Ruskinian naturalism. She had little sympathy with the deliberate imitation of archaic pictorial styles, and less with the attempt to revive medieval Catholicism; thus she once criticized Overbeck for evoking "all the barbarisms of the Pre-Raphaelite period." The Nazarene programme ran dead against George Eliot's belief in humanistic empiricism and evolutionary development.

Tempering this judgment with a characteristic admixture of sympathy, however, Eliot perceived many virtues in the Nazarene movement. She certainly admired the learning, energy, and commitment of its adherents. What she said of Overbeck in 1860 might well be applied to Naumann: "The man himself is more interesting than his pictures" (Cross, II, 158). Eliot agreed with Lewes's observation in Life and Works of Goethethat German revivalist art had not only "a retrograde purpose which was bad" but also a "critical purpose which was good (II, 216).

The critical purpose to which Lewes referred was the recovery of last traditions of Christian art, an educational endeavor which helped to overcome precisely the kind of ignorance displayed by George Eliot's description of Führich's Triumphzug According to Lewes, Overbeck and Cornelius '1ent real genius to the attempt to revive the dead forms of early Christian art" (II, 219). They did so not only in their own works but also by inspiring an important body of research into the history and iconography of European Pre-Raphaelite painting.

Such studies were no doubt in Lewes's mind when he spoke in 1855 of "the services rendered by Romanticism in making the Middle Ages more thoroughly understood" (Life and Works of Goethe, II, 220). By Romanticism in this context, he and George Eliot meant a German, Catholic, neomedieval movement whose "main feature ... was the exaltation of the Medieval above the Classic, of art animated by Christian spiritualism above the art animated by Greek humanism."

Largely published between 1835 and 1855, the scholarship inspired by Romanticism divided Dorothea's England of the first Reform Bill from George Eliot's of the second. Readers of Middlemarch are reminded that in Dorothea's day travelers to Rome did not often carry full information on Christian art either in their heads or their pockets; and even the most brilliant English critic of the day mistook the flower-flushed tomb of the ascended Virgin for an ornamental vase due to the painter's fancy. Romanticism, which has helped to fill some dull blanks with love and knowledge, had not yet penetrated the times with its leaven and entered into everybody's food; it was fermenting still as a distinguishable vigorous enthusiasm in certain long-haired German artists at Rome.... [19:287]

George Eliot's example of English ignorance is accurate and well-chosen. In Notes of a Journey through France and Italy (1826), a book Dorothea might well have carried to Rome, William Hazlitt grossly misreads the iconography of Raphael's The Coronation of the Virgin in the Vatican Museum. Referring indeed to a "vase of flowers," Hazlitt fails to recognize the Marian resurrection symbolism of the lilies and roses that spring from the Virgin's sarcophagus. And he describes the twelve apostles as a "crowd".

Readers of Middlemarch would almost certainly have possessed better "information on Christian art" than Hazlitt's. For example, Mrs. Jameson's popular Legends of the Madonna as Represented in the Fine Arts (1852) mentions five versions of the Coronation in which "the miraculous flowers" appear. Of Raphael's treatment Mrs. Jameson says: "Here we have the tomb below, filled with flowers; and around it the twelve apostles."[54] For such gains in precision George Eliot thanked the "long-haired German artists" of the early nineteenth century.

In Middlemarch Naumann dramatizes the educational function of Romanticism when he plays the kindly didact to Dorothea. Her pre-Romantic ignorance of the conventions of Christian art prevents her from appreciating the "walls ... covered with frescoes, or with rare pictures" that she sees in Rome (21:315). Although Dorothea's conscience is troubled by aesthetic apprehension per se, part of her difficulty is that often she simply does not know what the pictures represent. By explicating the iconography of his own neomedieval works, Naumann comes nearer than anyone else in the novel to teaching Dorothea how to look at traditional paintings which are not simple portraits or landscapes:

> The painter in his confident English gave little dissertations on his finished and unfinished subjects ... and Dorothea felt that she was getting quite new notions as to the significance of madonnas seated under inexplicable canopied thrones with the simple country as a background, and of saints with architectural models in their hands, or knives accidentally wedged in their skulls. Some things which had seemed monstrous to her were gathering intelligibility and even a natural meaning.

Although the narrator's dry tone suggests considerable sympathy with Dorothea's distaste for such subjects, the last sentence affirms a positive and welcome enlightenment. Here Naumann does in small what Romanticism will soon do for Europe at large: he gives "intelligibility and even a natural meaning" to symbols of Christian art that had come to seem unintelligible and unnatural.

Whether the conventions of medieval Christian art should determine the direction of nineteenth-century painting was, however, a different question in George Eliot's mind. On balance she felt they should not, because they distort more than they clarify. To teach Dorothea how to look at Madonnas is one thing; to paint her as one is another. Both Naumann and the narrator of Middlemarch present idealizing portraits of Dorothea as a Christian heroine, but the novel calls all such portraiture into doubt. One side of George Eliot's mind remained skeptical toward the pictorial idealization of character even as she was practicing it.

When Naumann first encounters Dorothea in the Vatican Museum, her "Quakerish" costume and meditative expression inspire him to paint her as a personification of the Christian spirit, "dressed," since Naumann is Catholic, "as a nun" (19:289). Then he sees Dorothea as a "perfect young Madonna," and eventually he settles for painting her as Santa Clara (19:290, 22:331). But Dorothea's figure and attitude resemble those of the statue of Ariadne near which she stands, so there are pagan elements in the scene which prompt Naumann to a more comprehensive definition. He envisions Dorothea as "antique form animated by Christian sentiment – a sort of Christian Antigone – sensuous force controlled by spiritual passion" (19:290). This formulation unites the classical and the medieval, reconciling the great antitheses of German aesthetic debate in a higher synthesis.

Though suggestive, Naumann's exalted and schematic vision is only partly valid. Will Ladislaw immediately warns his friend not to confuse a symbolic conception of Dorothea with her human reality. Actually Naumann's allegorizing distorts his subjects, much as the fantasies of the male egoists in Adam Bede distort Hetty. Ladislaw alludes to Naumann's egoism when he accuses the painter of "looking at the world entirely from the studio point of view" (21:317), of thinking that art perfects life, and of believing that his picture of Dorothea would be "the chief outcome of her existence – the divinity passing into higher completeness and all but exhausted in the act of covering [a] bit of canvas" (19:290).

This is a critique of the solipsistic tendency inherent in Romantic aestheticism. It no doubt reflects the many charges of spiritual pride which Ruskin laid against the Nazarenes. George Eliot quoted the third of these passages in her review of Ruskin, "Art and Belles Lettres," Westminster Review, 65 (1856), 628.

This critique may also entail a more contemporary reference to the Victorian philosophy of art-for-art's-sake that had begun to spin off from Pre-Raphaelitism by the later 1860s. The critique also aligns Naumann with one of the grand themes of the novel: the inescapable corruption of aspiration by egoism. Compare, for example, Naumann's description of Dorothea with Walter Pater's description of Leonardo's Mona Lisa; in both, the lady's beauty is a synthesis of the major phases of western civilization, an incarnation of the collective wisdom and experience of her kind. Pater's essay on Leonardo was first published in 1869; in 1870 George Eliot dined at Oxford with "Mr. Pater, writer of articles on Leonardo da Vinci, Morris, etc." (Letters, V, 100).

Naumann's Christianizing aestheticism, then, is one of the many modes of human intellection tested and found wanting in Middlemarch. Idealizing portraiture provides no coherent vision in this novel of incomplete insights. Ultimately Dorothea eludes all of the analogies that attempt to characterize her as Santa Clara, Santa Teresa, Santa Barbara, the Madonna, and a Christian Antigone, just as Mr. Casaubon more obviously eludes Naumann's vision of him as Saint Thomas Aquinas or Dorothea's comparison of him with "the portrait of Locke" (2:21).

In The Art of George Eliot (1969), W. J. Harvey has argued that in Middlemarch such comparisons border upon the mock-heroic (pp. 193-95; for a different interpretation of the mythological allusions in chapter 19 of Middlemarch, see Wiesenfarth, George Eliot's Mythmaking, pp. 194-97). George Eliot sometimes wished passionately to affirm the persistence of ideal types in everyday life (G. H. Lewes often called her "Madonna"), but at other times she was skeptical and satirical about just such affirmations; and her skepticism is by no means confined to Middlemarch. In Felix Holt, for example, she gently satirizes her own response to religious art in a scene between Felix and Esther Lyon: "He was looking up at her quite calmly, very much as a reverential Protestant might look at a picture of the Virgin, with a devoutness suggested by the type rather than by the image" (27:39).

Usually, of course, George Eliot tried to be as attentive to the image as to the type, and this attention often complicated her responses. She was, for instance, no indiscriminate admirer of Raphael's madonnas. Although she worshipped the Sistine Madonna, she disliked some of its earlier "sisters" for "their sheep-like look" (Cross, II, 189). In The Mill on the Floss she draws an unflattering analogy between these images and Mrs. Tulliver: "I have often wondered whether those early Madonnas of Raphael, with the blond faces and somewhat stupid expression, kept their placidity undisturbed when their strong-limbed, strong-willed boys got a little too old to do without clothing" (I, 2:15).

Eliot's ambivalent vision sometimes issued in contradictory treatments of the same picture. Raphael's Saint Catherine, for example, was an early favourite of hers. At the age of twenty-five she told a friend that "you are a bright spot in my memory, like Raphael's Saint Catherine" (Letters, I, 188); and she may well have had the same painting in mind when Arthur Donnithorne refers to Dinah Morris as "St. Catherine in a Quaker dress" (5:91), and when one of the characters in Romola says that the heroine is "fit to be a model for a wise Saint Catherine of Egypt". But Raphael's famous picture is treated much less reverently in Middlemarch when Dorothea, recuperating from her bereavement, begins to grow restless: "After three months Freshitt had become rather oppressive: to sit like a model for Saint Catherine looking rapturously at Celia's baby would not do for many hours in the day: (54:3-4). Viewed from this perspective, Raphael's saint seems posed and a bit silly.

George Eliot's ambivalence toward idealization also complicates her attitude toward sculpture. Her visit to Weimar in 1854 convinced her that she did not care for "classical idealising in portrait sculpture." She saw there several distasteful examples of the technique, including a "colossal statue of Goethe, executed after Bettina's design," which represents him "as a naked Apollo with a Psyche at his knee!"

Any work in which the "artist tells us that the ideal of a Greek god divides his attention with his immediate subject" must be taken, Eliot warned, with a grain of salt. She declared herself particularly "irritated with idealization in portrait when, as in Dannecker's bust of Schiller, one has been misled into supposing that Schiller's brow was square and massive, while, in fact, it was receding".

In other words, idealization must not exceed the bounds of phrenological realism. Yet in other moods Eliot was not at all averse to classical idealizing in portrait sculpture. She was particularly fond of heroic and monumental images of women, such as the cockle-woman she once saw at Swansea: "the grandest woman I ever saw — six feet high, carrying herself like a Greek Warrior, and treading the earth with unconscious majesty". This taste for massive, Amazonian figures also manifests itself in Eliot's admiration of several pieces of contemporary sculpture: August Kiss's Mounted Amazon Attacked by a Tiger and Ludwig Schwanthaler's Bavaria (Cross, II, 21-22). Given her predilection for grand, statuesque female forms, she naturally visualized her own heroines as imposing creatures.

Dorothea, for example, resembles the reclining Ariadne in the Vatican Museum, and the similarity is of amplitude as well as attitude. The full-grown Maggie Tulliver is a tall, queenly figure whose arm resembles either one of the Parthenon sculptures or a classical sculpture that George Eliot saw in Berlin. In "Janet's Repentance" we pause with the heroine's mother to admire Janet's "tall rich figure, looking all the grander for the plainness of the deep mourning dress, and the noble face with its massy folds of black hair, made matronly by a simple white cap. Janet had that enduring beauty which belongs to pure majestic outline and depth of tint".

In a word, Janet's beauty, like that of Isola Churchill, the heroine of G. H. Lewes's Ranthorpe, is "more sculpturesque than picturesque". In Daniel Deronda the heroine is visualized in terms of Roman colored sculpture: "Dressed in black, without a single ornament, and with the warm whiteness of her skin set off between her light-brown coronet of hair and her square-cut bodice, she might have tempted an artist to try again the Roman trick of a statue in black, white, and tawny marble. Seeing her image slowly advancing, she thought, 'I am beautiful"'. As usual, Gwendolen is the first to admire her own aesthetic effects.

Herein she differs from Mirah Cohen, who is all unconsciously transformed from "immovable, statue-like des" to "a coloured statue of serenity" (17:280, 52:159). On a smaller scale, Mirah is visualized as "an onyx cameo" (17:281), "a perfect cameo" (32: 144). As in the case of Mirah's suicidal despair, George Eliot often represents states of extreme emotional stress through an imagery of sculpture. See, for example, Adam Bede (27:10, 27:19, 43:223). Roman sculpture figures, too, in the presentation of Felix Holt: "Felix might have come from the hands of a sculptor in the later Roman period, when the plastic impulse was stirred by the grandeur of barbaric forms" (46:309). Although pagan sculptural idealization obviously does not involve the renewal of biblical types, it nevertheless serves much the same function as George Eliot's Christian pictorialism. Both modes of literary portraiture hallow character by associating it with venerated traditional norms.

Eliot also elicited exemplary values from her literary portraits by grouping them in contrasting pairs. For example, the description just quoted of Felix Holt as a late-Roman statue occurs in combination with a description of Harold Transome as "a handsome portrait by Sir Thomas Lawrence." The two Radicals, we are told, "certainly made a striking contrast" (46:309). A similar pairing takes place in Daniel Deronda: "Deronda, turning to look straight at Grandcourt who was on his left hand, might have made a subject for those old painters who liked contrasts of temperament" (15:240). Or again, in Adam Bede: "The family likeness between [Mrs. Poyser] and her niece Dinah Morris, with the contrast between her keenness and Dinah's seraphic gentleness of expression, might have served a painter as an excellent suggestion for a Martha and Mary" (6: 10',7).

In George Eliot's work such contrasts are usually moral as well as visual, and sometimes they border on the emblematic in their clear-cut, monitory juxtaposition of virtue and vice, altruism and egoism. In "Amos Barton," for example, Milly is compared in physiognomy and moral temperament with the Countess Czerlaski: "Look at the two women on the sofa together! The large, fair, mild-eyed Milly is timid even in friendship: it is not easy to her to speak of the affection of which her heart is full. The lithe, dark, thin-lipped countess is racking her small brain for caressing words and charming exaggerations" (3:48). Exemplary pairings of women may be found among George Eliot's earliest published writings (Essays, pp. 21-22), and as Constance Marie Fulmer points out in "Contrasting Pairs of Heroines in George Eliot's Fiction," they are an important device for unifying parallel plots in her mature fiction (Studies in the Novel, 6 (1974), 288-94).

Perhaps the best-known of Eliot's double portraits is the "Two Bed-Chambers" scene in chapter 15 of Adam Bede. Here Hetty Sorrel and Dinah Morris are contrasted in great visual and moral detail. Their surroundings, their appearances, and their physical and mental activities are set forth with a painstaking realism that emulates the spirit of Dutch painting. Yet these concrete descriptive details compose themselves into coherent symbolic patterns as well, so that Hetty's portrait incorporates many traditional symbols of vanity, whereas Dinah's abounds with familiar signs of contemplation [90/ 91] and spiritual rebirth. After describing the two women separately, George Eliot brings them together, as if joining two wings of a diptych.

What a strange contrast the two figures made! Visible enough in that mingled twilight and moonlight. Hetty, her cheeks flushed and her eyes glistening from her imaginary drama, her beautiful neck and arms bare, her hair hanging in a curly tangle down her back, and the baubles in her ears. Dinah, covered with her long white dress, her pale face full of subdued emotion, almost like a lovely corpse into which the soul has returned charged with sublimer secrets and a sublimer love. The uncharacteristic absence of predication in Eliot's syntax here reinforces the impression of static, juxtaposed icons.

Although vanitas symbolism is common enough in seventeenth-century Dutch genre painting, this sort of stark moral contrast is not common. Eliot's description is so emblematic that one critic has actually proposed a direct iconographic parallel with Francis Quarles's emblem III, 14. This is not a convincing analogy, however. R. T. Jones is closer to the mark when he compares the scene to a hypothetical nineteenth-century painting: "It might be called 'Sacred and Profane Love,' and it might have been painted by, say, Holman Hunt" (George Eliot, Cambridge: Cambridge University Press, 1970, p. 17). This is a perceptive suggestion, especially if Jones is thinking of Hunt's famous pair of moral pictures, The Light of the World and The Awakening Conscience.

Yet Hunt never depicted two women together in quite the way that Eliot does here. A better pictorial analogy for "The Two Bed-Chambers" scene, if one need be sought, is Wilhelm von Schadow's Pietas und Vanitas: Parabel der klugen und törichten Jungfrauen (1842), a painting displayed at the great Munich exhibition of 1858 within two months of George Eliot's visit to the Bavarian capital. Schadow's wise and foolish virgins are juxtaposed as if in a diptych, equipped with contrasting symbolic accoutrements and differentiated by the directions of their gazes. Although the painting does not resemble George Eliot's text in every detail, the correspondences are nonetheless suggestive. A comparable Victorian painting, though donc too late to have influenced Adam Bede, is Arthur D. Lemon's Pure Innocence and Pure in No Sense (ca. 1880); see Rodee, "Scenes of Rural and Urban Poverty," p. 141 and illus. 52.

This sort of contrast attains massive proportions in the structure of Daniel Deronda, where the English and Jewish parts of the novel incorporate two distinctive and antithetical modes of literary portraiture. Both modes involve the idealization of character and the reincarnation of sacred types, but the novel treats one mode as false and the other as true. Throughout Deronda, George Eliot regularly visualizes Gwendolen and the other English characters in terms of the English portrait tradition, and especially of the "fancy" portraits that were fashionable among the upper classes in the seventeenth and eighteenth centuries.

Conversely, Eliot visualizes Daniel and other Jewish characters in terms of Italian Renaissance painting, especially that of Titian and the Venetian school. The contrasts between these two schools of painting reflect moral contrasts between the two races and cultures represented. George Eliot's characteristic ambivalence toward the pictorial idealization of character finds a complex resolution in the double plot of Daniel Deronda: her ironic portraiture has full play in the English half of the novel, while her ennobling portraiture finds a more ardent and affirmative expression in the Jewish part than anywhere else in her fiction.

Gwendolen, as we have seen, likes to imagine herself as the central subject of attractive pictures. Her favourite attitudes in these imaginary self-portraits are borrowed from the allegorical society portraiture of the Van Dyck tradition. In the seventeenth and eighteenth centuries it was fashionable to idealize sitters by depicting them in costumes, poses, and settings that recall heroic, mythical, or religious figures from earlier works of art. Van Dyck popularized this technique of pictorial quotation in England when he transferred the baroque style of his Genoese religious work into his society portraiture. Thus he painted Lady Venetia Digby as Prudence, Rachel, Countess of Southampton, as Fortuna, and Mary, Duchess of Lenox, as Saint Agnes. Continuing the fashion,

Sir Peter Lely drew the Duchess of Cleveland as Juno, Mrs. Middleton as Pomona, Jane Kelleway as Diana, the Duchess of Rutland as Saint Agnes. Godfrey Kneller drew Anne, Lady Middleton, and Mrs. Voss and her daughter as Arcadian shepherdesses bearing staffs in their hands, and, on another occasion, the same Mrs. Voss as St. Agnes holding a prayer book in her hand and cuddling a lamb.

Reynolds, in his turn, portrayed Mrs. Quarrington as

St. Agnes, Mrs. Crewe as St Genevieve, The Daughters of Sir William Montgomery as the Graces Adorning a Term of Hymen, The Duchess of Manchester as Diana, Mrs. Blake as Juno, and the famous courtesan Kitty Fisher as Cleopatra.[74] Because they allude to the subjects of historical or "fancy" painting, these pictures are often referred to as "fancy portraits" (Tinker, Painter and Poet, p. 14). That George Eliot was familiar with the term is shown by the fact that Latimer, the narrator of "The Lifted Veil," has been "the model of a dying minstrel in a fancy-picture" (1:295).

It is with fancy portraits that Gwendolen is most prominently associated in Daniel Deronda. At the Archery Meeting in Brackenshaw Park, for example, it was the fashion to dance in the archery dress, throwing off the jacket; and the simplicity of [Gwendolen's] white cashmere with its border of pale green set off her form to the utmost. A thin line of gold round her neck, and the gold star on her breast, were her only ornaments. Her smooth soft hair piled up into a grand crown made a clear line about her brow. Sir Joshua would have been glad to take her portrait.... [11:170]

Clearly Sir Joshua would have entitled the portrait Miss Harleth as Diana. Earlier in the same scene, a comparable portrait is evoked when we are told that "Gwendolen seemed a Calypso among her nymphs. It was in her attitudes and movements that every one was obliged to admit her surpassing charm" (10:147). We are dealing once more with Ovidian mythological fantasies of the sort that were treated so ironically in Adam Bede and Romola. The self-indulgence of the fantasies is underlined by the fact that Gwendolen is critical of other women who might figure in the same sort of painting. After observing that Charlotte Arrowpoint "would make quite a fine picture in that gold-coloured dress," Gwendolen decides that the picture would be "perhaps a little too symbolical — too much like the figure of Wealth in an allegory" (10:151). Too many allegorical figures might crowd Gwendolen's canvas.

Gwendolen's most memorable borrowed attitudes are Hermione and Saint Cecilia. The famous tableau of Hermione in Daniel Deronda is indebted to a similar scene in Goethe's Die Wahlverwandtschaften, which was in turn inspired by the drawing-room attitudes of Lady Emma Hamilton. In her tableau Gwendolen chooses to imitate the attitude in which Mrs. Siddons and other eighteenth-century actresses regularly played the statue scene in The Winter's Tale: "Hermione, her arm resting on a pillar, was elevated by about six inches, which she counted on as a means of showing her pretty foot and instep, when at the given signal she should advance and descend" (6:85).

Edgar Wind, in his classic essay on English heroic portraiture in the eighteenth century, reproduces engravings of Mrs. Siddons and Miss Farren in the role of Hermione, holding precisely this pose. He shows that the attitude descends from classical representations of the Muses, and that it was "an established formula" for all actresses who played the statue scene in the eighteenth century.[77] Gwendolen, then, is imitating pictures of Mrs. Siddons as Hermione. As Wind notes, in society masquerades the ladies "often learned the attitudes which they assumed from actresses on the stage" ("Humanitatsidee," pp. 222, 224). Wind reproduces a drawing of Mrs. Siddons as Hermione from the sketchbook of a young lady, Mary Hamilton, who depicted the attitudes and costumes of Mrs. Siddons in a variety of roles, with a view to recreating them in private entertainments.

Gwendolen's Hermione is designed primarily to allow her to display "a statuesque pose" in her Greek dress (6:82). The planned effect perfectly exemplifies Ruskin's assertion in Modern Painters, vol. III that "the modern 'ideal' of high art is a curious mingling of the gracefulness and reserve of the drawing-room with a certain measure of classical sensuality" (V, 96). But it is Gwendolen's expression, not her attitude, that is affected by the sudden apparition of the prophetic picture of the dead face and fleeing figure. Instead of assuming the radiant face of comedy appropriate to the end of The Winter's Tale, Gwendolen unwittingly dons the mask of tragedy:

Gwendolen ... stood without change of attitude, but with

a change of expression that was terrifying in its terror. She looked like a statue into which a soul of Fear had entered: her pallid lips were parted; her eyes, usually narrowed under their long lashes, were dilated and fixed. [6:86]

The complacent beauty has now become a study in physiognomical expression, a sculpturesque representation of Terror, one of the two passions appropriate to Aristotelian tragedy. Instead of Miss Harleth as Hermione, we have, still in the Reynolds tradition, Miss Harleth as the Tragic Muse. The picture distinctly recalls Piero di Cosimo's picture of Tito as a terror-stricken reveller in Romola.

More to Gwendolen's taste is the attitude of Saint Cecilia:

"Here is an organ. I will be Saint Cecilia: some one shall paint me as Saint Cecilia. Jocosa (this was her name for Miss Merry), let down my hair. See, mamma!"

She had thrown off her hat and gloves, and seated herself before the organ in an admirable pose, looking upward; while the submissive and sad Jocosa took out the one comb which fastened the coil of hair, and then shook out the mass till it fell in a smooth light-brown stream far below its owner's slim waist. Mrs Davilow smiled and said, "A charming picture, my dear!" not indifferent to the display of her pet, even in the presence of a housekeeper. Gwendolen rose and laughed with delight. All this seemed quite to the purpose on entering a new house which was so excellent a background. [3:33-34]

Here the imaginary portrait is in the style of Kneller's Lady Elizabeth Cromwell as Saint Cecilia (1703), Reynolds's Mrs. Sheridan as Saint Cecilia (1775), or Reynolds's Mrs Billington as Saint Cecilia. The aristocratic life to which Gwendolen aspires is again presented as an eighteenth-century affair. The attitude of Saint Cecilia in society portraiture was familiar enough by 1735 to be an object of Pope's satire in Moral Essay II, "On the Characters of Women":

How many pictures of one Nymph we view,
All how unlike each other, all how true!

....

Let then the Fair one beautifully cry,
In Magdalen's loose hair and lifted eye,

Or drest in smiles of sweet Cecilia shine,
With simp'ring Angels, Palms, and Harps divine;
Whether the Charmer sinner it or saint it,
If folly grows romantic, I must paint it.81

Hagstrum's The Sister Arts cites this passage after listing the representations of Saint Cecilia best known in the seventeenth century. Fancy portraits were also satirized by Oliver Goldsmith in chapter 16 of The Vicar of Wakefield. Edgar Wind argues that English allegorical portraiture reflects a heroic conception of mankind, and other scholars have defended them. But Pope and George Eliot see in such portraiture mainly the affectation and folly of the social class depicted. Indeed, for the middle-class Victorian intellectual, fancy portraits must have epitomized all that was Dandy about the fashionable classes under George III and George IV.

Ruskin strikes the characteristic Victorian tone in the third volume of Modern Painters when he speaks of paintings which introduce pretty children as cherubs, and handsome women as Magdalens and Maries of Egypt, or portraits of patrons in the character of the more decorous saints; but more frequently, for direct flatteries of this kind, recurring to pagan mythology, and painting frail ladies as goddesses or graces, and foolish kings in radiant apotheosis. [V, 93-94]

The portraits in which Gwendolen loves to see herself do not in George Eliot's view truly idealize their subjects; they falsify in order to please the vanity of their subjects. Hans Meyrick temporarily resists Sir Hugo Mallinger's advice to take up portraiture because the sort of painter Sir Hugo has in mind "has a little truth, and a great facility in falsehood — [his] idealism will never do for gods and goddesses and heroic story, but it may fetch a high price as flattery" (52:152). That Hans has higher standards of truthfulness in portraiture is perhaps suggested by the fact that he is "christened after Holbein" and that "only to look at his pinched features and blond hair dangling over his collar reminded one of pale quaint heads by early German painters" (16:270).

Early German is not the only school to be contrasted with the English in Daniel Deronda Before discussing George

Eliot's Italian sources, we should glance briefly at her use of the Dutch school in the presentation of Mordecai. Eliot's idealization of Mordecai is pictorial and overtly typological. Daniel's first impression of the consumptive scholar is that "such a physiognomy as that might possibly have been seen in a prophet of the Exile, or in some New Hebrew poet of the medieval time" (33:165). Later Daniel sees Mordecai as "an illuminated type of bodily emaciation and spiritual eagerness" (40:327).

For Hebrew portraiture Eliot turned naturally to Rembrandt's pictures of rabbis. G. H. Lewes spoke of "a Rembrandtish background to her dramatic presentation" of the Jews in Daniel Deronda (Letters, VI, 196), and certainly a Rembrandtish chiaroscuro is suggested by the first glimpse of Mordecai's face, "with its dark, far-off gaze, and yellow pallor in relief on the gloom of the backward shop". Later Hans Meyrick, who is painting the picturesque figure, says: "Our prophet is an uncommonly interesting sitter — a better model than Rembrandt had for his Rabbi" (52:147).

It is difficult to know which of Rembrandt's so-called rabbis Hans has in mind, but perhaps he is referring to the only one in the collection of the National Gallery, purchased under the title A Jewish Rabbi in 1844. The picturesque caps of Rembrandt's sitters were probably in George Eliot's memory when she wrote of Mordecai: "he commonly wore a cloth cap with black fur round it, which no painter would have asked him to take off" (38: 298). Mordecai himself may be thinking of Rembrandt when he envisions his messiah "from his memory of faces seen among the Jews of Holland and Bohemia, and from the pictures which revived that memory" (38:300).

Nevertheless, Dutch art does not dominate the Jewish part of Daniel Deronda as completely as might be expected. It is an exaggeration to say, as Harold Fisch does in "Daniel Deronda, or Gwendolen Harleth?" that "the Jewish portraiture of Rembrandt" is "the true prototype" of George Eliot's treatment of the Jews (Nineteenth-Century Fiction, 19 (1965), 354-55). Except for Mordecai, no important character in the novel is associated with Rembrandt's portraiture. Eliot's use of Dutch painting is highly selective, no doubt because the idealization she wished to confer upon her Jewish characters was incompatible with her audience's preconceptions about the limitations of the Dutch school.

No one did more than Eliot herself had done in Adam Bede to foster the notion that the province of Dutch art is "the faithful rendering of commonplace things," and that it depicts "few prophets ... few sublimely beautiful women; few heroes" (17:270). In Adam Bede Dutch models sufficed for the mundane range of experience she wised to present. But in Daniel Deronda she ventures into precisely those extraordinary reaches of experience which she chose to avoid in Adam Bede. She could not make an extensive use of Dutch models because she shared with a substantial part of her audience the venerable prejudice that Dutch painting rarely achieves the sublime.

Instead she relies heavily upon Italian, especially Venetian, models. So persistently does she associate Jews with Italians that the Anglo-Saxon reader of Daniel Deronda is induced almost subliminally to grant the Jews whatever tolerance and respect he is accustomed to grant the Italians. It is as though George Eliot were saying to her Protestant English audience: you have learned to appreciate the Italians despite their ethnic, religious, and cultural foreignness; you can learn to appreciate the Jews in the same way: both peoples are of Mediterranean origin, both have distinguished non-Protestant religious traditions, and the Italian Renaissance painting you admire realizes many motifs of the Hebrew scriptures. (Disraeli's hero in Lothair (1870) makes a similar point when discussing the influence of "Semitism" upon "Aryan art" [chap. 29].)

Eliot's pictorialism, in other words, here becomes a sophisticated rhetorical device employed in the service of a liberal social vision. The Italian connection affects major and minor characters alike. An elderly man at the synagogue in Frankfurt, for example, has an "ample white beard and felt hat framing a profile of that fine contour which may as easily be Italian as Hebrew" (32:136). Of Klesmer, the Jewish pianist, the narrator says: "draped in a loose garment with a Florentine berretta on his head, he would have been fit to stand by the side of Leonardo da Vinci" (10:149).

Even Mirah Cohen is associated with Italians in Hans Meyrick's Titus and Berenice series; she is to be the model for the Jewish mistress of the prospective emperor of Rome. The series was originally suggested, as Hans explains, by "a splendid woman in the Trastevere — the grandest women there are half Jewesses — and she set me hunting for a fine situation of a Jewess at Rome" (37:276). The fusion of Jewish and Roman identities here is threefold: in Berenice, in the Trasteverina, and by association in Mirah.

Finally, Daniel Deronda himself, who learns in Genoa that he is a Jew, has "a face not more distinctively oriental than many a type seen among what we call the Latin races" (40:332). Gwendolen's mother says the same thing more concisely: "he puts me in mind of Italian paintings" (29: 83). That Deronda does not belong pictorially to the English school is made clear when Gwendolen notices that "hardly any face could be less like Deronda's than that represented as Sir Hugo's in a crayon portrait at Diplow" (29:84).

Of the regional schools of Italian painting evoked in Daniel Deronda, the most prominent is the Venetian. Venetian painting regained its prestige in England in the 1860s and 1870s after the rage for Pre-Raphaelite styles had run its course. Ruskin's revaluation of the Venetian school in the last volume of Modern Painters (1860) concludes that "the Venetian mind ... and Titian's especially, as the central type of it, was wholly realist, universal, and manly.... In all its roots of power, and modes of work ... I find the Venetian mind perfect" (VII, 296-98.). Earlier in the same work Ruskin contrasted Venetian Renaissance portraiture to modern English portraiture in terms that parallel George Eliot's handling of the two schools in Daniel Deronda:

the first step towards the ennobling of any face is the ridding it of its vanity; to which aim there cannot be anything more contrary than that principle of portraiture which prevails with us in these days, whose end seems to be the expression of vanity throughout, in face and in all circumstances of accompaniment; tending constantly to insolence of attitude, and levity and haughtiness of expression, and worked out farther in mean accompaniments of worldly splendour and possession ... whence has arisen such a school of portraiture as must make the people of the nineteenth century the shame of their descendants, and the butt of all time. To which practices are to be opposed both the glorious severity of Holbein, and the mighty and simple modesty of Raffaelle, Titian, Giorgione, and Tintoret, with whom armour does not constitute the warrior, neither silk the dame. And from what feeling the dignity of that portraiture arose is best traceable at Venice.

According to Ruskin, painting done before 1600 embodies a greater purity of religious spirit than painting done since, and the Venetians "were the last believing school of Italy" (VII, 286). Hence the Venetian school is appropriate to the Jewish characters in Daniel Deronda, who have preserved a vital contact with their ancient religion; whereas the modern school is appropriate to the English characters, who are vain and worldly. In characterizing modern portraiture as an art of vanity, Ruskin anticipates George Eliot's pictures of Gwendolen.

Among the Victorians the chief technical excellence of the Venetian painters was generally held to be their colour. In The Stones of Venice Ruskin spoke of "that mighty spirit of Venetian colour, which was to be consummated in Titian," and argued that there is always a "connexion of pure colour with profound and noble thought" (X, 64, 174. In Deronda George Eliot draws upon the pure colour values of Venetian painting when she describes Daniel's visit to the family of Ezra Cohen:

When she showed him into the room behind the shop he was surprised at the prettiness of the scene.... The ceiling and walls were smoky, and all the surroundings were dark enough to throw into relief the human figures, which had a Venetian glow of colouring. The grandmother was arrayed in yellowish brown with a large gold chain in lieu of the necklace, and by this light her yellow face with its darkly-marked eyebrows and framing roll of grey hair looked as handsome as was necessary for picturesque effect. Young Mrs Cohen was clad in red and black, with a string of large artificial pearls wound round and round her neck: the baby lay asleep in the cradle under a scarlet counterpane; Adelaide Rebekah was in braided amber; and Jacob Alexander was in black velveteen with scarlet stockings. As the four pairs of black eyes all glistened a welcome at Deronda, he was almost ashamed of the supercilious dislike these happy-looking creatures had raised in him by daylight.

Here the Venetian aura of colour in the group portrait dignifies the London Jewish family in Deronda's eyes and is meant to have the same effect upon the reader. Structurally, the scene is a conversation piece. It may recall Simeon Solomon's "Illustrations of Jewish Customs," The Leisure Hour, vol 15 (1866). Once again we see "Hebrew dyed Italian" (55:213). No doubt the coloristic style of Venetian painting seemed to George Eliot more exotic, more "oriental," and therefore more appropriate to her Jewish characters than did the linear styles of other Italian schools.

If Reynolds dominates the English portraiture in Daniel Deronda, then Titian dominates the Jewish. "One can," says Jean Hagstrum, "almost always count on a literary Englishman's admiration of Titian" (SisterArts, p. 164). In a sense, the entire novel was inspired by a Titian painting — the Annunciation at the Scuola di San Rocco in Venice, which gave George Eliot the theme she developed first in The Spanish Gypsy and later in Deronda. In "this small picture of Titian's," she found "a great dramatic motive": a young person chosen to fulfil a great destiny ... chosen, not by any momentary arbitrariness, but as a result of foregoing hereditary conditions ... I came home with this in my mind, meaning to give the motive a clothing in some suitable set of historical and local conditions.

Here is an excellent example of the typological thinking that underlies so much of Eliot's art. Titian's handling of a traditional biblical type inspires Eliot to reincarnate the same type in a more contemporary setting. Small wonder, then, that the literary portraiture of George Eliot's hero derives principally from two of Titian's paintings.

In the early part of the novel, before he has accepted his Zionist mission, Daniel is associated with a secular portrait in the Louvre — The Young Man with a Glove. In the later part of the novel, after his destiny has been revealed, Daniel is associated with a religious painting at Dresden — The Tribute Money. The change of portraits symbolizes Daniel's progression from a life of aimless upper-class ease to a life of religious commitment. Deronda comes to exemplify G. H. Lewes's belief that "a well-painted face, with a noble expression, is the highest reach of art" ("Realism in Art," p. 499). Earlier in the novel the Meyrick girls create their own portrait of "Deronda as an ideal" when they set about "to paint him as Prince Camaralzaman," hero of one of the Arabian Nights.

The Young Man with a Glove is evoked in chapter 17 as Deronda rows on the Thames:

Look at his hands: they are not small and dimpled, with tapering fingers that seem to have only a deprecating touch: they are long, flexible, firmly-grasping hands, such as Titian has painted in a picture where he wished to show the combination of refinement with force. And there is something of a likeness, too, between the faces belonging to the hands — in both the uniform pale-brown skin, the perpendicular brow, the calmly-penetrating eyes.

George Eliot might have seen this portrait during visits to the Louvre in 1859 and again in 1864 (Cross, II, 96 and "Italy 1864," Beinecke Library, entry 6 May). Here is Deronda as handsome young gentleman, idle perhaps but potentially energetic and less affected than he might be if he belonged to the English school. The young man's potential is fully realized in the painting that represents Deronda's later, more spiritual aspect. Titian's [102/103] The Tribute Money is evoked immediately after Deronda is recognized by Mordecai as the incarnation of his messianic vision:

In ten minutes the two men, with as intense a

consciousness as if they had been two undeclared lovers, felt themselves alone in the small gas-lit book-shop and turned face to face, each baring his head from an instinctive feeling that they wished to see each other fully.... I wish I could perpetuate those two faces, as Titian's "Tribute Money" has perpetuated another type of contrast. Imagine — we all of us can — the pathetic stamp of consumption with its brilliancy of glance to which the sharply-defined structure of features reminding one of a forsaken temple, give already a far-off look as of one getting unwillingly out of reach; and imagine it on a Jewish face naturally accentuated for the expression of an eager mind-the face of a man little above thirty, but with that age upon it which belongs to time lengthened by suffering, the hair and beard still black throwing out the yellow pallor of the skin, the difficult breathing giving more decided marking to the mobile nostril, the wasted yellow hands conspicuous on the folded arms.... Seeing such a portrait you would see Mordecai. And opposite to him was a face not more oriental than many a type seen among what we call the Latin races: rich in youthful health, and with a forcible masculine gravity in its repose, that gave the value of judgment to the reverence with which he met the gaze of this mysterious son of poverty who claimed him as a long-expected friend.

The scene in the bookshop is analogous, not identical, to the scene in The Tribute Money. In particular, Mordecai does not resemble the tax-collecting Pharisee through whom Jesus renders unto Caesar what is Caesar's. Yet Titian's Christ looks enough like The Young Man with a Glove to resemble Deronda as well, and Deronda is bearded. Probably we are meant to visualize Deronda in terms of Titian's Christ. "In this way," to borrow a remark made by Albert R. Cirillo in another context, "Eliot fleshes out Daniel's portrait as a paragon, as a symbol, or personal savior." That Daniel's Portrait involves a form of typological incarnation is strongly suggested by the language of the novel. Deronda is "the antitype of [the] visionary image in Mordecai's mind" (41:352).

An antitype is not the opposite of a type but its fulfillment. As soon as he meets Daniel, Mordecai is struck by "a face and frame which seemed to him to realise the long-conceived type ... Deronda had that sort of resemblance to the preconceived type which a finely individual bust or portrait has to the more generalised copy left in our minds after a long interval" (38:307-08). The type in question reveals its virtues through its expression; it has "a face at once young, grand, and beautiful, where, if there is any melancholy, it is no feeble passivity, but enters into the foreshadowed capability of heroism" (38:298).

This face, at once contemplative and active, belongs both to Mordecai's messiah and to Titian's Christ in The Tribute Money. In effect, Eliot seeks to make Deronda a convincing postfiguration of Christ in her secular religion of humanity by contrasting his unconscious pictorial fulfillment of the role with Gwendolen's self-conscious fulfillment of the pictorial roles of saints and goddesses in fashionable society portraiture.

Deronda's literary portrait associates him with one of George Eliot's favourite paintings in all the world. During her extended stay at Dresden in the summer of 1858, she and G. H. Lewes visited the Gemäldegalerie "three mornings in the week" and "looked at the Zinsgroschen (Titian's), too, every day" (Cross, II, 47). In an essay written that summer, Lewes explained their reasons for admiring the picture. He cites The Tribute Money to illustrate the compatibility of idealism with realism in art:

Titian's unsurpassable head of Christ, in the famous "Christo del Moneta," if compared with all other heads by other painters, will likewise be found to have its profound significance and idealism in the wonderful reality of the presentation: the head is more intensely human than that of any other representation of Christ, but the humanity is such as accords with our higher conceptions.

In other words, The Tribute Money is a supreme example of the ideal in the real. It successfully achieves the idealization which fancy portraits fail to achieve when they depict their sitters as saints or mythological divinities. And it realizes a higher conception of humanity than does The Young Man with a Glove, as Lewes made clear when he ranked the two paintings on a Ruskinian scale of "greatness" in "The Principles of Success in Literature":

> Titian's portrait of "The Young Man with a Glove" is a great work of art, though not of great art. It is infinitely higher than a portrait of Cromwell, by a painter unable to see into the great soul of Cromwell, and to make us see it; but it is infinitely lower than Titian's "Tribute Money," "Peter the Martyr," or the "Assumption."

During the story, Deronda traverses the spiritual distance that separates The Young Man with a Glove from The Tribute Money on Lewes's scale. Deronda moves from a secular to a religious life, from a poised sitter in a portrait to a dramatic actor in a sacred history painting.

With this bold pictorial affirmation George Eliot's career as a novelist ends. The techniques we have observed call into doubt Henry James's influential description of George Eliot's idealization in his review of Cross's Life. We feel in her, always," wrote James, that she proceeds from the abstract to the concrete: that her figures and situations are evolved, as the phrase is, from her moral consciousness, and are only indirectly the products of observations. They are deeply studied and elaborately justified, but they are not seen in the irresponsible plastic way. [Atlantic Monthly, 55 (May 1885); rpt. Carroll, ed., George Eliot: The Critical Heritage, p. 498.]

James's metaphors do not provide an altogether accurate account of the process which produced such characters as Dinah Morris, Romola, Mordecai, and Daniel Deronda. To be sure, these figures were evolved from Eliot's moral consciousness; but they were also seen in a plastic way virtually from the moment of their conception. They are not abstract or indirectly observed in any visual sense of the terms; on the contrary, as Ian Milner has observed, they are highly particularized and often modeled upon specific, identifiable pictures (The Structure of Values in George Eliot (Prague: Universita Karlova, 1968), p. 121). If we judge the characters to be failures, our verdict may be based upon our distaste for exemplary typological characterization rather than upon George Eliot's failure to achieve presentational concreteness.

Chapter 15

Inheriting the Empire After Morant Bay

When we reflect on the nineteenth century, the mid-1860s does not immediately spring to mind as a moment of great crisis in British domestic and imperial affairs. The mobilization that led up to the Second Reform Bill in 1867 lacks the revolutionary drama of the first round of Reform agitation and the great Chartist movement in the 1830s and 40s; the Morant Bay uprising in Jamaica in late 1865 was hardly on the same scale as the Sepoy Rebellion in India in 1857 or the Anglo-Boer War that brought the Victorian age to an end.

Nevertheless, social commentators and cultural critics of the 1860s believed themselves to be living through a period of major upheaval. And although some anticipated a positive outcome from the winds of change they sensed blowing through musty old Britain, others saw only threats and possible catastrophe. Thomas Carlyle, for instance, blustery as ever in his old age, fired off a letter in August 1866 promising support for the Eyre Testimonial and Defence Fund, set up to defend the governor of Jamaica against criticism of his methods in suppressing the Morant Bay rebellion:

The clamour raised against Governor Eyre appears to me to be disgraceful to the good sense of England; and if it rested on any depth of conviction ... I should consider it of evil omen to the country, and to its highest interests, in these times.... The English nation never loved anarchy; nor was wont to spend its sympathy on miserable mad seditions, especially of this inhuman and half-brutish type; but always loved order and prompt suppression of seditions. (Workman 91-2) The shift to the past tense in the second of Carlyle's sentences here nicely conveys the sense that anarchy may actually be the new order of the day, and the disturbing fact that the opposition to Eyre not only rested on strongly held convictions but also had mass appeal.

This second sentence also recalls (anachronistically, as it turns out) that most famous statement of the troubles of the 1860s, Matthew Arnold's *Culture and Anarchy* , first published as a series of magazine essays in 1867-68 and printed in book form in 1869.

In the conclusion to that work, writing about the disorder in Hyde Park in 1866 during a massive rally for Reform, Arnold demonstrates his firm conviction that seditions of any kind must be put down forcefully:

For us the framework of society, that theatre on which this august drama has to unroll, is sacred; and whoever administers it ... we steadily and with undivided heart support them in repressing anarchy and disorder; because without order there can be no society, and without society there can be no human perfection. (180-1)

In the original magazine version of this essay, and in the first edition of *Culture and Anarchy,* this passage is immediately followed by these notorious lines:

With me, indeed, this rule of conduct is hereditary. I remember my father, in one of his unpublished letters of more than forty years ago, when the political and social state of the country was gloomy and troubled and there were riots in many places, goes on, after strongly insisting on the badness and foolishness of the government, and on the harm and dangerousness of our feudal and aristocratical constitution of society, and ends thus: "As for rioting, the old Roman way of dealing with that is always the right one; flog the rank and file and fling the ringleaders from the Tarpeian Rock!" (qtd. in Super 526)

In later editions of the book, Arnold deleted this passage, for reasons that have never been entirely clear. Perhaps the country seemed less gloomy and troubled by the time of the second edition (1875), and thus less in need of Thomas Arnold's lawgiving. Or perhaps Matthew revised his text in response to the answer, now lost, that his mother gave to this letter that he sent to her on July 25, 1868:

In the passage quoted from Papa, [Arthur Penrhyn] Stanley's impression is that Papa's words were "Crucify all the slaves" instead of "Flog the rank & file"—but as the latter expression is the milder, and I have certainly got it in my memory as what he said, I have retained it. Do you remember which the words were, and in what letter they occur? (qtd. in Super 455)

Buried deep within Arnold's text, we find a connection between the unrest in the Caribbean—"Crucify all the slaves"—and the sometimes unruly agitation for working-class enfranchisement and parliamentary reform—"Flog the rank and file." [3] It is this conjuncture, this alchemy of race and rights, that forms the subject of this essay. I argue that what has come to be known, rather misleadingly, as the Governor Eyre controversy enabled the articulation of the discourses of class, race, and empire in Britain, discourses that were all in a state of major transition. It was these connections, more or less explicitly made, that gave the Jamaica uprising such a disproportionate significance at the time, and produced the sense of crisis that Arnold and Carlyle felt compelled to respond to. And it is out of this sense of crisis, I argue, after the Morant Bay rebellion, that the modern notion of the British Empire as a single conceptual, territorial, and political unit emerges.

Jamaica in the 1860s had been in serious economic decline for half a century; the days when ownership of a Jamaican sugar plantation was virtually a licence to print money were a distant memory. The Afro-Jamaican labouring classes, however, were beginning to leave behind the legacies of chattel slavery, establishing an internal island economy based on foodstuffs grown on small plots of land (often the same fields cultivated during slavery days, known as provision grounds). A combination of drought and ruling-class attempts to push squatters and poor tenants from abandoned estate lands led, in the southeast of the island in the mid-1860s, to a volatile situation.

In October 1865, a group of Afro-Jamaicans, led by Paul Bogle, rescued one of their friends from punishment before the hated magistrates in the nearby town of Morant Bay; then they overwhelmed the police sent to arrest them the following day; finally, several hundred of them marched on the town to demand justice. The local worthies, expecting trouble, had called out the volunteer militia; shots were fired, and several rebels were killed; then the rebels laid siege to the courthouse and took over the town, killing eighteen and wounding dozens, predominately whites. The insurgents, however, were never well organized, and they were no match for the might of the colonial military machine once it rolled into action. The British governor of the island, Edward Eyre, declared martial law in the district, and in the month-long suppression of the abortive uprising that followed, upwards of 400 people were killed, most without trial, hundreds were flogged, and a thousand houses were burned. Bogle, along with the other leaders of the rebellion, was quickly captured and executed.

The response to the Jamaica events in England was initially predictable: the governor was generally praised for saving the island from destruction. It seemed unlikely that much controversy would ensue; this was just another in a long line of colonial rebellions put down with brutal force and then conveniently forgotten—except by its victims. But as more details began to emerge, opposition from liberals in England began to grow against Eyre's handling of the crisis, and by the end of 1865 the "Governor Eyre Case" had become the hottest topic of national debate.

A coalition of antislavery activists, radical politicians, and lawyers formed the Jamaica Committee, chaired by John Stuart Mill; public pressure led to the government sending a Royal Commission of inquiry to Jamaica to gather evidence on the uprising and its suppression. It delivered its report in April 1866, and while it broadly exonerated Eyre, it concluded that British and Jamaican troops had often used excessive force. The controversy raged throughout 1866, coinciding with the intense debates over parliamentary reform and the enfrancisement of the working classes in England—indeed, this was a connection that was frequently made at the time.

I argue in this essay that the relationship between national and imperial histories needs to be rethought. With "Britain"—or, still worse, "England"—no longer the unexamined organizing principle of cultural and historical studies, events in "the colonies" will have a relevance beyond their traditional marginal locations.

Affairs in the colonies will no longer be relegated to the discrete field of "imperial history" and to those rare moments in British national history when they happen to illuminate English questions. Thus, reversing the usual polarity of such comparisons, I suggest below that debate over the Second Reform Bill was so intense because it represented the entrance, however surreptitiously, of a new discourse of racial formation into the social fabric of England.

The 1860s were a time when constructions of race and class were undergoing substantial changes. A new scientific interest in race and descent combined with renewed political emphasis on equality of birth and the "rights of man" to produce a highly contradictory, unstable situation. An older discourse of "blood" and "breeding," associated with the "feudal and aristocratical constitution of society," as Arnold put it, was being replaced by a newer rhetoric of "citizenship" and "rights," a rhetoric which, nevertheless, incorporated elements of the older discourse in its emphasis on the "natural" disposition of particular groups, especially those which could be marked as racially other. Thus, by a circuitous route, "blood" made its reappearance in the new science of anthropology at precisely the moment it appeared to have lost its explanatory value in descriptions of English society: to quote Arnold again, "science has now made visible to everybody the great and pregnant elements of difference which lie in race".

The career of George Eliot exemplifies this transition, I might suggest, as she moved from the early novels' engagement with the domestic inheritance plot to the emphasis in her last novel, *Daniel Deronda* , on international and racial questions in which, paradoxically, individual destiny is more a question of blood and breeding than it ever was in *Silas Marner* . In the penultimate section of this essay I analyse her 1866 novel, *Felix Holt* , as enacting this transition from one literary and intellectual mode to the other.

This is also the movement that Etienne Balibar charts so accurately in an essay on the complex relationship between race and class in modern Europe:

The "bourgeois revolutions"... had raised the question of the political rights of the masses in an irreversible manner.... The idea of a *difference in nature* between individuals had become juridically and morally contradictory, if not inconceivable. It was, however, politically indispensable, so long as the "dangerous classes"... had to be excluded by force and by legal means from political "competence" and confined to the margins of the polity—as long, that is, as it was important to *deny them citizenship* by showing ... that they constitutionally "lacked" the qualities of fully fledged or normal humanity. Two anthropologies clashed here: that of equality of birth and that of a hereditary inequality which made it possible to re-naturalize social antagonisms. ("Class Racism" 209-10, emphasis in the original)

A quick glance at the pages of the *Anthropological Review* (founded 1863) will confirm that forcefully racist arguments were being made that people of African descent in particular "lacked the qualities of fully fledged or normal humanity." One effect of these arguments was to produce a racialized white Englishness, which allowed the white working class to be enfranchised at the expense of the black working class: citizenship and its concomitant rights were defined by racial (as well as national and class) demarcation. This is what Balibar means when he goes on to say that "the introduction of universal suffrage is moving the boundary line between 'citizens' and 'subjects' to the frontiers of nationality".

The Morant Bay rebellion, occurring at a moment of intense debate over the status and characteristics of "the negro," ensured the subjection of the Afro-Jamaican labouring classes; I hope to show that this is intimately connected to the granting of citizenship to English working-class men.

MORANT BAY AND THE EMERGENCE OF "HEREDITARIAN RACIALISM"

The revolt of October 1865 in and around the town of Morant Bay, on the southeastern coast of Jamaica, has garnered increasing attention from cultural critics and historians. Belatedly, critics have begun to move away from earlier polemics that hinged on the actions and character of the governor, Edward Eyre, in the suppression of the revolt. Philip Curtin, Bernard Semmel, and, more recently, Catherine Hall and Gad Heuman have laid the groundwork for a more careful analysis of the events in Jamaica and their aftermath that situates them in the context of contemporary debates over race, slavery, labour, and empire—debates in which Eyre himself appears more as symptom than as cause.

Such analyses, while avoiding the histrionics of earlier readings of "the Governor Eyre controversy," tend to agree that Morant Bay was an extremely significant event in British imperial history, despite being relatively minor in terms of numbers of casualties. Although the Sepoy Rebellion (the so-called Indian Mutiny) of 1857 and the New Zealand Land Wars (once called the Maori Wars) of the mid-1860s were far bloodier, it was Morant Bay that crystallized debate in Britain about the imperial mission itself.

Thus postcolonial scholars are coming to accept that Morant Bay was as important as people believed it to be at the time. The journalist and historian Justin McCarthy remembered in the 1870s that back in 1866, "for some weeks there was hardly anything talked of, we might almost say hardly anything thought of, in England, but the story of the rebellion that had taken place in the island of Jamaica, and the manner in which it had been suppressed and punished" (qtd. in Semmel 13). This was not mere journalistic hyperbole: it is indeed remarkable the extent to which a local rebellion in a British colony that had long ceased to be of the highest economic significance galvanized most of the major public figures of the day to take a stand on one side or the other. Defending the governor's methods on the executive committee of the Eyre Testimonial and Defence Fund were Ruskin and Carlyle, with Dickens offering vocal but more passive support.

On the other side, the chairman of the Jamaica Committee, set up to condemn the slaughter by British and Jamaican troops that followed the initial rebellion, was John Stuart Mill, who spent much of the next two years trying unsuccessfully to bring Eyre to trial on murder charges for the execution under martial law of the Jamaican politician George William Gordon. Supporting Mill were Huxley, Darwin, and Goldwin Smith, among others.

The events in Jamaica generated such an intense response, I would suggest, because they connected a longstanding concern in English middle-class society over the consequences of the abolition of slavery with newer debates around working-class enfranchisement and citizenship. Of course, these issues had never been entirely separable, as the ubiquity of the rhetoric of slavery and freedom in Chartist texts of the 1840s amply demonstrates. Indeed, the period of agitation leading up to the first Reform Bill of 1832 exactly coincided with the movement towards the abolition of slavery in all British territories (which itself followed a major slave revolt in the west of Jamaica).

This connection was sharpened by English responses to the U.S. Civil War, which was all too easily coded as a struggle between a modern, industrialized North and an antiquated, paternalistic South, in which the abolition of chattel slavery came to represent the triumph of all the forces of Progress, that imaginary Victorian behemoth. But beyond this historical link between abolition and liberal progress, what was new in the conjuncture of the mid-1860s was a widespread interest in questions of race, heredity, and breeding, which were then, after the publication of Darwin's *On the Origin of Species* in 1859, being transformed into *scientific* questions.

However, this was a moment of transition, and these scientific concerns continued to be marked by their former prominence in the realm of the literary romance genre, their realization in the tropes of inheritance, bloodlines, and genealogy. And it could even be argued that these new theories were doubly literary, because, as Gillian Beer argues in her magisterial analysis of the Darwinian revolution:

> Most major scientific theories rebuff common sense. They call on evidence beyond the reach of our senses or overturn the observable world. They disturb assumed relationships and shift what has been substantial into metaphor.... When it is first advanced, theory is at its most fictive. The awkwardness of fit between the natural world as it is currently perceived and as it is hypothetically imagined holds the theory itself for a time within a provisional scope akin to that of fiction. (*Darwin's Plots* 3)

It is this instability in meaning that allows us to locate and analyse these discourses of descent—of species, races, nations, families, individuals—in a whole range of mid-Victorian texts, from novels and cultural criticism to popular journalism and scientific articles. Such an analysis will serve as a kind of cross-section of a crucial moment in modern British history.

Morant Bay occurred at a moment when what we might call the "romantic" and the "scientific" understandings, to risk a convenient shorthand, of blood, race, and inheritance still overlapped. And at their point of intersection in the mid-1860s stood the figure of "the negro." Africans—especially those Africans who laboured under the legacies of chattel slavery—occupied a particular place in the emergence at this moment of what George Stocking has aptly called "hereditarian racialism" (*Victorian Anthropology* 142): that is, the notion that difference is hereditary (and therefore more or less fixed) and that the name for that difference is "race."

In 1863, a group of scientists led by James Hunt founded the Anthropological Society of London, bringing into the open a split within the older Ethnological Society of London, a division explicitly based on the status of "the negro," in particular, and on the importance of "race" in general. Hunt's inaugural address to the new body was at pains to stress the scientificity of the new discipline of anthropology, its adherence to a Gradgrindian positivism that sought only the facts and resisted the charms of non-scientific prejudices. Hunt's speech staked a claim for a huge field of inquiry: "Anthropology is ... the science of the whole nature of Man," he declared ("Introductory Address" 2). But within this field, the position of "the negro" is closed off before the inquiry has even begun:

Whatever may be the conclusion to which our scientific inquiries may lead us, we should always remember, that by whatever means the Negro, for instance, acquired his present physical, mental, and moral character, whether he has risen from an ape or descended from a perfect man, we still know that the Races of Europe have now much in their mental and moral nature which the races of Africa have not got.

As Hunt continued his address, he made it clear that when it came to "negroes" his fellow scientists were at liberty to disregard the conclusions to which their scientific inquiries might lead them—in particular, he wanted to avoid the "vulgar error that the Negro only differs from the European in the colour of his skin and peculiar hair". Quickly, the disingenuousness of that "for instance"—as in "the Negro, for instance"—becomes clear. The "negro" (and, as we shall see, the Jamaican "negro" in particular) was not merely one example among many in this new science; "he" became the very foundation of the science itself, in his exclusion from the project of civilization.

The political goals of the Anthropological Society were thus explicit from the start: the society claimed the mantle of science in an overt rejection of an older discipline linked to the antislavery movement. The Ethnological Society from which Hunt and his followers felt compelled to distance themselves had been founded back in the 1840s as an offshoot of the Aborigines Protection Society, one of the abolitionist and philanthropic organizations that formed the backbone of middle-class dissenting culture from the late eighteenth century onwards.

The motto of the APS was "*ab uno sanguine* " (of one blood), a reference to the biblical emphasis on the essential unity of humankind. There is obviously much common ground between this sentiment and the better known slogan of the abolitionist movement in Britain: "Am I not a man-and a brother?" (inscribed on images of an African man kneeling in chains). But by the time of Morant Bay in the mid-1860s a new idea of race had arrived to disrupt the Victorian antislavery consensus; the founding of the Anthropological Society was one example of this cultural shift. Homilies on the oneness of the human race were out of fashion. *The Morning Herald* , finding the time for analysis of the events in Jamaica as early as November 1865, discovered that a great change had taken place in English attitudes, because "the world-renowned question, once thought so convincing, of 'Am I not a man and brother?' would nowadays be answered with some hesitation by many—with a flat negative to its latter half by those who regard the blacks as an inferior race" (qtd. in Lorimer 198-9).

Delivering his annual presidential address to the Anthropological Society of London shortly after the outbreak at Morant Bay, James Hunt declared that:

We anthropologists have looked on, with intense admiration, at the conduct of Governor Eyre.... The merest novice in the study of race-characteristics ought to know that we English can only successfully rule either Jamaica, New Zealand, the Cape, China, or India, by such men as Governor Eyre.

Such revolutions will occur wherever the Negro is placed in unnatural relations with Europeans. Statesmen have yet to be taught the true practical value of race-distinctions, and the absolute impossibility of applying the civilisation and laws of one race to another race of man essentially distinct. Statesmen may ignore the existence of race-antagonism; but it exists nevertheless. ("Presidential Address" lxxviii)

This period witnessed the re-emergence of the long discredited theory of polygenism, which held that the various races of humankind had separate origins, and had developed as separate species which, all evidence to the contrary notwithstanding, were not fertile with one another. The ASL expended a great deal of intellectual energy on proving that races—especially the black and white races—were "essentially distinct." The irony, however, was that the hereditarian racialism peddled by the likes of Hunt relied heavily on the romantic concept of blood so central to the abolitionist movement they despised, and to the ethnologists they had split from.

A cartoon from *Punch*, contemporary with the Morant Bay controversy, conflating race, class, affiliation and national duty.

So analysis of the Jamaica events often had more in common with the inheritance plot of the romance novel than with the science of anthropology. *The Times* declared on November 18, 1865 that "though a fleabite compared with the Indian mutiny, it [Morant Bay] touches our pride more and is more in the nature of a disappointment.... Jamaica is our pet institution, and its inhabitants are our spoilt children" (qtd. in Bolt 77). A fortnight earlier, on November 4, 1865, as the first sketchy reports of the events in Jamaica were arriving in Britain, *The Times* recoiled at the ingratitude of the "negro":

> He, who has come in as the favoured heir of a civilization in which he had no previous share—he, petted by philanthropists and statesmen and preachers into the precocious enjoyment of rights and immunities which other races have been too glad to acquire by centuries of struggles, of repulses, and of endurance—he, dandled into legislative and official grandeur by the commiseration of England,—that he should have chosen ... to revolt ... this is a thing so incredible that we will not venture to believe it now. (qtd. in Bolt 87)

A great deal is condensed in this quotation. Since Carlyle's now notorious "Occasional Discourse on the Nigger Question" (1849) had popularized the figure of "Quashee" eating pumpkins and refusing to work, the myth of the lazy freedman had rapidly gained ground in Britain, carrying with it the literally incredible notion that Africans in the Caribbean had been "favoured" by emancipation. Included in this potent myth was the false perception that Africans had been given the vote in large numbers in those Caribbean islands, such as Jamaica, where some form of representative government was in operation ("dandled into legislative and official grandeur").

This motif of favouritism also refers to the idea that British abolitionism and philanthropy had concerned themselves with the poor and dispossessed overseas while ignoring British poverty "at home" (the ridiculous figure of Mrs. Jellyby in Dickens' *Bleak House* being the perfect example of this). Here the whole question of Caribbean wage labour in the post-emancipation period is displaced onto the discourse of family inheritance, with Afro-Jamaicans as the "favoured heirs" of British middle-class culture who fail to recognize their privilege. Their "precocious" access to the "rights and immunities" of civilization is explicitly contrasted with the hard labour ("struggles ... repulses ... endurance") of other, white races. Here the language of filiation and inheritance sits uneasily with the language of citizenship and rights; the romance novel vies with the science of political economy.

Thus we can begin to see how complicated is the relationship between the discourses of racial difference and working-class enfranchisement. The debate over the decline of the Jamaican economy, which was engaged once again after Morant Bay, concerned itself fundamentally with questions of capital and labour: after emancipation, did sugar plantations continue to fail because Afro-Jamaicans were unused to the discipline of wage labour, or because the planters failed to pay wages regularly and failed to invest capital in modernizing agricultural and industrial practices? When the black population withdrew its labour from the estates, were they working against their own economic interests or were they establishing themselves as an independent peasantry by saving money to buy small parcels of land and growing their own crops to sell in the Jamaican internal market?

However, these economic questions were constantly being supplemented by questions of race—did the Afro-Jamaican "character" disprove the fundamental tenet of political economy, that men would work to further their economic self-interest? And the emergence of the dogmatic physical anthropology of writers like James Hunt meant that this "character" could now be scientifically explained as a question of unmodifiable racial inheritance—Stocking's "hereditarian racialism." Such theories left "the negro" doomed by bloodlines to remain at the bottom of a static taxonomy of racial "types."

It is important to recognize that such a taxonomy implies the racialization of the white English also, and that the intersection of Reform and Jamaica only makes sense when viewed in this light. Edward Beesly, a prominent figure both on the Jamaica Committee and in the labour movement (and a close associate of Marx's in the First International), wrote to the labour newspaper *The Bee-Hive* in November 1865 the following response to the uprising in Morant Bay:

I protest I am no negro-worshipper. I don't consider a black man a beautiful object, and I daresay he sings psalms more than is good for him. Some negroes may be men of ability and elevated character, but there can be no doubt that they belong to a lower type of the human race than we do, and I should not really like to live in a country where they formed a considerable part of the population. But there is no reason why the negro should work cheaper for us because he is ugly. If the white labourer has a right to put a price on his labour, so has the black labourer. (qtd. in Lorimer 191)

The identity of the white and black labourers—the fact that capital treats them both as labour power from which value can be extracted—is riven by the assumption that black labourers "work for us," where "we" includes the white labourers whom Beesly claimed to represent. Thus Beesly can consider himself fortunate that he lives in a country where white labourers form a considerable part of the population. Here we might recall Etienne Balibar's contention that the extension of the franchise was "moving the boundary line between 'citizens' and 'subjects' to the frontiers of nationality" ("Class Racism" 210); the subjection of the Jamaican workers, who are of a lower racial "type," ensures the fantasmatic stability of the frontier of the country of England (from which blacks are happily absent). And inside these racial and national frontiers there opens up the possibility of citizenship for "white labourers."

GENEALOGY, ANTHROPOLOGY, AND HYBRIDITY

Ten years after Edward Beesly's comments in *The Bee-Hive,* George Eliot published *Daniel Deronda* , in which the following passage occurs, with its odd echoes of Beesly's letter:

The talk turned on the rinderpest and Jamaica.... Grandcourt held that the Jamaican negro was a beastly sort of baptist Caliban; Deronda said he had always felt a little with Caliban, who naturally had his own point of view and could sing a good song; Mrs Davilow observed that her father had an estate in Barbadoes, but that she herself had never been in the West Indies; Mrs Torrington was sure she could never sleep in her bed if she lived among blacks; her husband corrected her by saying that the blacks would be manageable enough if it were not for the half-breeds; and Deronda remarked that the whites had to thank themselves for the half-breeds.

This passage provides striking evidence of the prominence of the debate over Morant Bay at the time: ten years after the controversy had died down, Eliot could be reasonably sure that a brief allusion to Jamaica would allow her readers to date the conversation at Grandcourt's estate as late 1865 or early 1866, the last time that Jamaica had taken centre stage in British culture. Many of the issues addressed in this essay are contained within this intellectually allusive piece of narrative.

It is especially important here to trace the discourse of the inheritance of the "estate" in the debates over Jamaica, since this connects with my earlier claim that this older language of a caste privileged by blood returns in descriptions of racial formation in the 1860s. I think this language can be glimpsed in Beesly's patrician assumption that Afro-Jamaicans should be working "for us." And in Eliot's passing reference to Morant Bay in *Daniel Deronda* we can clearly see how the polite chatter at Grandcourt's estate connects plantation life in the West Indies with the world of the English aristocracy (and lesser gentry), in which the question of breeding and pedigree intersects with the question of miscegenation ("the whites had to thank themselves for the half-breeds").

This George Eliot passage bears striking witness to the mid-Victorian fascination with hybridity, in all its forms. In his book *Colonial Desire,* Robert Young has assembled a mass of cultural and historical evidence as proof that across a wide range of discourses, from the biological sciences to Victorian poetry, the spectre of the "hybrid" haunted the mid-nineteenth-century imagination in Britain. In particular, the new scientific racism dwelt at length on the troubling figure of the "mulatto." Paul Broca's influential work on human hybridity laboured mightily to show that the offspring of unions between Europeans and Africans were infertile with each other, although they were said to be fertile with either "parent race" (Broca 28-39).

This was a variant on the popular theory that hybrid human forms "reverted" to pure races after two or three generations, a theory invoked in an attempt to prove the permanence of racial "types," or, in extreme versions of this argument, to prove that different human "races" were in fact different species (the theory of polygenism). James Hunt, who modelled the Anthropological Society of London on Broca's Société anthropologique de Paris, argued torturously that it was not yet proven that "the offspring of all the mixtures of the so-called races of man are prolific.... At present it is only proved that the descendants of some of the different races of man are temporarily prolific; but there is the best evidence to believe that the offspring of the Negro and the European are not indefinitely prolific" (*Negro's Place* 24-5).

For Hunt, however, this desire to wish away the offspring of mixed race unions clashed with his belief in the improving powers of European blood. He explained the intelligence of Africans in the United States (which he "fully admit[ted]") as "owing to the mixture of European and Negro blood" rather than being explicable by environmental factors (*Negro's Place* 33), since the theory that human racial groups developed because of the social and climatic conditions they lived in was associated with the liberal abolitionist movement he so strenuously opposed. The debate between these two positions on racial formation was engaged most frequently and most explicitly at this time in writings on the Caribbean; we can see both sides of the argument conflated in Anthony Trollope's travelogue *The West Indies and the Spanish Main* (1859), which provides further evidence of this mid-Victorian obsession with the mulatto:

> My theory ... is this: that Providence has sent white men and black men to these regions in order that from them may spring a race fitted by intellect for civilization; and fitted also by physical organization for tropical labour....
>
> When civilization, commerce, and education shall have been spread; when sufficient of our blood shall have been infused into the veins of those children of the sun; then, I think, we may be ready, without stain to our patriotism, to take off our hats and bid farewell to the West Indies.

Trollope, in his outlandish celebration of the Jamaican "coloured" class, seems unable to decide between explanations based on environmental factors (civilization, commerce, education) and those based on mixing of blood. He is unsure whether to adopt an analytic framework based on the English class system, in which the "coloureds" would play the heroic role of a rising bourgeoisie, and one based on the new science of race, in which blood determines character and destiny.

Trollope's position may have appeared idiosyncratic, but in fact it was essentially the same as the Jamaica policy followed by the Colonial Office after emancipation was completed in 1838, although the ultimate goal of the British government was undoubtedly not Jamaican decolonization, as Trollope here suggests. Tired of the West India lobby's power in Parliament, and of the constant clashes between the Jamaican planters (who dominated the local House of Assembly) and the governor about who should have day-to-day control over the island's affairs, the Colonial Office tried to promote the interests of the island's merchant and professional class, the majority of whom were "coloureds," as a counterweight to the anachronistic power of the white planters.

This involved a delicate balancing act, since extending the franchise, for instance, to include more "coloureds" also risked empowering those elements in Jamaican society more sympathetic to the interests of the black peasantry. Thus there developed the anomalous situation that while the property qualifications for voting rights were gradually reduced (although the percentage of the population eligible to vote in Assembly elections remained minuscule at the time of Morant Bay), the restrictions on who could stand as candidates remained as onerous as ever. The number of African and multiracial Jamaicans holding Assembly seats never rose above fifteen out of 45; at the time of the 1865 rebellion, that number had been reduced still further, to twelve.

The controversy surrounding the events in Jamaica in October 1865 hinged on the execution of George William Gordon, a wealthy merchant and landowner renowned in Jamaica for his outspoken support for the black masses. Gordon was the representative in the House of Assembly of the district of St. Thomas-in-the-East where the uprising took place, an ardent and vocal opponent of the governor, Edward Eyre, and, significantly enough, a "coloured." After the governor had imposed martial law in the east of the island on hearing of the uprising, he had Gordon arrested in Kingston (where martial law was not in place) and transported by boat to Morant Bay where he stood trial before a court martial, with the flimsiest of evidence against him, was sentenced to hang, and then duly executed on Eyre's personal orders.

It was Eyre's scant regard for legal niceties, the perception that he had taken advantage of a chaotic situation to rid himself of a troublesome adversary, that outraged liberals and radicals in England and Jamaica. Thus the debate tended to focus on the character, and especially the family history, of George William Gordon, son of a planter father and a slave mother, who had been cast out of his father's house, had pulled himself up by his bootstraps and made his fortune at an early age, and then rescued his father from ruin when his sugar estate fell into bankruptcy. The uprising, about which Gordon apparently knew nothing in advance, was characterized crudely as a kind of personal feud between the governor and the radical politician.

The real story of the rebellion remained all but untold: the severe drought that had brought St. Thomas-in-the-East to the brink of famine; local dissatisfaction with the magistrates, who all represented planter interests, and punished petty crimes like crop theft severely (crimes that had increased as poverty grew); the desire of poor smallholders to maintain their tenuous hold on land to which they often held no legal title, versus wealthy landowners' attempts to extract rent from them and evict them if rent was not forthcoming.

All of this was lost in the polemics over Gordon's execution. His final letter to his wife (a highly respectable white woman) was a major propaganda coup for Eyre's critics in England; in it he declared his allegiance to the Queen, demonstrated Christian forgiveness for his persecutors, and generally behaved himself like a gentleman. The Baptist minister Wriothesley Noel felt "compelled to conclude that the hatred which hunted him to death was like that which crucified the Lord of glory as a blasphemer and a traitor". In only marginally more prosaic terms, Noel quotes Gordon's mother-in-law: "The late Mr. Gordon was bold as a lion in the cause of truth, but in domestic life, few, if any, could surpass him in urbanity of manner and kindness of disposition".

Rev. David King cites a fellow Presbyterian minister, Rev. H. Renton, as saying, "I never knew a man who seemed to me actuated by more honourable and unselfish and purer motives. He had an enthusiastic admiration of the British Constitution, and an exalted estimate of the dignity, rights, and privileges of British citizenship" (qtd. in King 8). Men such as these had no doubt, as an anonymous member of the Jamaican Assembly put it in a letter to the *Daily News* on February 5, 1866, that "Jamaica had a worthy and faithful son in him" (qtd. in Noel 6).

The language of filiation and inheritance seemed

inescapable in the furor over Gordon's death. In particular, opinion was sharply divided over Gordon's relationship with his father. On one hand, there were accounts of Gordon's filial devotion, despite his father's alleged hostility to his non-white children (which some claimed included banishment from his house). David King asserted that: "Through the reverses of the colony the father, from being very rich, came to lose all; and the coloured son bought his estate: not, however, to deprive him of it, but to leave him in occupancy, surrounded by the comforts he had been accustomed to enjoy. He always spoke to me with deferential regard for his father" (qtd. in Noel 3-4).

On the other hand, in an anonymous letter to *The Times*, "one who knew him for 21 years" claimed that "Mr. G.W. Gordon was a singular compound of opposites, a great pretender in religion, but one who altogether ignored the claims of truth and honesty. One who could expatiate eloquently on the sins of the people, and at the same time beat his own father and defraud all those who were so unfortunate as to place confidence in him" (Great Britain 245). And, as if to demonstrate that Gordon's dubious lineage had its corollary in his willingness to disinherit a child, Governor Eyre included among the 170 pages of documents vilifying Gordon that he gave to the Royal Commissioners a copy of an anonymous letter to the Jamaican *Colonial Standard*, claiming that Gordon had purchased half of "a thrown-up sugar estate," the other half of which was being held in trust "on behalf of an infant."

The letter maintained, moreover, that Gordon had proceeded to dismantle the sugar works and everything else "that was convertible into money" without even informing the trustees of his actions. The letter writer narrated this story to "expose what is really known of this said-to-be martyr." He concluded: "All feelings of delicacy towards Gordon's family must subside" (Great Britain 174).

This letter, showing by negation at least that the Gordon family romance was a story in the public domain, was published in Kingston on January 13, 1866. Three days later, on January 16, the gentlemen of the Anthropological Society of London held their fortnightly meeting (ladies were not allowed to become members of the ASL; in fact, the proposal that the Ethnological Society permit women to join had been one of the reasons for the split that had produced the ASL in 1863). There President Hunt informed the gathering that ASL stalwart William Pritchard "had been appointed special commissioner from the Anthropological Society of London, to inquire into the causes of the recent negro insurrection in Jamaica" ("Minutes" lxxxii).

Reassured that their views on the rebellion would be made known in official circles, therefore, the members sat back to listen to a scholarly paper entitled "Remarks on Genealogy in Connexion with Anthropology," by George Marshall. In his paper, later published in the *Memoirs* of the society, Marshall claimed that: "Genealogy, or the tracing of descent of individuals, and through them of nations, from some common progenitor, is a subject of vital importance to a society which includes among its various objects that of investigating the laws of man's origins and progress" (Marshall 68). It is no coincidence, I would maintain, that the public fascination with George William Gordon's "pedigree" is mirrored in this exactly contemporaneous debate on the uses of genealogy, as mid-Victorians attempted to work through the connection between the "descent of individuals" and of races and nations.

Balibar argues in his essay "The Nation-Form" that one of the striking features of a modern national culture is that, "except for a few genealogy 'fanatics' and a few who are 'nostalgic' for the days of the aristocracy, genealogy is no longer either a body of theoretical knowledge or an object of oral memory.... Today *it is the state which draws up and keeps the archive of filiations and alliances*" (101; emphasis in original). While this statement seems more persuasive in the French than the British context, as a general description of an historical shift it is unarguable.

What are we to make, therefore, of Marshall's assertion that "a taste for genealogy is a passion inherent in the whole human race. In all nations, civilised and uncivilised, in all times, ancient as well as modern, we find mankind carefully preserving the names and relationship of those from whom they claim descent"?

In fact, it seems clear that Marshall's paper is an attempt to graft a discipline in decline onto the new science of anthropology—another indication that the new scientific racism buttressed itself with the narratives of a passing hereditary aristocracy (which we can properly call "nostalgic"):

It is admitted that ethnology is an important part of anthropology; and are not ethnology and genealogy essentially the same? Have not the ethnologist and the genealogist the same object in view? If they differ, is it not only in this, that the ethnologist studies man by grouping him into different large races; whilst the genealogist seeks to know him more completely by studying him in individual families? The genealogist is, in fact, the architect who builds up the structure of the science of man, stone upon stone, and story upon story. He is the author who compiles the history of man, of which the ethnologist, like a reviewer, presents to the public a general sketch of the contents.

The literary metaphors ("author," "reviewer") and the emphasis on "story" demonstrate once more the superimposition of the "romantic" and "scientific" accounts of human descent.

The responses to Marshall's paper—as recorded in the minutes of the ASL—make fascinating reading. "Dr. Beigel observed that genealogy ... was in reality anthropology. What had hitherto been considered genealogy was nothing more than the determination of what man was the ancestor of another; what relation, in short, Tom was to Harry. But when they proceeded to consider what the physical condition of Tom was, that subject of inquiry became anthropology" ("Minutes" lxxvi). Rev. Dunbar Heath disagreed: "In considering the question, they should view the influence of lineal descent, as well as other influences distinct from it.... The external life of the mother, independent of the father, had no doubt great influence, but was there not something more than that? Was there not something in the race?" (lxxxvi-

lxxxvii). The role of the mother, so rarely even acknowledged in these discussions, is something I will return to in my analysis of *Felix Holt* ; here it serves momentarily to break apart the constellation of individual and "racial" descent, the bizarre assumption that heredity is a question of paternity only.

But other participants in the meeting failed to take up Heath's point, and continued to conflate the history of noble families with the make-up of human groups or "races." Augustus Goldsmid thought genealogy could usefully "show what influences that affect man's nature may be said to depend on external circumstances, and what are innate properties" (lxxxviii). The cases that he suggested might benefit from this genealogical analysis were, not surprisingly, those of noble families:

> One fact deserving of notice ... he would mention, the thickness of the lip of the members of the House of Hapsburg ... [which] was observable in almost every branch of the family. Another instance was that of a gentleman belonging to a great aristocratic family, who had one white lock of hair, though his hair was generally dark, which peculiarity had been transmitted to him from a distant ancestor. ("Minutes" lxxxviii)

Goldsmid's suggestions were immediately taken up by William Pritchard (who had just been appointed to take charge of the ASL's special mission to examine the causes of the Morant Bay rebellion, of course), who executed an apparently seamless transition from great aristocratic families to "natives":

> Mr. Pritchard stated that among the natives of the Pacific he had met with individuals who had a white lock amongst the surrounding dark hair, which was said to be hereditary. With respect to the question of consanguinity, he stated that there are many of the small or *atoll* islands in the Pacific where the natives trace back their origin through three or four hundred years to the few persons who, drifting from their homes, originally landed there. (lxxxviii)

Despite Dunbar Heath's note of caution, most of those

present found no difficulty in marrying their brand of physical anthropology (based largely on questions of blood and breeding) to the protocols of genealogical research. The meeting then adjourned, with President Hunt calling the members' attention to a special meeting of the ASL, "at which Captain Bedford Pim would read a paper on the causes of the Negro insurrection in Jamaica" ("Minutes" lxxxix). Demand for tickets had been so great that a larger room would have to be obtained for the meeting, Hunt proudly declared.

This intersection of genealogy, anthropology, and responses to the Morant Bay rebellion, I am suggesting, rests on more than a temporal coincidence. The flood of pamphlets, letters, and speeches about Jamaica in late 1865 and throughout 1866 occurred in the context of existing debates about the relation between the descent of individuals and races/nations. As William Pritchard suggested, the "question of consanguinity" became critical at this moment, where inheritance through blood was perceived to explain human culture in all its variety. Thus, at the moment when the Reform movement and the opposition to Governor Eyre were giving public weight to the figure of the citizen-subject and the rights of man, others were falling back on the premodern discourse of bloodlines and inheritance, which, after Darwin, bore the modern stamp of scientific method and enabled the citizen and the subject to be prised apart on the basis of racial difference.

I want to turn now to an examination of George Eliot's novel *Felix Holt*, a text in which this constellation of genealogy, inheritance, political rights, and race is everywhere strikingly apparent without ever being resolved into the simple binary oppositions that marked the polemics of the pamphleteers and anthropologists with whom she shared the public sphere.

READING FELIX HOLT AFTER MORANT BAY

George Eliot's novel *Felix Holt, the Radical* was first published in May 1866, at the height of the controversy over the suppression of the Morant Bay rebellion. By turning to *Felix Holt*, we can shed light on some of these entangled problems of race, genealogy, and descent. We can also show that this complex tale of English Reform intersects in more than fleeting ways with the questions raised by the events in Jamaica, despite the fact that Eliot never refers to the Caribbean in the novel. Eliot's engagement with the debate over the extension of the franchise turns, I argue, on the racially hybrid figure of Harry Transome, who inherits the country estate in the novel but cannot be allowed to inherit that larger and more precious estate, England. Thus this essay will return to the relationship between "slaves" and the "rank and file" with which it began.

Critics, if they have paid attention to *Felix Holt* at all, have tended to see it as a flawed, transitional novel of Eliot's, the subsidiary term in comparisons to the better novels which come before and after it. Thus the discovery that Esther is the true heir to the Transome estate, despite her humble station as Rev. Lyon's adopted child, is a recapitulation of Eppie's story in *Silas Marner*. Eliot's attempt to capture the web of relations in the provincial town of Treby Magna in the period of the First Reform Bill is seen as a precursor to the magnificence of *Middlemarch*. Raymond Williams expresses well the dissatisfaction most modern critics have felt in reading *Felix Holt*.

He observes that the novel "is made to turn on the inheritance of an estate, and this is a crucial surrender to that typical interest which preoccupied the nineteenth-century middle-class imagination". But this "surrender" is not the same as the easy, casual way that Trollope, for instance, handles the traditional settlements of the romance genre; rather it deforms the structure of the novel: "George Eliot, by contrast [with Trollope], questioning in a profoundly moral way the real and assumed relations between property and human quality, accepts the emphasis of inheritance as the central action, and then has to make it external, contradictory, and finally irrelevant".

The basic point here is that it is the very convolutedness of the inheritance plot that reveals its failure, in the 1860s, as symbol of the transmission of the national heritage. In

Disraeli's *Sybil, or the Two Nations* , to which *Felix Holt* is often compared, the hidden aristocratic lineage of Sybil must lead to the restitution of the estate to her: blood eventually "tells." In Eliot's novel, by contrast, the relationship between property and virtue has been irrevocably severed, and the whole edifice of patrilineal inheritance appears to be crumbling.

Not only does Esther ultimately reject her inheritance of the Transome estate, preferring the virtuous existence of an artisan's wife, but she is not even "really" a Transome, her legal claim stemming from her descent from the Bycliffe family, who have no "natural" claim to inherit the Transome estate. As Catherine Gallagher writes, in the best modern reading of the novel:

Indeed, Frederic Harrison, who advised Eliot on the legal intricacies of the plot, implored her to make Esther a real Transome so that her claim would carry the weight of nature as well as that of legality, but Eliot insisted on grounding Esther's claim also in legal conventions. Thus, although *Felix Holt* resembles *Sybil* in that a young woman is discovered, in the aftermath of a popular uprising, to be the heir to an estate, it reverses *Sybil* by making that young woman no more the natural heir to the estate than is the family she has the power to dispossess.

Disraeli needed to bind the naturally virtuous status of Sybil and her Chartist father to the institutional structures of the hereditary aristocracy; twenty years later, by contrast, George Eliot felt no compunction in poking fun at the claims of good breeding. The last surviving real Transome, poor, mad Tommy Trounsem, claims that "'I allays felt it inside me as I was somebody, and I could see other chaps thought it on me too'". However, this is patently false in the logic of the novel: although a certain pathos clings to Tommy, his fundamental role is to be trampled to death in the election-day riot so that Esther's non-natural right to the estate can be established.

Thus Eliot disregarded the advice of Frederic Harrison, a young barrister whom she met while working on the novel, and who advised her, as Gallagher notes, on the law of entail (that branch of inheritance law on which the plot of *Felix Holt* depends). The extended correspondence between the two is well known: not only does it provide rare insights into Eliot's thoughts during the composition of a novel, it also engages some key intellectual concerns of both Eliot's and Harrison's, especially the question of Comtism.

But critics have failed to notice the fact that at exactly the same time as Harrison was providing legal counsel to George Eliot, he was also serving on the executive committee of the Jamaica Committee, the body led by John Stuart Mill that protested the suppression of the Morant Bay uprising. Soon after *Felix Holt* was published, Harrison began his series of essays on martial law—a key question in the Jamaica events—later published as number 5 in the Jamaica Papers series: *Martial Law: Six Letters to the "Daily News"* (1867). So although Eliot and Harrison do not refer to the Jamaica rebellion in their letters, there is strong circumstantial evidence that the inheritance of the Transome estate in *Felix Holt* and the troubles in Jamaica must be connected.

The novel opens with Mrs Transome nervously awaiting the return from "the East" of her son Harold to take over the running of the Transome estate, now that her wild, "savage" older son Durfey has finally died and Harold is the heir apparent. (Harold has spent the last fifteen years acquiring a fortune in Smyrna, technically part of the Ottoman Empire but under de facto British control.) Mrs Transome's anxiety is magnified because Harold has only recently informed her "that he had been married, that his Greek wife was no longer living, but that he should bring home a little boy, the finest and most desirable of heirs and grandsons"; his mother's response to Harold's revelation of this long-kept secret was to tear up the letter "in a rage".

Mrs Transome's anger at this suppression of the place of women in questions of descent is in fact bitterly appropriate, since the reader eventually discovers that the arriviste lawyer Jermyn is Harold's biological father, and thus Harold's (and Harry's) descent and inheritance are entirely dependent on Mrs Transome. Thus right at the outset the novel undermines the traditional claims of patrilineal inheritance—Harold's belief that his mother was "a good elderly lady, who would necessarily be delighted with the possession on any terms of a healthy grandchild". The return of the prodigal son to take over the estate and save the nation is made possible by the relegation of Mrs Transome, who has been managing the estate up to this point, to the role of domestic ornament. Harold says to his mother, "'Ah, you've had to worry yourself about things that don't properly belong to a woman .... We'll set that right. You shall have nothing to do now but to be grandmamma on satin cushions'". Behind this suppression is the silent (and convenient) death of Harold's Oriental wife.

Harold returns from the Orient darker, wealthier, with a taste for spicy food, and with new ideas about politics and the role of women. These threads are all entangled in Eliot's Orientalism: Harold's decision to become a Radical shocks his Tory mother "as if her son had said that he had been converted to Mahometanism at Smyrna, and had four wives, instead of one son". Similarly, Harold's corruptibility, the fact that his Radicalism (unlike Felix Holt's) is veneer rather than a deeply held commitment, is signalled by his seduction by the delights of Oriental women: "Western women were not to his taste.... Harold preferred a slow-witted, large-eyed woman, silent and affectionate, with a load of black hair, weighing more heavily than her brains.

He had seen no such women in England, except one whom he had brought with him from the East". The narrator makes this observation at the moment when the possibility arises of Harold and Esther getting married, thus resolving the problem of the inheritance plot with a union straight out of the romance genre. But Eliot refuses the easy way out: Harold's Orientalism is utterly incompatible with Esther's independence of spirit. She is tempted, "but it was a fact that Harold's previous married life had entered strongly into her impressions about him. The presence of Harry made it inevitable". Harold tries to woo her: "'You don't suppose, I hope, that any other woman has ever held the place that you could hold in my life?'"; as proof of this sentiment he delivers the revelation that opens up *Felix Holt* to the debates over Morant Bay: "'Harry's mother had been a slave—was bought, in fact'".

The careful use of the pluperfect tense—"had been"—and the passive voice—"was bought"—leaves nicely ambiguous Harold's proprietary relationship to his wife. On the one hand, Harold is aligned squarely with the slaveholding planters of the Caribbean who kept, and indeed owned, black mistresses but eventually married respectable white women of their own class. On the other hand, the syntax allows the reader to interpret Harold's relationship with his wife as an act of abolitionist philanthropy, a white man saving a native woman from Oriental despotism.

Although slavery is displaced from the Caribbean to Turkey in Eliot's novel, the "presence of Harry" in the novel comes from the same source as the controversy over George William Gordon and the Jamaica uprising. In February 1866, while George Eliot was finishing *Felix Holt* and England was convulsed by the Governor Eyre case, Dr. Hyde Clarke delivered a paper at the Anthropological Society of London entitled "On Anthropological Investigations in Smyrna," where he was the ASL's local secretary and where Harold Transome made his fortune and met his wife:

Many examples of mixed races are found here, particularly of Negro mulattoes and Levantines, or the mixture of Europeans with the natives of the country. The latter afford the most beautiful women in the first, and occasionally in the second, generation; but there is undoubted evidence that neither of the mixed races is permanent.... It is curious that, though the Levantine is a cross-breed chiefly among the Indo-Europeans, the third and fourth generations produce many of the phenomena of Negro cross-breeds, as seen in the West Indies and South America.

Unwittingly, no doubt, George Eliot finds herself sharing the same field as the new physical anthropologists, with their heavy-handed Orientalism and their fascination with the figure of "the negro." In other words, the trouble with Harry is that he is a mulatto. Eliot gives very little narrative time to the ultimate heir of the Transome estate, but in Harry's irregular appearances he is consistently portrayed as violent and wild. We see him first through the eyes of the Debarrys (sole representatives of the old aristocracy in *Felix Holt*): Lady Debarry initially mistakes him for "'a charming little fellow...[a] round-cheeked cherub'".

But she is soon disabused, as Harry sinks his teeth into Mrs Transome's arm: "'What a little savage!'", Lady Debarry quickly corrects herself; and then, when she has had time to reflect a little: "'That savage boy—he doesn't look like a lady's child'". Lady Debarry is right the second time around. It may no longer be possible, in the age of Reform and industrialization, to be sure what a lady's child looks like; we cannot rely on genealogy to tell the truth about good breeding any more. But there can be no doubt, in the age of anthropology, as to the characteristics of the savage.

The problem this poses for the novel, however, is insuperable. Although Harry's filiation is almost the only line of descent in the book that is not in doubt, there is such uneasiness about Harry that he and his father almost never appear together. When Harold first arrives back at Transome Court and his mother asks him about his son, Harold replies casually, "'O, I left him behind in town.... My man Dominic will bring him, with the rest of the luggage'". In this narrative distancing, I think we can read the trace of George William Gordon's expulsion from his father's house.

The overelaborate inheritance plot that takes up so much of *Felix Holt* is ultimately resolved by the estate being passed on to Harry, but the novel makes so little of this denouement that the reader is forced to conclude that this half of the book's plot is finally irrelevant, as Raymond Williams put it. Once we recognize that Harry is the son of a slave, however, we are in a better position to read this narrative incoherence. In a climate in which *The Times* could write scathingly of Afro-Jamaicans as the "favoured heirs" of British middle-class culture, George Eliot shows the ultimate worthlessness of the country house as a symbol for the national heritage by having its heir be the son of a slave mother.

Thus *Felix Holt* ends by proving the truism delivered by the coachman in the "Author's Introduction" to the novel, that "property didn't always get into the right hands". Such a reading would seem to divide the novel in two: first, the Transome Court plot, with its roots in the traditional inheritance narrative and its branches intersecting with contemporary race theory; second, the Felix and Esther plot, which concerns itself most directly with Reform and political rights for the English working classes. But, as I have argued throughout this essay, questions of class and citizenship in the mid-1860s cannot be kept separate from questions of race and breeding.

Thus Felix applauds the Chartist speaker who gets up in front of the crowd at Treby Magna and denounces the "slave's share" the workers have at present, calling instead for a "freeman's share" of the nation's wealth. However, for Felix Holt, and for George Eliot, rights ought not to accrue to men simply on the basis of their being born free. Felix follows the Chartist speaker up on to the podium and proceeds to lecture the assembled masses on the dangers of premature democracy, exhorting them not to mistake the benefits of the vote—which he calls, in perfect Arnoldian language, a mere "engine"—for the more lasting gifts of wisdom, education, and virtuous living.

As he comments to Esther a little while earlier, "'I want to be a demagogue of a new sort; an honest one, if possible, who will tell the people they are blind and foolish, and neither flatter them nor fatten on them'". Catherine Gallagher argues that Felix represents a vision of Matthew Arnold's "best self," the man of culture he idealizes in *Culture and Anarchy* (Gallagher 244). And this speech of Felix's sounds uncannily like the lecture Matthew Arnold delivered a year later at Oxford, entitled "Culture and Its Enemies," later to become the first chapter of *Culture and Anarchy* :

Culture ... does not try to teach down to the level of inferior classes; it does not try to win them for this or that sect of its own, with ready-made judgments and watchwords. It seeks to do away with classes; to make the best that has been thought and known in the world current everywhere.... This is the social idea; and the men of culture are the true apostles of equality.

However, Felix differs from Arnold's man of culture in that he does not become the déclassé "alien" of *Culture and Anarchy*. Instead, Felix continually insists on his class identity; his virtue lies in his determination to remain an artisan: "'I mean to stick to the class I belong to'". His status as *artisan* is crucial here. The factory hands and agricultural labourers of Treby Magna represent the emergence into the public sphere of a new class, the proletariat; George Eliot's worker-hero represents an anachronistic understanding of caste that owes more to the outmoded language of blood and breeding than to the language of rights and citizenship that accompanies advanced capitalism.

So that when Felix continues his speech to Esther about wanting to be a new type of demagogue by saying "'I have my heritage—an order I belong to. I have the blood of a line of handicraftsmen in my veins'", we know that this is an anachronistic sentiment, a trace of nostalgia for a vanishing segment of the population. But I want to push this line of thinking one step further. The invocation of blood here, in the section of the novel primarily concerned with domestic Reform, is also a statement transposed from the new hereditarian discourses of race that I analyzed above.

And so we can argue that the two halves of *Felix Holt* are not as distinct as they have seemed to most critics and readers. The "blood of a line of handicraftsmen" that Felix embodies is not so different from the wild blood that determines the character of young Harry, whose inheritance of the estate is eclipsed by the birth of "a young Felix" on the last page of the novel.

The new way of talking about race in the mid-1860s allows "blood" to resurface as a meaningful concept; it even reflects back onto those class distinctions it would seem unable to explain now that "family" and "breeding" are no longer self-evidently positive. Thus the narrator comments on Esther's anticipation of the problems she will encounter in talking to

Harold Transome about Felix: She had a native capability for discerning that the sense of ranks and degrees has its repulsions corresponding to the repulsions dependent on differences of race and colour; and she remembered her own impressions too well not to foresee that it would come on Harold Transome as a shock, if he suspected that there had been any love-passages between her and this young man, who to him was of course no more than any other intelligent member of the working class.

The differences between Harold Transome, who represents the English gentry's inability to adjust to the changes associated with Reform, and Felix, the new symbol of honest, hard- working Englishness, can most easily be explained by comparison with "differences of race and colour"—and these distinctions, the narrator implies, are not open to question. This is the equivalent of Matthew Arnold's statement that "science has now made visible to everybody the great and pregnant elements of difference which lie in race", a statement, we should recall, in the service of the author's classification of the English class system into Barbarians, Philistines, and Populace.

Thus we have found, in the unlikely setting of *Felix Holt* 's study of provincial life, proof of the saturation of discourses of citizenship and Reform by questions of race, genealogy, and descent. We have traced the outlines of the debate over the Jamaica rebellion in George Eliot's novel, providing further evidence of the complex and interlocking relationship between "slaves" and "the rank and file" in the British Empire of the mid-1860s.

INHERITING THE EMPIRE

The third quarter of the nineteenth century often used to be characterized by historians as the period of "anti-imperialism," when prominent intellectual figures like John Bright and Goldwin Smith publicly called for the independence of "the Colonies," which were seen as a financial and military drain on the resources of England. This notion of anti-imperialism has more recently given way to an understanding of the continuities in British imperial policies, the fact that the empire expanded throughout the nineteenth century (in both its formal and informal incarnations), and a recognition that those who advocated the independence of the white settler colonies never even considered the possibility that British dependencies peopled predominately by non-whites ought to govern themselves.

However, without wanting to endorse the idea of mid-Victorian anti-imperialism, I would suggest that this period needs to be rethought once more in the light of the Jamaica events and the responses to them. In short, it is my argument here that when the possibility emerges of the end of British rule over the declining colony of Jamaica, the spectre of the end of imperial hegemony arises. And the response to this threat is to conceive, for the first time, of the Empire as a whole, no longer insisting on the distinctions between the Colonial Empire, the Indian Empire, Crown Colonies, and other dependencies.

It is only in the mid-1860s that Victorian writers began to talk of the British Empire in the sense that seems so familiar to us now. Richard Koebner, in his meticulous study of the changing significance of the word "imperialism," notes that during the first 30 years of Queen Victoria's reign the term "British Empire," if it was used at all, "was governed by the interpretation which related the name to the United Kingdom of the British Isles and to England in particular" (Koebner and Schmidt 45). The common phrase "Imperial Parliament" referred primarily to England's hegemony over Scotland, Wales, and, more particularly, Ireland, which after the Act of Union of 1800 sent "representatives" to sit in the House of Commons in London.

Thus, in a way which seems distinctly counterintuitive to those of us at the other end of the British Empire, "the Colonies and the Indian Empire were regarded as dependent on the British Empire rather than being parts of it" (Koebner and Schmidt 37). In 1865, Jamaica was in the anomalous position of being a colony not generally included in the phrase "the Colonies," which tended to encompass only the white settler territories (although administratively it was part of the domain of the Colonial Office). Paradoxically, therefore, the fact that Jamaica was unassimilable to the standard contemporary discourses of imperialism enabled it to become the locus of the construction of the Empire.

The Morant Bay uprising, far more than the Sepoy Rebellion of 1857 to which it was (and is) often compared, crystallized concern on questions of governance, citizenship, and rights, both "domestic" and "imperial," and in so doing inaugurated the new era of "the Empire." Perhaps we can read this awkward transition in the letter from Carlyle I alluded to in the opening paragraph of this essay. After opining that "penalty and clamour are not the thing this Governor merits from any of us, but honour and thanks, and wise *imitation* (I will farther say) should similar emergencies arise, on the great scale or on the small, in whatever we are governing!" (Workman 91-2), Carlyle goes on to pledge his active support for the campaign so that

> by wise effort and persistence, a blind and disgraceful act of public injustice may be prevented [i.e., the prosecution of Eyre brought by the Jamaica Committee]; and an egregious folly as well,—not to say, for none can say or compute, what a vital detriment throughout the British empire, in such an example set to all the colonies and governors the British Empire has.

Here, as Carlyle piles clause upon clause with his characteristic rhetorical abandon, we can detect the instability of meaning between the lower-case "empire"—which seems to approximate the more modern concept—and the capitalized "Empire"—which "has" colonies and governors that, nevertheless, do not seem to be a part of it.

The solution that Carlyle proposes to this crisis of British imperialism is a throwback to the romance inheritance plot that George Eliot struggled to leave behind in *Felix Holt*. In *Shooting Niagara: And After?* (1867), his tirade against democratic government and the "knot of rabid Nigger-Philanthropists" who made up the Jamaica Committee, Carlyle devotes several pages to the island of Dominica. ("Jamaica," he claims implausibly, "is an angry subject, and I am shy to speak of it".) He elaborates a fantasy scenario, in which

the Queen "in Council"...[will] pick out some gallant-minded, stout, well-gifted Cadet, - younger son of a Duke, of an Earl, of a Queen herself ... and say to him...., "See, I have scores on scores of 'Colonies,' all ungoverned, and nine-tenths of them full of boa-constrictors, rattlesnakes, Parliamentary Eloquences, and Emancipated Niggers ripening towards nothing but destruction: one of them *you* shall have, you as Vice-King; on rational conditions, and *ad vitam an culpam* it shall be yours (and perhaps your posterity's if worthy)."

Carlyle suggests a model of governance based on the protocols of inheritance rooted in the structural power of the hereditary aristocracy in England; I have argued in this essay that this residual conception of society fueled the emergent discourses of anthropology and racial science. However, the new concept of Empire marks the beginning of the end of the inheritance plot as a trope for what we must now call governmentality. Joseph Howe, in a little pamphlet called *The Organization of the Empire* (1866), signals the end of this older discourse of empire, one which assimilates the relationship between "mother" country and colony to a family affair. Some people, he says, argue that colonies "grow up" and should therefore receive independence:

The parental relationship is assumed to sanction this policy. Young men grow, and, when they are of age, marry and set up for themselves, and why should not colonies do the same. But the analogy is not perfect. One house would not hold all the married members of a large family, nor one estate maintain them. They scatter that they may live. They are kept in friendship by the domestic affections, and personal ties, which in respect of distant communities, do not exist, and at the death of the founder of the family there is an estate to divide.

Not so with Colonies. Their life begins at a distance from the homestead. There are few personal attachments. There is no estate to divide, and no security that when they separate they may not drift into antagonism to each other, and to the parent colony. The old metaphors are worn out, Howe is arguing. The inheritance of an estate, be it Transome Court, an "ungoverned colony" like Jamaica, or the estate of "the Empire," can no longer signify the mode of English power after the 1860s. Instead, the practice of imperialism, in its late Victorian manifestation of a mission to educate and civilize "backward peoples," emerges, paradoxically enough, in the writings of those mid-Victorian liberals who advocated equal rights for whites and blacks and the extension of the franchise and citizenship to the working classes in England. Frederic Harrison, for instance, George Eliot's collaborator on *Felix Holt* , can be heard bringing this new Empire into being in his treatise on martial law written to protest the suppression of the Jamaica revolt:

> In the name of the people, of the great family of citizens of the British empire, it again becomes vital to crush the pretensions of the executive abroad; it becomes necessary to vindicate beyond the seas the first principles of civil liberty.... This is why an association of Englishmen has undertaken to bring this cause to an issue [i.e., by prosecuting Eyre]... simply to hear from the lips of an English judge what is the right to civil justice of English citizens, what are the safeguards of life throughout the breadth of our vast empire.

The repetition of Englishness here (Englishmen, English judge, English citizens) appears to be in opposition to the principle of formal equality that Harrison celebrates. The "people," the "family of citizens"—the genealogical term persists as a link to the discourses Harrison was ostensibly refuting—for whom these "Englishmen" speak are marked as subjects as well as citizens in this unstable equation. Defended against the unlawful force of the executive power, they become subject to a new kind of discipline, one formed through education, church missions, public health policies, and the apparatus of civil law: "The precise issue we raise is this—that throughout our empire the British rule shall be the rule of law; that every British citizen, white, brown, or black in skin, shall be subject to definite, and not to indefinite powers".

In this strategy for managing what he calls "our vast

unresting empire", Harrison is taking up the definition of empire of his fellow executive committee member of the Jamaica Committee, Goldwin Smith. Back in 1863, Smith had written in the foreword to a collection of his pieces from the *Daily News* , given the title *The Empire* for its book publication:

The term Empire is here taken in a wide sense, as including all that the nation holds beyond its own shores and waters by arms or in the way of dominion, as opposed to that natural influence which a great power, though confining itself to its own territories, always exercises in the world. In the case of our Empire this definition will embrace a motley mass of British Colonies, conquered Colonies of other European nations, conquered territories in India, military and maritime stations, and protectorates, including our practical protectorate of Turkey [where Harold Transome struck it rich, of course], as well as our legal protectorate of the Ioanian islands. These various dependencies stand in the most various relations to the Imperial country.

Koebner and Schmidt comment on the novelty of this definition, arguing that "by making the name of Empire the comprehensive headline of a critical survey of colonial, Indian, and certain external affairs, the author [Smith] was not so much referring to an established terminology as intending to create such usage on his own account". I would argue that the better known beginnings of the imperial federation movement in the late 1860s—for instance the founding of the Colonial Society in 1868, with its motto "United Empire"—are made possible by the efforts of liberal thinkers such as Smith and Harrison; that the call for an integrated empire begins with the invocation of formal equality before the law.

This gesture may even be explicitly anti-imperialist, as when Goldwin Smith argues for the independence of Canada, but covertly the expansion of English law around the empire works to consolidate the very inequalities that English rule works by at the same time as it establishes a formal discourse of equality, rights, and citizenship. That this new imperial apparatus of discipline and surveillance emerges in the aftermath of the controversy over Morant Bay can be seen clearly in the writing of Charles Roundell, who had acted as secretary to the Royal Commission of inquiry while it collected its thousands of pages of evidence in Jamaica in 1866.

Later that same year, he published a pamphlet of his own, *England and Her Subject Races, with Special Reference to Jamaica*, in which he extrapolated from the Jamaica situation to provide a blueprint for the organization of the Empire as a whole. The rebellion of 1865, he concluded, showed the need for "an impartial and trusted administration of justice" and a system of "regulating native settlements":

> The principal agents for effecting these primary requirements will be an efficient police, the enactment of a bastardy law, a systematic registration of births and deaths, the establishment of hospitals and a well-organized system of medical supervision, the construction of roads, the instruction of the people in improved methods of agriculture, and, above all, a system of industrial, compulsory, unsectarian education.

The problem of descent, inheritance, and miscegenation will be handled by a bastardy law, the state will take over the genealogical enterprise of recording births and deaths, and the emphasis on compulsory state education is in line with the thinking of Matthew Arnold; here we can see the outlines of a theory of late Victorian high imperialism. From the minor rebellion at Morant Bay, via the agitation for parliamentary reform, there emerges this checklist for the constitution of a new (but to us familiar) figure: the citizen-subject of the British Empire.

Following the critical and popular success of *Scenes of Clerical Life* in 1858, George Eliot (pseudonym of Mary Ann, or Marian, Evans) published *Adam Bede* to further acclaim. Having gained recognition for the realistic characters and situations in the three sketches comprising *Scenes*, Eliot again sought to create complex characters who display a range of traits, neither all good nor all bad. A pastoral novel, *Adam Bede* is set at the turn of the nineteenth century and presents realistic images of daily life in a quiet rural community. However, within this apparently peaceful, simple country world, Eliot's character-narrator tells a story of unfulfilled love and selfishness resulting in tragedy and hard-won self-awareness. Through the narrator, the middle-class reading audience is encouraged to look upon the novel's lower-class characters with the same sensibility and sensitivity as they would their peers. Rather than expressing superiority or contempt for the rural people in the novel, readers are invited by the narrator to set aside class or economic biases and view the characters in *Adam Bede* in light of their humanity and goodness.

Discussing *Adam Bede* in her personal journals, Eliot cautiously confessed that the character of Adam was inspired by her own father's early life, and the character of Dinah was drawn from her Methodist Aunt Samuel. She insisted, however, that the novel was not biographical beyond those initial inspirations. These same journals, along with her published essays and reviews, have led critics to argue that *Adam Bede* reflects themes in other literary works with which she was familiar, including Milton's *Paradise Lost*, Hawthorne's *The Scarlet Letter*, and the Greek Tragedies, among others. However, according to Eliot, she did not intend *Adam Bede* as a memoir or even as historical fiction; it was her most earnest intent to write realistic fiction at a time when realism was "out of fashion." *Adam Bede*, considered by her contemporaries to display "a touch of genius," has been overshadowed in twentieth-century criticism by the more mature *Middlemarch*. Nevertheless, its reputation has remained untarnished and many scholars regard *Adam Bede* as one of the finest examples of realistic fiction of its time.

Adam Bede is set in the rural community of Loamshire, England, in the summer of 1799. Adam Bede, the eponymous main character, and his younger brother Seth are employed as carpenters. Seth is well-meaning and generous while Adam, who serves as foreman to the crew of rustics who assist him, is serious and hard-working. Outwardly, Adam is a role model for the community, but inwardly he is plagued by resentment towards his alcoholic father and annoyance with his ever-complaining mother. Seth is a devout Methodist who practices his religion over the objections of both his family and the larger community. He is in love with Dinah Morris, a solemn Methodist preacher who, though demure and feminine, refuses to allow her religious mission to be compromised by her gender. Her quiet confidence attracts significant attention in Loamshire, and, in part, fuels Seth's affection. Meanwhile, Adam hopes one day for the financial security to be able to ask Hetty Sorrel, a distractingly beautiful and childishly self-centered young woman, to be his wife. While Dinah refuses Seth's romantic affections believing her duty is to minister to the unsaved, Hetty is deliberately distant and coquettish, while at the same time encouraging Adam's hopes for an eventual union. Although the two women are entirely different in character and morals, their lives are nevertheless entwined; both are orphaned cousins staying with their relations, the Poysners, a prominent tenant farming family.

Like the Poysners, the entire community operates under the patronage of the elderly landowner, Squire Donnithorne. His grandson Arthur, without an income of his own as long as his grandfather remains alive, looks benevolently upon Loamshire as his birthright. He imagines himself making improvements to the land and gaining the love of all his tenant farmers through his generosity and earnestness. But until he gains his inheritance, he is powerless and becomes bored and frustrated with his grandfather's mismanagement of the land. Seeking distraction, he discovers Hetty. While he is drawn to her beauty, she is equally drawn to his social position and the promise of being rescued from domestic servitude to live as the wife of a wealthy, respected man.

Hetty becomes deluded about the nature of their relationship, and Arthur is torn between his determination to live up to his social position and his desire for the young woman. At a pivotal moment, the couple is caught in an embrace by Adam who, despite his inferior social standing, challenges Arthur over the indiscretion. Adam, heartbroken, loses his faith in his long-time friend Arthur, but becomes more protective of Hetty. Shortly after Adam's discovery, Arthur ends the affair and leaves town, and Hetty turns to Adam for comfort. He takes her back, and joyously plans their life together. However, haunted by her scandalous behaviour, Hetty discovers that she is pregnant and, unable to take responsibility for her actions, runs away.

Alone, Hetty gives birth to a child, whom she abandons in the wilderness. Her crime is discovered, and she is sentenced to death for infanticide. Adam refuses to believe she could have committed such a crime, and Hetty herself refuses to confess. Arthur, who left the country immediately following the affair, has not been heard from, and Hetty is left with only the comfort of her cousin Dinah. Arthur returns with a stay of execution just in time to save Hetty from death. Through the course of his love and loss of Hetty, Adam learns sympathy and forgiveness, and thus becomes a better person than he was at the start of the novel. With this change, Adam is rewarded with marriage to Dinah, who gives up her ministry in favour of domestic life.

While *Adam Bede* centers around the title character's progress from a calloused sense of moral superiority to a state of sympathy and understanding for others, there are several other significant themes. *Adam Bede* is widely recognized as a pastoral novel dealing with rural farm life and country people. Attentions to the everyday details of butter-making, berry-picking, and cattle-herding, far away from the political and economic changes of an industrialized society, lend the story a sense of innocence and peacefulness. However, as England crossed from the eighteenth to nineteenth century, the pastoral peace enveloping the Loamshire countryside is disrupted by Hetty and Arthur's affair. The pastoral setting underscores the transition of English society from relative innocence to experience, leaving Eliot's readers nostalgic for simpler times.

In addition, issues of religion, while not at the forefront of the novel, are nonetheless present. Dinah's evangelical Methodist preaching is set against Reverend Irwine's staid traditional church leadership. In the midst of this doctrinal difference, moral weaknesses abound and neither religious leader is able to save Hetty and Arthur from their lack of moral judgement. While Eliot avoids religious sermonizing, the lack of spiritual intervention on behalf of the lovers demonstrates her greater concern with the state of religion in nineteenth-century England and hints at her own religious dissent.

Eliot's use of realism in the novel is also significant. The realistic portrayal of both her characters and situations is reinforced by her pointed description of Dutch genre painting in Chapter 17 of the novel. Dutch painting was considered a low art form by Eliot's contemporaries, not because the technique was inferior, but because the subject matter failed to conform to the aesthetic ideal of beauty so favored by critics and consumers alike. By embracing this genre of painting, where commoners engaged in common tasks were presented in great detail, Eliot attempted to justify her own representation of "common, coarse people."

Immediately recognized as a significant literary work, *Adam Bede* has enjoyed a largely positive critical reputation since its publication. An anonymous review in *The Athenaeum*in 1859 praised it as a "novel of the highest class," and *The Times* called it "a first-rate novel." Contemporary reviewers, often influenced by nostalgia for the earlier period represented in *Bede*, enthusiastically praised Eliot's characterizations and realistic representations of rural life. Charles Dickens wrote: "The whole country life that the story is set in, is so real, and so droll and genuine, and yet so selected and polished by art, that I cannot praise it enough to you." In fact, in early criticism, the tragedy of infanticide has often been overlooked in favour of the peaceful idyllic world and familiar personalities Eliot recreated.

Other critics have been less generous. Henry James, among others, resented the narrator's interventions. In particular, Chapter 15 has fared poorly among scholars because of the author's/narrator's moralizing and meddling in an attempt to sway readers' opinions of Hetty and Dinah. Other critics have objected to the resolution of the story. In the final moments, Hetty, about to be executed for infanticide, is saved by her seducer, Arthur Donnithorne. Critics have argued that this deus ex machina ending negates the moral lessons learned by the main characters. Without the eleventh hour reprieve, the suffering of Adam, Arthur, and Hetty would have been more realistically concluded. In addition, some scholars feel that Adam's marriage to Dinah is another instance of the author's/narrator's intrusiveness. These instances have been found to directly conflict with the otherwise realistic images and events of the novel.

This act of textual suppression was singularly unsuccessful, because J. Dover Wilson restored the excised lines in the edition of *Culture and Anarchy* that has remained the most popular since its publication in 1932.

Arthur Penrhyn Stanley was Thomas Arnold's biographer. The letter in question does not appear in Stanley's *Life and Correspondence of Thomas Arnold*.

Robert Young, in his compelling analysis of Matthew Arnold, also hears the trace of rebellion in Jamaica in these lines: "Though Arnold refused to take sides in the bitter controversy about Governor Eyre's conduct, his comments in *Culture and Anarchy* about the correct way to deal with rioting ('flog the rank and file and fling the ringleaders from the Tarpeian Rock!') more or less describes what happened to those in Jamaica after the Morant Bay uprising four years previously". The connection between Jamaica and Reform is reinforced by the passage in *Culture and Anarchy* immediately following the deleted lines, in which Arnold declares that "monster-processions in the streets and forcible irruptions into the parks ... ought to unflinchingly forbidden and repressed," even when they are in support of "undoubtedly precious" causes "such as the abolition of the slave-trade". Matthew Arnold, like his father before him, was strongly opposed to slavery; the same could not be said of Thomas Carlyle.

The best accounts of Morant Bay in the context of Jamaican history are Heuman and Holt; see also Curtin and Bakan. V.S. Reid's novel *New Day* is a fine fictionalized account of Morant Bay, celebrating the uprising as the awakening of Jamaican national resistance to British imperialism; *New Day* is often one of the set texts for Jamaican secondary school literature exams. The standard account of the Eyre case in England, although it now appears rather dated, remains Semmel. The best historiographical work on this intersection of Jamaican and British affairs in the 1860s is the writing of Catherine Hall, especially her essay "Rethinking Imperial Histories." Although our theoretical approaches are different, Hall's work has greatly influenced the development of my own.

Robert Young has written the best account to date of the ways in which Arnold's classification of English social classes into Barbarians, Philistines, and Populace is heavily indebted to the racial (and racist) theories of Renan, Gobineau, and de Thierry—the same writers who are constantly cited by the British anthropologists of the 1860s I discuss below.

This connection, however, is not as clear cut as Balibar implies in his neat formula. The Second Reform Bill by no means instituted "universal suffrage," as Balibar seems carelessly to imply here. John Stuart Mill's amendment to the Bill replacing the word "man" with "person" was easily defeated in Parliament, and a property qualification remained in place, showing that women and the poor were still considered inherently incapable of exercising political responsibility.

The committee was later renamed the Eyre Defence and Aid Fund. Although accounts often assume that Carlyle was the driving force behind the group, in fact he left much of the day-to-day running of affairs to others, especially Ruskin and Hamilton Hume, Eyre's first biographer. See Workman; Hall, "Economy."

On Mill's involvement see Hall, "Economy"; Semmel.

On the connections between working-class and black emancipation, see Gallagher, especially Chapter 1, "Workers and Slaves: The Rhetoric of Freedom in the Debate over Industrialism."

On the Anthropological Society of London, see below. Good historical accounts of the society can be found in Stocking, "What's in a Name?"; Rainger; and Young.

Robert Young develops a similar argument in his analysis

of Gobineau, whose *Essay on the Inequality of Human Races* (1853-5) was just becoming known to English audiences at this time. Gobineau's book, Young suggests, "rests on a clever fusion of the implications of the older and newer uses of the word 'race': the traditional meaning involves bloodlines, the 'lineage' of an ancient family, with an aristocratic pedigree like a thoroughbred horse. The line of such a family is distinguished by its breeding, by the blood that flows through its veins through the act of procreation from father to son. Gobineau adapts this aristocratic notion of race as ancient stock to the modern notion, derived from linguistic families, of families of races, and assumes that however large they too are distinguished by their 'breeding,' by a particular blood that flows through their veins, passed on through the act of reproduction from generation to generation". Young's work, especially *Colonial Desire*, has been central to the articulation of the ideas in this essay.

One of the consequences of the Jamaica rebellion was the abolition of the Jamaican House of Assembly and the imposition of direct rule from London (Jamaica became a Crown Colony after 1866), thus ending even the pretense of self-government in the British West Indies.

"The old pre-emancipation claim that the Jamaican worker would not follow his own economic interest —would not behave like the 'economic man'—was brought out again. It was held that the Jamaican had such limited desires, that he would work only for a bare subsistence. When he had earned it he would stop. If this was generally true, it would reverse the traditional supply curve for labour—the higher the wages, the less labour would be offered".

It should be noted here that these national and racial boundaries are in fact not stable at all, despite the apparent certainties of Beesly's racial typology. In particular, the question of Ireland disrupts any simple claims to national or racial purity. After the Act of Union of 1800, Ireland was juridically part of Britain, although on the ground it continued to be governed more like a colony than a regional entity. Persistent attempts to racialize the Irish might be read as responses to the dangerous incorporation of Ireland into the English nation. I would like to acknowledge the importance of fruitful conversations with Amy Martin on the question of Ireland.

Space constraints preclude a detailed reading of *Daniel Deronda* here, although it should be noted that this reported conversation carries the weight of wider debates in the novel: for instance, we could trace the connection between Deronda's identification with the downtrodden Calibans of the world and his eventual discovery that he is Jewish and racially "pure." For a good reading of the novel, see Gillian Beer's analysis in her *George Eliot* .

For a powerful analysis of the ways in which this debate turned on competing versions of middle-class masculinity, see Hall, "Economy." The real leader of the rebellion, Paul Bogle (who was a kind of political agent for Gordon in the district around Morant Bay), remained all but invisible in contemporary accounts of the uprising and its suppression. The status of Morant Bay as a founding event in Jamaican national history has ensured that Bogle's role is now more fully acknowledged: see especially Heuman.

Such a narrative works as a kind of allegory of the parental model of British imperialism, in which the colonies figure as children who will be guided slowly towards maturity (i.e., self-government and capitalism) while retaining their sense of responsibility towards their British fathers. For more on this particular trope, see the final section of this essay.

"When I speak of a man 'having a pedigree,' I mean to say that some two or three generations at least of his fathers have been in better circumstances than the generality of their fellow men" (Marshall 69).

The meeting was held at St. James's Hall on February 1, 1866. Pim's paper was later published in the ASL's *Popular Magazine of Anthropology* and as a separate pamphlet, *The Negro and Jamaica* . Pim, a major landowner in the Caribbean and Central America, thanked "that vigorous and fearless body, the Anthropological Society of London" for giving him the opportunity to share with the public his collection of racial stereotypes. In amongst his scientific analysis of the unchanging degraded character of "the negro" since antiquity, he found space to make a connection to the Reform debates: "I make bold to say that 50 million of blacks have not been placed on this magnificent globe of ours for no purpose; it is therefore our duty, by wise legislation, to utilize this large mass of human beings. They must be dealt with from no sentimental standpoint, but from a knowledge of their nature and characteristics, discarding at once the theory of equality. We do not admit equality even amongst our own race, as is proved by the state of the franchise at this hour in England! and to suppose that two alien races can compose a political unity is simply ridiculous".

Darwin in fact says almost nothing about humankind, let alone about race, in *On the Origin of Species* , but of course he says a great deal about descent in general: "Propinquity of descent,—the only known cause of the similarity of organic beings,—is the bond, hidden as it is by various degrees of modification, which is partially revealed to us by our classification". Although, as Beer points out in *Darwin's Plots,* this theory actually "muddied descent, and brought into question the privileged 'purity' of the 'great family'", opening up the possibility of "an uncouth progenitor hard to acknowledge as kin", many of the new race theorists adapted a crude version of natural selection to their notions of fixed racial "types" defined by blood relations.

This series of pamphlets was published by the Jamaica Committee in an attempt to influence public opinion in Britain over Morant Bay. Other Executive Committee members included Mill, Huxley, Spencer, and E.B. Underhill, whose letter to Governor Eyre in early 1865 about the desperate condition of the island's population had led to the so-called Underhill meetings throughout the island, at which grievances were expressed and the beginnings of a resistance movement can be discerned.

There is only one, fleeting, reference to Harrison's work with the Jamaica Committee in their correspondence: on February 5, 1867, Harrison wrote to Eliot, "I sent you as you asked the letters on Martial law. The Prosecution commences at once". When Eliot replied a fortnight later, she did not even acknowledge receipt of Harrison's pamphlet. The prosecution Harrison was referring to was the private case brought by the Jamaica Committee against Colonel Alexander Nelson and Lieutenant Herbert Brand, the presiding officers at George William Gordon's trial, on charges of wilful murder. Although the Lord Chief Justice, Sir Alexander Cockburn, delivered a famous address to the grand jury virtually instructing them to proceed with the trial, the jury refused to indict the two officers. In March, the Committee began the first of its two unsuccessful attempts to secure a conviction of Edward Eyre, the first time on murder charges, the second time for "high crimes and misdemeanours".

Of course, this does not prevent Mrs Transome herself clinging to the very notion of breeding that the novel in general, and her own life in particular, renders obsolete: "Poor Mrs Transome, with her secret bitterness and dread, still found a flavour in this sort of pride [of family and blood]; none the less because certain deeds of her own life had been in fatal inconsistency with it. Besides, genealogies entered into her stock of ideas, and her talk on such subjects was as necessary as the notes of the linnet or the blackbird. She had no ultimate analysis of things that went beyond blood and family—the Herons of Fenshore or the Badgers of Hillbury".

Gillian Beer comments: "The book opens with the suppression of a woman's [Mrs Transome's] independence, a suppression which has been previously put at her [Eliot's] works' conclusion, and therefore out of reach of question". Harold's deceased wife has attracted little or no attention from critics.

This revelation also raises the intriguing possibility that the "woman from the East" whom Harold brings to Transome Court—who is mentioned nowhere else in the novel, and is certainly never seen—is in fact Harry's mother, and that the story about her death is a convenient fiction. This suppressed narrative of the "native" woman hidden in the country house would make *Felix Holt* an explicit reworking of *Jane Eyre* , and would consolidate the claims made here for the connections between George Eliot's novel and Jamaica. Unfortunately, pursuing this comparison is beyond the scope of this essay.

The imaginary stagecoach of the Introduction makes its way through Treby Magna and on to the reader's first view, through the eyes of the coachman, of "Transome Court, a place there had been a fine sight of lawsuits about. Generations back, the heir of the Transome name had somehow bargained away the estate and it fell to the Durfeys, very distant connections, who only called themselves Transomes because they had got the estate.

But the Durfeys' claim had been disputed again and again; and the coachman, if he had been asked, would have said, though he might have to fall down dead the next minute, that property didn't always get into the right hands". Characteristically, this information is conveyed through an unnamed, minor character. Bruce Robbins' groundbreaking book *The Servant's Hand* , which analyzes the centrality of these apparently marginal figures in English fiction, contains a fine reading of *Felix Holt* : "Throughout the novel, the news that 'property doesn't always get into the right hands,' as the coachman of the introduction puts it, is specifically and almost obsessively placed in the hands of propertyless servants".

It would be more accurate, in fact, to say that writers began to use the term "British Empire" once again, since it had been current before the American Revolution in discussions about the possible loss to England of the thirteen colonies although it is doubtful whether the term encompassed all of England's dependencies overseas, including what was coming to be known as the Indian Empire. I believe that this point in fact strengthens my argument that it is only at the moment of possible loss of imperial hegemony that the Empire as such comes into being.

Bibliography

Modern Critical Interpretations: George Eliot's The Mill on the Floss. Ed. Harold Bloom. New York: Chelsea House, 1988.

Draper, R.P. (ed.). George Eliot's The Mill on the Floss and Silas Marner: A Casebook. London: Macmillan, 1977.

Hardy, Barbara. "*Implication and Incompleteness: George Eliot's Middlemarch.*" The Victorian Novel, ed. Ian Watt. New York: Oxford University Press, 1971. Pp. 289-310

Harvey, W. J. "*The Intellectual Background of the Novel: Casaubon and Lydgate.*" The Victorian Novel, ed. Ian Watt. New York: Oxford University Press, 1971.

Knoepflmacher, U.C. "*Middlemarch: Affirmation through Compromise.*" Laughter and Despair: Readings in Ten Novels of the Victorian Era. Berkeley: U of California Press, 1971.

Middlemarch: Critical Approaches to the Novel. ed. Barbara Hardy. London: The Athlone Press, 1967.

Alley, Henry. "*Silas Marner and the Balance of Male and Female.*" Victorians Institute Journal 16 (1988): 65-73.

Bonaparte, Felicia. "*Carrying the Word of the Lord to the Gentiles: Silas Marner and the Translation of Scripture into a Secular Text.*" Religion and Literature 23, 2 (Summer, 1991): 39-60.

Cohen, Susan. "'*A History and a Metamorphosis': Continuity and Discontinuity in Silas Marner.*" Texas Studies in Language and Literature 25, 3 (Fall, 1983): 410-26.

Fisch, Harold. "*Biblical Realism in Silas Marner.*" Identity and Ethos, ed. Mark H. Gelber. New York: Peter Lang, 1986. Pp. 343-360.

Hawes, Donald. "*Chance in Silas Marner.*" Journal of the

English Association 31, 141 (Autumn, 1982): 213-218.

Knapp, Shoshana, "*George Eliot and W. S. Gilbert: Silas Marner into Dan'l Druce.*" NCF 40 (1985): 438-459.

John, Joseph. "*Aspects of George Eliot's Characterization.*" Unisa English Studies 26, 1 (April 1988): 8-13.

Levine, George. "*George Eliot Studies: 1980-84.*" Dickens Studies Annual 16 (1987): 377-407.

Marks, Louis. "*Silas Marner: Filming the Novel.*" George Eliot Fellowship Review 18 (1987): 18-23.

Preston, John. "*Silas Marner: The Community of the Novel.*" George Eliot Fellowship Review 11 (1980): 109-130.

Rechelson, Meri-Jane. "*The Weaver of Raveloe: Metaphor as Narrative Persuasion in Silas Marner.*" Studies in the Novel 15, 1 (Spring, 1993): 35-43.

Roberts, Janene. "*Literature on PBS: Three 'Masterpiece Theatre' Productions of Nineteenth-Century British Novels.*" Text and Performance Quarterly 9, 4 (Oct., 1989): 311-21.

Shuttleworth, Sally. "*Fairy Tale or Science? Physiological Psychology in Silas Marner.*" Languages of Nature: Critical Essays on Science and Literature, ed. L. J. Jordanova. New Brunswick: Rutgers University Press, 1986. Pp. 244-288.

Swindon, Patrick. Silas Marner: Memory and Salvation. Twayne's Masterwork Studies. New York: Twayne, 1992.

Wiesenfarth, Joseph. "*Demythologizing Silas Marner.*" ELH 37 (1970): 226-244.

[illegible] Association [illegible] 1980 [illegible]
[illegible] Snobbism [illegible] and [illegible]
[illegible]

Jehn, Joseph. "Aspects of George Eliot's Comedy [illegible]" [illegible] English Studies 26 [illegible]
[illegible] Studies Annual 16 (1987): 37 [illegible]

Marks, Louis. "Silas Marner: Filming the novel." George Eliot Fellowship Review 18 (1987): 18-24

[illegible] John. "Silas Marner: The Continuance of the Needs [illegible]" George Eliot Fellowship Review 11 (1980): [illegible]
[illegible] "The Weaver of Raveloe [illegible]"
[illegible]

[illegible]
[illegible] Collection [illegible] Nineteenth-Century [illegible]
Pennsylvania's Quarterly 4, 4 (Oct. [illegible]): 211-21

Shuttleworth, Sally. "Fairy Tale or Science? Physiological [illegible] in Silas Marner." Languages of Nature: Critical [illegible] on Science and Literature, ed. L. J. Jordanova. New [illegible] Rutgers University Press [illegible]
[illegible]